Reference
and Essence

Reference and Essence

Nathan U. Salmon

Basil Blackwell • Oxford

First published in Great Britain by
Basil Blackwell, Publisher, Limited
108 Cowley Road
Oxford OX4 1JF

British Library Cataloging in Publication Data

Salmon, Nathan U.
    Reference and Essence
    Reference (Philosophy)
    I.   Title
    149'.946   B105.R25

    ISBN 0-631-13004-7
    ISBN 0-631-13005-5 Pbk

This book has been composed in Linotron Times Roman

Printed in the United States of America

To my parents,

Mair and Rebecca Ucuzoglu,

without whom *dthat*(the author of this work) would be possible, but only possible.

Contents

I
THE THEORY OF DIRECT REFERENCE

ONE. The Theory of Singular Direct Reference

TWO. The Theory Extended to General Terms

Contents

II
THE PROGRAM TO DERIVE ESSENTIALISM FROM THE THEORY OF REFERENCE

Contents

Preface

On October 11, 1974, I attended a talk given by Keith Donnellan at a meeting of the UCLA Philosophy Colloquium (Donnellan, 1974b). The talk, entitled "Rigid Designators, Natural Kinds, and Individuals," was an expansion of a commentary (Donnellan, 1973b) on Hilary Putnam's "Meaning and Reference" (Putnam, 1973b), both originally delivered at the 1973 American Philosophical Association Eastern Division Symposium on Reference. I was already familiar with the basic tenets of what has come to be called the "new" or "causal" theory of reference, having attended numerous lectures by three of the theory's main exponents and proponents, Donnellan, David Kaplan, and Saul Kripke. Following Kaplan, I shall call this theory *the theory of direct reference*. I was aware at the time that Kripke and Putnam had argued in connection with this theory, as it applies to natural kind terms, that though it could only have been an empirical discovery that water is H_2O, it is nevertheless a necessary truth that water is H_2O. By the theory, it follows that the substance water is such that it *has to* have the chemical structure that it actually has. Similarly, I had also read an argument of Kripke's concerning concrete things like tables and lecterns which seemed to show that certain nontrivial forms of essentialism followed from his theory of proper names in conjunction with certain trivial assumptions. These were exciting claims in and of themselves. But there was something new and marvelous in Donnellan's talk concerning the relation between the theory of direct reference and these essentialist claims. It might have been more perspicuously entitled "How to Derive Essentialism from the New Theory of Reference." For the first time I was made to appreciate the subtleties of the enterprise. Donnellan was doing more than merely performing feats of magic. Kripke and Putnam, it seemed, had done that much already. Donnellan was *explaining how* to pull the rabbit out of the hat. He provided a general mechanism allegedly employed by Kripke and Putnam for this purpose, and broke the mechanism down into its component pieces in order to show precisely where the philosophy of language, and where scientific or empirical principles, came into the picture.

This made the rabbit trick look easy, but instead of removing the mystery, it only increased it. The mechanism seemed to involve things in addition to the magician's top hat, i.e., the theory of direct reference, but still no deeply metaphysical rabbit-parts. The practical question was answered: How do you extract nontrivial essentialism from the philosophy of language? You use this mechanism. But the deeper and more puzzling problem remained: How is it *possible* to extract a rabbit from an empty hat? I was determined to get to the bottom of the mechanism, and uncover its hidden props. It was Donnellan's talk in 1974 that provided the impetus for the research which culminates in the present work.

Putnam's work, on which Donnellan's paper was originally a commentary, has deservedly received a great deal of attention since its appearance in 1973. Donnellan's paper has remained unpublished. With Donnellan's permission, I have attempted to present some of the central ideas of his paper in Section 17 below. The reader is hereby cautioned, however, that I do not know to what extent these ideas form part of his present view on the subject.

The present book was written in widely separated periods. Much of it was written between mid-1977 and mid-1978 in my native city of Hawthorne, California, as part of my doctoral dissertation. Further work had to wait until the summers of 1979 and 1980, to be done in the sweltering humidity of Princeton, New Jersey. My labor consisted largely in putting down in pencil the details of an extended argument that I had been thinking through since Donnellan's talk in 1974.

The interim has seen a veritable explosion of literature on the "new" or "causal" theory of reference, though relatively little is concerned with one of the main issues with which the present book is concerned, the relation of the theory to essentialism. Some of the published criticisms of the theory are mentioned in Part I below, but those that are mentioned are brought in only as a means for elaborating the theory. No attempt is made here to construct a complete defense of the theory against its critics, or to resolve all of the well-known difficulties that the theory encounters with certain referentially opaque constructions and with nondenoting names. I argue that these phenomena do not disprove the theory, but it is not my objective here to show how the apparent difficulties are ultimately to be resolved.

The bibliography was compiled primarily with an eye to listing those works actually referred to in the text or actually consulted in preparing the book. It does not constitute a complete list of important works dealing with the theory of direct reference or essentialism. In particular, a significant part of the critical literature on the theory of direct reference is conspicuously missing, though much of the rest is included.

All page references to Kripke's *Naming and Necessity* given throughout this book are to the 1980 book edition (Harvard University Press or Basil Blackwell). Given a page number n in the text of that edition, the reader with a calculator at hand can easily arrive at the approximate page in the Davidson and Harman edition by using the formula: $(n - 21) 0.67 + 252$. All page references to Putnam's "The Meaning of 'Meaning'" are to his *Philosophical Papers II* edition (1975d). The conversion formula for the *Minnesota Studies VII* edition is: $(n - 214) 1.1 + 130$. Conversion formulae for the opposite direction are obtained by solving for n.

Throughout the work, many complex expressions are referred to time and again. These expressions have been labeled for easy reference, and an index of the labeled expressions is provided at the end.

I thank *The Journal of Philosophy* for allowing me to incorporate portions of my "How *Not* to Derive Essentialism from the Theory of Reference" (Salmon, 1979b) as well as portions of my review of Leonard Linsky's *Names and Descriptions* (Salmon, 1979a) into the present work. I am grateful to Saul Kripke for permission to quote extensively from *Naming and Necessity* and to Hilary Putnam and the University of Minnesota Press for permission to quote extensively from Putnam's essay "The Meaning of 'Meaning'" (Putnam, 1975a). A portion of the cost of typing and copying was supported by a grant from Princeton University's Committee on Research in the Humanities and Social Sciences, for which I am also grateful.

Several individuals have contributed in various ways to the successful completion of this project. I owe a profound debt of thanks to David Kaplan for his helpful, detailed comments on the 1977–78 draft, and for countless hours of delightful and illuminating discussion on the topics raised in the present work. Thanks are due also to Tyler Burge, Keith Donnellan, Graeme Forbes, William Hively, Saul Kripke, the anonymous reviewers of my manuscript, and the participants in my seminars on the philosophy of language and metaphysics at Princeton University in the fall semesters of 1978 and 1980 for their valuable comments and suggestions. Further thanks are due to still others too numerous to mention.

Special thanks are owed to Keith Donnellan, for reasons made evident in the first three paragraphs. Very special thanks go to Eileen Conrad for her substantial donation of time and energy in assisting me in preparing the manuscript, and for her love—though not in that order.

Princeton, New Jersey
1980

*Reference
and Essence*

Introduction

A great deal of philosophical attention has recently been devoted to an important area in the philosophy of semantics commonly referred to as the theory of reference. In the present work a number of philosophical issues arising from current theories of reference are examined and clarified. The theories of reference in question were not fully developed at the time that the present work was undertaken, but several versions were partly developed, to a considerable extent independently, by several contemporary philosophers of semantics, most notably Keith Donnellan, David Kaplan, Saul Kripke, and Hilary Putnam. Donnellan's early pioneering efforts were concerned mainly with a common use of definite descriptions, the so-called referential use, with later attention given to proper names and natural kind terms such as 'water' and 'tiger'.[1] Kaplan has begun to develop a theory of so-called indexical expressions, i.e., certain context-sensitive expressions such as 'I', 'here', and 'this'.[2] Putnam has constructed a theory of natural kind terms and physical magnitude terms, e.g., 'energy', which he extends to artifact terms, e.g., 'pencil', and some other forms of speech.[3] Kripke has formulated a widely discussed account of proper names,[4] and he also extends his account to natural kind terms and terms for natural phenomena, e.g., 'heat'. Despite differences in scope and emphasis, these several theories bear striking similarities to one another, enough so that a sort of composite theory has been discussed as the "new" or "causal" theory of reference.[5] Simply put, this theory asserts that the referential expressions mentioned above are nonconnotative appellations, and not disguised or abbreviated descriptions which achieve reference through the mediation of a Fregean *Sinn,* or sense. We shall attempt to clarify this further in Part I. Since the theory asserts that

---

[1] In Donnellan, 1966, 1978, 1972, 1974a, 1973b, and 1974b.
[2] In Kaplan, 1970, 1973a, 1973b, and 1975.
[3] In Putnam, 1970, 1973b, 1975a, and 1973a.
[4] In Kripke, 1971, 1972a, 1979a, and 1979b.
[5] See for instance the introduction to Schwartz, 1977.

3

certain expressions refer directly, we shall call it *the theory of direct reference.*

Kripke's papers on the subject have attracted the most attention. In setting out his theory of reference, Kripke puts forth a number of important and exciting views, and supports them with artful and cogent argument. Fascinating issues that are related, often in an unobvious way, to the theory of direct reference are raised throughout his discussion. From a relatively simple base—the assertion that proper names are nonconnotative appellations, together with this assertion's supporting arguments—Kripke launches into issues concerning the reference of proper names in modal and epistemic contexts, the possibility of contingent *a priori* truth and necessary *a posteriori* truth, *de dicto* and *de re* modality, essentialism, and even the Cartesian mind-body problem. Thus, although many of the issues raised by Kripke involve concepts familiar to philosophical semantics, such as necessary truth and *de dicto* and *de re* modality, much of his discussion touches on issues that seem to belong more to metaphysics than to the philosophy of language.

That Kripke is able to bring a relatively simple theory about the reference of proper names to bear on classical metaphysical problems is a testimony to the power of the theory. But the path from the philosophy of language to metaphysics is a slippery one. It is often difficult to tell whether one of the views being put forth is a straightforward consequence of Kripke's theory of reference (taken together with trivial or uncontroversial premises), whether it is related to the theory of reference in some less direct way, or whether it is entirely and simply independent of the theory of reference. Sorting these matters out is a delicate task. It is often difficult to determine when an argument depends on an unobvious connection between related theses, and when it uses a nontrivial suppressed premise connecting what are in fact unrelated and independent theses.

The need to clarify the consequences of the theory of direct reference is especially pressing with regard to Kripke's espousal of *essentialism,* the doctrine that certain properties of things are properties that these things could not fail to have, except by not existing. Kripke holds for instance that a table which was in fact originally constructed from a certain hunk of wood is such that it *could not* have originated from a sample of water hardened into ice, and that any particular pain sensation is such that it *could not* have had the feel of a tickle. Indeed, the latter view is crucial to Kripke's discussion of mind-body identity theory. Kripke's essentialism seems to go hand in hand with his theory of reference.

It is surprising, at least initially, that a simple theory about a very basic aspect of language could have this much metaphysical import. A proper theory of reference, one would think, should be concerned only with the nature of the semantical relations that hold between certain linguistic expressions and the objects for which they stand, and ought to be indifferent to the question of whether the objects referred to have certain of their properties essentially. A major project of the present work is to investigate the extent to which essentialism is indeed a *consequence* of the theory of direct reference.

The book is divided into two parts. In Part I a careful attempt is made to clarify, to elaborate, and sometimes to develop further the theory of direct reference, along with its supporting arguments and an important immediate consequence, rigid designation.[6] It will be argued that a trivial form of essentialism is, as it were, built into the theory and is in a certain sense derivable from it, viz., the doctrine that every object is such that it could not fail to be itself. In Part II, a recent attempt by Putnam, as elaborated by Donnellan, to substantiate the claim that certain nontrivial forms of essentialism concerning natural kinds are also consequences of the theory of direct reference is presented and analyzed. It will be argued that this program is flawed in that it begs the crucial question by relying on nontrivial essentialist premises that are quite independent of the theory of reference. A related argument of Kripke's which uses the theory of direct reference to prove a version of essentialism concerning the origins of concrete artifacts is also analyzed, and also found to rely on an independent essentialist premise.

In addition, there are two appendices. The first is an exploration into certain cross-world identification principles at work in Kripke's argument for a version of essentialism. The second arbitrates a

---

[6]There are aspects of the theory of direct reference that are not directly relevant to the issues concerning modality and essentialism with which the present work is chiefly concerned. The historical or casual account given by Donnellan and Kripke for determining the reference of a proper name in a given speaker's idiolect, and Putnam's sociolinguistic hypothesis concerning the division of linguistic labor, for instance, are not as important for the concerns of Part II as is the phenomenon of so-called rigid designation. Part I is mainly an attempt to clarify those aspects of the theory of direct reference that may be directly relevant to the question of whether the theory has any nontrivial essentialist import.

disagreement between Donnellan and Kripke concerning the epistemological and theoretical status of the crucial essentialist premises involved in some of the relevant arguments. The result of this investigation taken together with the results of Part II will be seen as supporting the contention that nontrivial essentialism concerning natural kinds and concrete individuals is an intrinsically metaphysical doctrine, or set of doctrines, not reducible to, or obtainable as a product of, the philosophy of language or science.

I
THE THEORY OF DIRECT REFERENCE

ONE · *The Theory of Singular Direct Reference*

1. A FORMULATION OF THE THEORY

1.1 The Orthodox Notion of Sense

The theory of direct reference is reactionary. It takes as its point of departure a rejection of the orthodox, Fregean philosophy of semantics, urging a return to the naive view held by Mill, and to some extent by Russell, that certain expressions, in particular proper names, are nonconnotative appellations.[1] The contrast between the orthodox theory and the theory of direct reference is clearest in the case of purported denoting expressions, or (definite) *singular terms,* expressions like 'Shakespeare', 'the world's wealthiest plumber', 'this', etc., which are to be taken as denoting, or standing for, a single thing.

On the orthodox picture, received from Frege, every singular term has in addition to its *denotation,* or the object denoted by the term, a *Sinn,* or sense, which is the manner in which the term presents its denotation to the listener or reader. Pairs of co-referential terms, i.e., terms having the same denotation, may present their denotation in different ways. Thus, for instance, the terms 'the inventor of bifocals' and 'the author of *Poor Richard's Almanac*' have the same denotation, Benjamin Franklin, but differ in sense. Pairs of strictly synonymous terms, i.e. terms having the same sense, such as (perhaps) 'Socrates' thinnest enemy' and 'the skinniest foe of Socrates', are *a fortiori* co-referential terms, since they present the same individual in precisely the same way. The sense of a term thus provides a criterion for identifying the referent of the term, thereby determining who or what the referent of the term is to be. The sense of a singular term is something which a speaker mentally *grasps* or *apprehends* and which forms a part of any belief (or assertion, thought, hope) whose expression involves the term. The sense of a term is a concept,

---

[1]See Mill, 1843, and Russell, 1918 and 1911, especially pp. 216, 224.

9

whereas the denotation or referent of a term is whoever or whatever uniquely fits the concept.[2]

On the orthodox theory, all singular terms are assimilated to the model of a definite description (in attributive use). The sense of the expression is usually thought of as supplying a set of conditions, or properties, and the denotation, if any, is whatever uniquely satisfies those conditions.[3] The sense of an expression is often identified with a "conjunction" of properties. However, according to certain refinements of Frege's account, such as Searle's, an expression denotes whatever object *best* fits the conceptual representation contained in the sense. On this modified Fregean picture, the sense of an expression is identified with a "cluster" of properties, rather than a conjunction.[4] Other refinements have been proposed, as for instance in Linsky (1977),[5] but each of these rival theories does little more than add epicycles to Frege's original scheme. The general picture of descriptive denotation mediated by a concept consisting of properties remains essentially unchanged. The term expresses a concept, and the concept in turn *determines* an object, namely whatever object uniquely fits, or best fits, the concept. The *denoting* relation is thus an indirect relation between a term and an object; it is the relative product of the relation of *expressing,* which holds between the term and a concept, and the relation of *determining,* which holds between

---

[2]See Frege, 1892 and 1918.

[3]See Donnellan, 1966 and 1978, on the distinction between the so-called referential and attributive uses of definite descriptions. Roughly, a speaker uses a definite description referentially when he or she uses it simply as a device for calling attention to a predetermined individual that the speaker has in mind, wishing to say (ask, etc.) something about it, as for instance 'the man in the far corner drinking champagne', uttered with the intention of referring to someone whom the speaker sees and believes to be a man in the far corner drinking champagne. According to Donnellan, such uses of definite descriptions succeed in referring to the intended individual even if the description itself, qua literal description, is a misdescription of the intended referent and, coincidentally, a correct description of an unintended individual, e.g., if the intended man is drinking water though someone else in the far corner is in fact drinking champagne. By contrast, a speaker uses a description attributively when the speaker intends to refer to whoever or whatever literally fits the description, as for instance 'the thief (whoever he or she may be) who stole my lunch'. See also Prior, 1971, pp. 152–153.

[4]See for instance Searle, 1958 and 1967.

[5]Part I, especially pp. 84–111. On Linsky's view, which he derives from Wittgenstein, the sense of a proper name is generally vague and shifty, remaining indeterminate among a number of individual concepts, as expressed by distinct definite descriptions. See Wittgenstein, 1953, part I, section 79, pp. 36–38.

the concept and an object. A singular term does not have any intrinsic affinity to denote a particular object independently of that object's meeting certain conditions. Speaking metaphorically, the term lets its sense rummage through the existing things of a possible world at a given time in search of a uniquely suitable denotation, whoever or whatever that turns out to be.

The orthodox view is especially satisfying because it provides a plausible solution to the puzzles of reference which concerned Russell and Frege—a solution to Frege's puzzle about the informativeness of identity statements, to the failure of substitutivity in modal and propositional attitude contexts, to the problem of negative existentials, and to the more general problem of the significance and truth-value of statements involving nondenoting singular terms. Each puzzle may be resolved by noting that the proposition expressed, or information conveyed, by a statement or clause involving a singular term is a function of, or partly consists of, the sense of the term rather than its denotation. The success of the orthodox view in handling these puzzles of reference probably accounts for its widespread philosophical appeal. Proponents of the orthodox view include such notables as Rudolf Carnap, Alonzo Church, Michael Dummett, Leonard Linsky, John Searle, and P. F. Strawson.

By contrast, it is often said that the theory of singular reference espoused by Donnellan and Kripke is the theory that denies that proper names have a sense, contending instead that proper names are no more than "empty tags" which merely label objects, and for which reference is determined not by way of any conceptual content in the name but by tracing back along some sort of causal chain leading originally from the object to a speaker's use of its name.[6] Hence, this theory of reference is often called *the causal theory of reference.* So understood, an obvious criticism of the theory would be that it is refuted by the puzzles of reference. But this involves a mistake.

Although it is true that the theory of direct reference, in some sense, rejects the idea that proper names have a Fregean *Sinn,* it is neither helpful nor illuminating to see the central issue as a question of whether proper names have sense. As Linsky points out (1977, p. 75), the Fregean concept of sense "is a notion with [considerable] structure and part of a rather elaborately articulated theory." Tyler Burge (1977, p. 356) has discerned three distinct functions that Frege's concept of sense was designed to fill. Among these three,

---

[6]See for instance Ackerman, 1979a and 1979b, and Linsky, 1977, throughout part I.

The Theory of Direct Reference

even finer distinctions may be drawn. Roughly following Burge's trifurcation, at least the following three attributes of a term ought to be distinguished.

Sense₁. The purely conceptual representation of an object which a fully competent speaker associates in a particular way with his or her use of the term. Sense₁ is a psychological or conceptual notion. The sense₁ of a term is something that a subject "grasps." It includes only purely qualitative properties (this notion will be explained below); external things cannot "occur as constituents" of sense₁. Instead there are only conceptual representations thereof.

Sense₂. The mechanism by which the reference of the term (with respect to a possible world and a time) is secured and semantically determined. Sense₂ is a semantical notion.

Sense₃. The information value of the term; the contribution made by the term to the information content of sentences containing the term. Sense₃ is a cognitive or epistemic notion. The sense₃ of a term forms a part of any belief expressed by means of the term, and is relevant to the epistemological status (*a priori, a posteriori,* trivial, informative) of sentences containing the term.[7]

[7]This trifurcation departs from Burge's in ways that Burge does not accept. Burge's 'sense₁' combines our sense₁ with at least part of our sense₃. Burge's sense₃' may be seen as yet a fourth attribute of the Fregean *Sinn* of a term, namely, the entity denoted by occurrences of the term within 'that'-clauses and other oblique contexts. It seems likely, however, that this notion and our notion of sense₃ can, for most purposes, be safely collapsed into one.

There is yet another kind of "sense" for a term which is a close variant of our sense₁. This is the set or cluster of properties (achievements, identifying characteristics, etc., and perhaps other things such as emotional attitudes) which a speaker associates in a certain way with his or her use of a term. Philosophers often speak of this as a "mental file" attached to the term. (See for instance Lockwood, 1971, pp. 208–209. The notion is also closely tied to Putnam's notion of a "stereotype.") Call this mental file the *sense₁'* of a term. The major difference between sense₁ and sense₁' is that the latter is not, in general, purely qualitative or conceptual, and may involve nonintensional entities as constituents. As such, it is a notion which Frege would reject as playing no part in his notion of *Sinn*.

The temptation to assimilate either sense₁ or sense₁' with sense₃ must be resisted, and for much the same reasons. See Salmon, 1979a, for an argument that sense₁ ≠ sense₃. It may help to think of sense₃ as being defined as *whatever it is* that correctly solves Frege's puzzle about identity; that aspect of a term τ in which τ and a co-designative term τ' must differ if $\ulcorner\phi(\tau)\urcorner$ is to convey different information from $\ulcorner\phi(\tau')\urcorner$, for any sentential matrix $\ulcorner\phi(\ )\urcorner$. With this in mind, one may generalize Frege's strategy for showing that the sense₃ of a term is not the same thing as its

12

On any Fregean theory, these three attributes of terms are conflated. For any meaningful singular term, it is assumed that the sense$_1$ of the term is the sense$_2$ of the term is the sense$_3$ of the term. This three-way identification, though perhaps natural and satisfying, constitutes a very strong theoretical claim, a claim that warrants at least some careful consideration before it is given our unqualified approval. There are certain singular terms, to be sure, for which an identification of sense$_2$ and sense$_3$ seems unquestionably correct. These are definite descriptions in attributive use. If in addition the description does not contain any proper names or indexicals (e.g., 'the shortest spy'), a full three-way identification of sense$_1$, sense$_2$, and sense$_3$ may be warranted. But these are very special sorts of expressions. In the absence of any justification for an across-the-board three-way identification for singular terms generally, Fregean arguments that demonstrate the need to acknowledge such a thing as the sense$_3$ of a proper name as distinct from its reference do nothing toward showing that we must also countenance something that is simultaneously the sense$_1$ and sense$_2$ of a proper name. Faced with Frege's identity puzzle, it is difficult indeed to maintain that the names 'Hesperus' and 'Phosphorus' make precisely the same contribution to the information content of sentences that contain either one. Such a claim would be extremist. But the theory of direct reference, the theory defended by Kripke in *Naming and Necessity* and by others elsewhere, does not make such a claim. Kripke's theory is not even entirely friendly to such a claim, since he held (1972a, pp. 101–105) that 'Hesperus is Phosphorus' is necessary and *a posteriori* whereas 'Hesperus is Hesperus' is necessary and *a priori*. (But see 1979b, pp. 269, 281 n. 44.) Criticisms of the direct reference theory that focus on the need to acknowledge that proper names have one of the three kinds of "sense" betray a serious misunderstanding of the

---

reference (viz., find a pair of terms α and β which share a common reference, but which are such that $\ulcorner \alpha = \beta \urcorner$ is informative, whereas $\ulcorner \alpha = \alpha \urcorner$ is not) to show that the sense$_3$ of a term is also not the same thing as its sense$_1$ or sense$_{1'}$.

Other writers have drawn similar distinctions among the components of the notion of sense or meaning. See for instance Blackburn, 1975; Kripke, 1972a, p. 59; and Putnam, 1973b.

In calling sense$_1$ a "psychological" notion, I do *not* mean that the sense$_1$ of a term is like a private subjective experience, accessible to the mind of only one subject. The sense$_1$ of a term is a conceptual entity, intersubjective, graspable by different people and by the same person at different times. Sense$_1$ is a psychological notion in that, as Frege stressed, the conceptual content of an expression is mentally "grasped" or "apprehended."

main thrust of the theory. In point of fact, the central theses of the theory of direct reference do not reject any one of the three kinds of "sense" as distinct from the reference of proper names. The view is not primarily concerned with denying that proper names have any one of these three kinds of "sense," or the ordered triple consisting of all three. Insofar as the central theses are opposed to admitting sense at all, they oppose the full-blown Fregean notion of *Sinn* as applied to proper names, the idea that that which fills one of these three functions for a proper name fills the cther two as well.[8] If that is the sort of thing that the *sense* of a term is supposed to be, then perhaps *some* definite descriptions do indeed have sense. Proper names and indexical singular terms, on the other hand, certainly do not.

1.2. Descriptional Singular Terms

Isn't a concession of any one of these three kinds of sense as distinct from reference for proper names just a Fregean theory after all? If the theory of direct reference does not oppose $sense_1$, $sense_2$, or $sense_3$, in what significant respect is it anti-Fregean? I propose to answer this question by introducing a technical notion. Let us say that a singular term α is *descriptional in the Carnap way* if there is associated with α (as part of its $sense_{1}$) a set of properties such that the denotation of α with respect to a possible world w and a time t is determined by semantics alone to be whoever or whatever uniquely has all these properties in w at t, if there exists an individual uniquely having all these properties in w at t, and to be nothing if there does not. (See footnote 7 concerning the $sense_{1}$ of a term.) This definition does not literally accord with other notions of sense for proper names, such as those offered in the theories of Searle or Linsky. Insofar as these rival sense-theories have been adequately specified, it is also possible to define the corresponding notion of *descriptional in the Searle way, descriptional in the Linsky way,* and so on. In order to accommodate Searle's "cluster" notion of sense, for instance, we have to allow the possibility that the denotation is identified with

---

[8]The theory's acknowledgment of $sense_2$ might be seen as indicating that 'the theory of direct reference' is strictly a misnomer. The phrase is intended as suggesting the idea of reference without the semantical mediation of a full-blown Fregean sense, and should not be taken as denying that such reference is accomplished by means of *something* connecting the term and the thing denoted. It may help to think of the words 'direct reference' not as a description but as a name for the phenomenon of reference without sense, or more accurately, for the phenomenon which we are about to call 'nondescriptionality'.

whoever or whatever has "sufficiently many"[9] of these properties, though perhaps not all.[10] We shall say that a singular term is *descriptional* (*simpliciter*) if it functions either in the Carnap way or in accordance with any one of these different variations on the original Fregean theme.[11] A descriptional term is one that denotes by way of properties. It is a term which expresses a way of conceiving something (as its sense$_{1'}$), and its referent, with respect to a possible world and a time, is secured *indirectly* by means of this concept or "sense." (A descriptional term is one whose sense$_2$ may be identified with its sense$_{1'}$.) It will be assumed throughout the present work that definite descriptions, or at any rate definite descriptions in attribu-

[9]The notion of something "best satisfying" a set of conditions, or satisfying "sufficiently many" of a set of conditions, is a vague one. The definition given below of a descriptional singular term, as well as that of a descriptional general term, is intended to include so-called cluster terms, however the latter notion is to be made precise.

[10]In order to accommodate Linsky's notion of sense, we need to consider also the possibility of fuzzy sets of such properties, or perhaps fuzzy sets of sets of such properties, together with a clause stipulating that each of these properties, in the case of a proper name, is a modally indexed property of *actually having the property P*, or *having P in the actual world*, and some sort of indeterminacy as to precisely which of these properties determines reference. See footnote 5. In attempting to give a precise definition for *descriptional in the Linsky way*, one finds that Linsky owes the reader considerably more detail than he gives. An important question which he leaves unanswered is how the reference is supposed to be determined when the shifting senses determine different objects. However Linsky fills out his view, the epistemological and semantical arguments raised below will apply.

[11]I prefer the adjective 'descriptional' to the more commonly used 'descriptive' for several reasons. The adjective 'descriptive' has a primary nontechnical sense which need not suggest the *semantical* properties of definite descriptions, whereas our adjective 'descriptional' is a quasi-technical term. There is a clear and ordinary sense in which demonstrative descriptions such as 'that tall basketball player' have some descriptive content, though they are probably nondescriptional in our technical sense. Similarly, there is a clear sense in which expressions formed by attaching Kaplan's '*dthat*'-operator to a definite description have descriptive content, though such terms are nondescriptional in our sense. Another difficulty in using the term 'descriptive' is this. Diana Ackerman, a critic of the theory of direct reference, puts forth the view in each of her works listed in the bibliography that proper names express a "non-descriptive connotation" or a "non-descriptive sense." She means by this that proper names are descriptional, though generally there are no (non-hokey) "purely qualitative" general terms, or predicates, which could be combined with the definite descriptions operator ('the' in the singular) to provide an exact synonym. Independently of the question of whether her view about proper names is correct, it must be acknowledged that, at any rate, there could be expressions which are descriptional in the technical sense, but which would not ordinarily be called 'descriptive' because of the difficulty or impossibility of providing description-like synonyms.

tive use, are descriptional in the sense defined here.[12] Indeed, the clearest case of a descriptional singular term is a definite description in attributive use. But not all descriptional singular terms need function in precisely the same way as a definite description. Singular "cluster terms," if there are any, are also descriptional in this sense.

We may say that a nondescriptional singular term is *directly referential,* and that it *directly denotes* its referent, since its denotation is not mediated by a descriptive sense.[13] The paradigm of a nondescriptional, directly referential, singular term is an individual variable (in a free occurrence). A free individual variable is a singular term that does not denote *simpliciter,* but denotes *under an assignment of values to individual variables.* The denotation, with respect to a possible world and a time, of a variable under such an assignment of values to variables is semantically determined directly by the assignment, and not by extracting a conceptual mode of presentation from the variable.

Using this notion of a descriptional denoting expression, the central and primary thesis of at least one version of the theory of direct reference might be simply stated thus: Certain sorts of singular terms held to be descriptional on the orthodox theory are in fact nondescriptional. In particular, ordinary uses of proper names and demonstratives, which are alleged by the orthodox theory to function in a manner rather like a definite description in attributive use, function instead in a manner more like a free variable, with an assigned value.

This is a simple thesis indeed. What could be more obvious than the observation that some terms do not denote by seeking whatever uniquely meets certain conditions, but purposely refer directly to an independently selected individual in order to allow the speaker to say (ask, etc.) something directly about it? But one must not be deceived by the simplicity and obviousness of this initial thesis. The wording conceals more than it reveals. This thesis lays the groundwork for an amazingly rich and powerful philosophical point of view. Unforeseen

---

[12]Accordingly, we shall allow the domain over which bound individual variables range to vary from possible world to possible world. The domain over which variables range *with respect to a possible world w* consists of just those (possible) individuals that "exist" in *w*.

[13]A possible exception to this claim is the case of demonstrative descriptions such as 'that tall basketball player' or 'this dusty manuscript'. Such expressions do indeed seem to convey some concepts, or to express a "sense," though they are nondescriptional. See footnote 11.

16

consequences are drawn from it, consequences that have been brought to bear on central questions in almost every branch of analytic philosophy from value theory to logic, including such unlikely areas as aesthetics, the philosophy of mathematics, epistemology, the philosophy of science, the philosophy of religion, and the philosophy of mind.

In Part II of the present work we shall investigate the question of whether this theory of direct reference has certain consequences claimed by some of its propounders for a notoriously difficult metaphysical problem, the problem of *essentialism*. Though the answer we shall give is largely negative, it is a striking fact that this question must be posed in the first place. The question cannot be discussed in a fruitful way, however, until we have gained a more extensive understanding of this theory of direct reference and have explored its contrast with the orthodox theory. This is the business of the remainder of Part I.

1.3. *Relationally Descriptional Singular Terms*

As we have seen, a descriptional singular term expresses a particular kind of "sense" consisting, in a certain way, of properties or conditions. The paradigm of a descriptional singular term is the definite description in attributive use. Let α be a nondescriptional singular term, and let R be any two-place relational predicate. Then on ordinary assumptions the open formula

$$R(x,\alpha)$$

expresses a definite condition, and the definite description

$$(\imath x)R(x,\alpha)$$

is therefore a descriptional term, one having a nondescriptional component. Such a definite description differs in an important way from what might be called a *thoroughly descriptional* term.[14] For example, if α is a nondescriptional name denoting Bertrand Russell, then the description ⌜the father of α⌝, though descriptional, is not thoroughly so. The property expressed is not one like that of *being a father of the only philosopher who ever held such-and-such a doctrine,* but rather a property that involves direct reference to

---

[14]Actually, in light of the applicability of the direct reference theory to nearly all single words (a point noted by Kaplan in 1973a, p. 518, n. 31), it becomes doubtful whether there exist any thoroughly descriptional terms. As we shall see, this contrasts sharply with the orthodox theory.

Russell; it is one in which Russell himself, to use his phrase, "occurs as a constituent," the property of *being a father of this very individual.*[15] Thoroughly descriptional terms, on the other hand, e.g., perhaps, 'the wealthiest plumber', express only purely conceptual properties, properties that do not involve direct reference to an individual.

The difference between a thoroughly descriptional term and one involving nondescriptional elements is most striking if we let R be the predicate of identity and contrast the resulting definite description, $\ulcorner(\imath x)(x = \alpha)\urcorner$, or $\ulcorner$the individual who is $\alpha\urcorner$, with a descriptional term that does not involve any component nondescriptional singular terms, e.g., 'the wealthiest plumber'. As we shall see in Section 3.2, a nondescriptional singular term α may function differently in modal and temporal contexts from its descriptional facsimile $\ulcorner(\imath x)(x = \alpha)\urcorner$, but for many purposes these differences are negligible.

To understand the issue between the orthodox and the direct reference theories, it is important that we sharply distinguish descriptional expressions with nondescriptional elements from thoroughly descriptional expressions. Unfortunately, this distinction cannot be made solely in terms of purely syntactic features, even if all nondescriptional expressions have been syntactically catalogued. Not all descriptional expressions need wear their components on their sleeves. Such phrases as 'the resurrection' and 'the immaculate conception', for instance, probably suppress nondescriptional reference to Christ.[16] It need not even be true that our language is rich enough to provide for every descriptional expression an exact synonym that reveals any nondescriptional components. It is proposed here to make the crucial distinction in patently metaphysical terms.

[15]Russell speaks primarily of individuals occurring as constituents of propositions, but the idea extends straightforwardly to those properties, relations, and other intensional entities whose formal expression involves the use of a genuine name. The idea of individuals occurring as constituents of propositions may be found in several places in Russell's writings. See for example 1905, pp. 55–56 of Russell, 1956; 1911, pp. 216–221; 1912, pp. 54, 57; and 1918, pp. 242–243 of 1956. We shall follow Kaplan (1970) in calling such propositions, having individuals as constituents, *singular propositions*.

[16]One possible view of so-called incomplete or indefinite definite descriptions, such as 'the table' (see Donnellan, 1968, p. 204) is that they all involve suppressed nondescriptional reference, though perhaps not always to an individual. Thus, for instance, 'the table' might be regarded as roughly synonymous with 'the table relevant to S', where 'S' is a name directly referring to a *situation*, as delineated by the surrounding context of use.

The distinction between descriptional and nondescriptional singular expressions is defined in terms of the notion of a *property* or *condition*. Traditionally, two sorts of properties may be distinguished: relational properties, i.e., properties built from some relation, such as the property of *loving Russell,* and nonrelational properties, such as the quality of *being green in appearance.* Let us reshape this traditional distinction and define a *relational property* as one that involves reference to an individual, i.e., in giving a standard gerund specification of the property in question (⌜the property of *X-ing*⌝), one makes reference to an individual by way of a properly contained singular term.[17] Some relational properties may be said to be *intrinsically relational* in that they seem to involve *direct* reference to an individual. That is, in many cases, in giving a standard gerund specification of a certain property one must make reference to an individual by way of some device other than a descriptional singular term, so that reference to the individual cannot be eliminated, or "analyzed away," by the method of Russell without significantly changing the property so designated.[18] The property of *being in love with England's greatest playwright ever,* for instance, involves reference to Shakespeare but does not involve direct reference to anyone, since it is in some sense equivalent to the property of *loving an English playwright who surpasses all others.* That this is a different property from that of *loving x,* where the value of '*x*' is Shakespeare (the property of *loving him,* said with direct reference

---

[17]This is intended not as a precise definition, but more as a rough-and-ready explanation of the notion. (Problems arise, for example, over the possibility of properties without standard gerund specifications and properties with more than one standard gerund specification.) According to this explanation, the property of *being married to someone in particular,* e.g., the property of *being married to Bertrand Russell,* counts as a relational property, whereas the more general property of *being married (to someone or other)* does not, since it does not involve reference to anyone in particular. The latter property does, however, involve the marriage relation, as does the former property. Two senses of the phrase 'relational property' may be distinguished: We may say that a property is *relational₁* if it satisfies the "definition" given here, and that a property is *relational₂* if its standard gerund specification involves either reference to a particular individual or quantification (universal or existential) over individuals, e.g., the property of *trusting no one*). The second notion of a relational₂ property is not important for present purposes, and will be assimilated to the nonrelational properties.

[18]For an illuminating and precise account of the notion of a property involving direct reference, and related notions, within the technical framework of possible-world model theory, see Fine, 1977b.

to Shakespeare), is established by noting the resulting difference in extension if, for instance, Shakespeare had never written a play and Sir Francis Bacon went on to become England's greatest playwright. Let us call properties that do not involve direct reference to an individual *purely qualitative* or *general properties.*

Relational properties that involve direct reference to an individual are like Russell's singular propositions in that they are intensional entities, but include nonintensional individuals rather than only concepts as constituents. Following a suggestion of Donnellan and Kaplan, we might represent one of Russell's singular propositions as an ordered couple consisting of an individual and a property, or more generally as a sequence of $n + 1$ terms consisting of n individuals and an n-ary relation. In conformity with this mode of representation, an intrinsically relational property might be represented as a sequence of n terms consisting of $n - 1$ individual relata and the relevant n-ary relation, the initial sequence of relata numbering one less than the number of places in the relation. The property of *studying under* α, where 'α' directly denotes Bertrand Russell, is thus represented as the ordered couple

⟨ Russell, the *studies under* relation ⟩,

and the proposition that directly predicates this property of Ludwig Wittgenstein is represented as the sequence[19]

⟨ Wittgenstein, Russell, the *studies under* relation ⟩.

Let us say that a descriptional singular term is *relationally descriptional,* or simply *relational,* if some of the expressed descriptional conditions involve direct reference to an individual, and let us say that it is *thoroughly descriptional* otherwise.[20] We shall also say

---

[19]This sequence representing the proposition may be "parsed" in either of two ways:

⟨Wittgenstein⟩⌐⟨Russell, *studing under*⟩,

indicating a simple single-subject-monadic-predicate analysis, and

⟨Wittgenstein, Russell⟩⌐⟨*studying under*⟩,

indicating a binary relational analysis.

[20]Cf. Adams, 1979. The definitions of a general *property* and of a *thoroughly descriptional* term are intended to have a provisional status. They will be modified in Section 4.1 to accommodate properties whose standard specifications involve nondescriptional general terms.

that a relational descriptional term is descriptional *relative to* the thing or things to which its expressed properties involve direct reference. Descriptional expressions involving nondescriptional singular term components are relationally descriptional. Descriptional expressions that express only general properties are thoroughly descriptional.

If α is a nondescriptional singular term which denotes an individual i, then the open formula $\ulcorner x = \alpha \urcorner$ "expresses" a special kind of property. This property is what Robert Adams, following Duns Scotus, calls the *haecceity* ("thisness") of i. It is the property of *being this very thing i*, which is represented by the ordered couple $\langle i, \text{identity} \rangle$.[21]

1.4. Orthodox Theories and the Theory of Direct Reference

A descriptional theory of singular terms would hold that all singular terms, and in particular even proper names and demonstratives, are descriptional. Frege seems to have held a particularly strong version of this theory. Whether he held that all proper names are synonymous with definite descriptions is a moot point. Whatever his view about the matter, it seems clear that he held that all proper names are thoroughly descriptional. On Frege's theory, if 'St. Anne' is analyzable as 'the mother of Mary', it must be in some sense analyzable even further, since the name 'Mary' is also supposed to be descriptional, whether or not it has a synonym in some definite description. But even 'the mother of the mother of Jesus' must be, in this sense, further analyzable, in view of the occurrence of the name 'Jesus', and so on. Refinements of Frege's original theory such as those suggested by Searle or Linsky do not make any significant departure from this fundamental Fregean thesis. Thoroughly descriptional terms are precisely the sorts of terms for which the three kinds of "sense" collapse, and so it is that any Fregean theory

---

[21]This property should not be confused with the nonrelational property of *being self-identical*, or self-identity, denoted formally by the expression '$\lambda x[x = x]$', where 'λ' is used as a variable-binding property abstraction operator ("the property of *being an individual x such that* ..."). The property of self-identity is a universal general property, one had by every individual whatsoever. The haecceity of a particular individual i, on the other hand, is an intrinsically relational *particularized* property, one had only by the individual i and nothing else. An individual "occurs in" its haecceity "as a constituent," whereas self-identity is a purely general property, if anything is.

of the reference of proper names involves the positing of a highly structured and theory-laden notion of *sense.*[22]

A more precise statement of the primary and central thesis of the theory of singular direct reference propounded by Donnellan, Kaplan, Kripke, and others can now be given: It is precisely that certain singular terms which are alleged by the orthodox theory to be thoroughly descriptional, in particular proper names and indexical singular terms, are in fact entirely nondescriptional—unless they are descriptional only in the trivial sense of being relationally descriptional in terms of the special property of *being x,* where *x* is the referent of the term. Thus, for instance, the theory of direct reference would hold that a proper name like 'Shakespeare' is not shorthand for any description such as 'England's greatest bard', but is in fact entirely nondescriptional, or else descriptional only in terms of Shakespeare's nonqualitative haecceity, his property of *being that very individual.* A strong version of the theory holds that names and indexical singular terms are altogether nondescriptional, period, and not even descriptional in terms of the property of *being this particular individual.* It is this strong version of the theory which is usually intended, and with which the present work is chiefly concerned.[23]

In either case, the central thesis of the direct reference theory,

[22]Russell's theory of what he calls *logically genuine proper names* admits the existence of a few nondescriptional names for special items to which a speaker has intimate epistemic access: private sensations, ideas, universals, and perhaps oneself. This would apparently allow for the possibility of relationally descriptional designators were it not that his Theory of Descriptions, taken as a solution to the puzzles of reference, involves an ultimate elimination of all singular terms other than individual variables and a very select group of additional nondescriptional names (see 1905; 1911; 1912, chapter V, pp. 46–59; and 1918). If one retained Russell's theory of logically genuine proper names while rejecting his Theory of Descriptions—a move which Stephen Schiffer (1978) at least partially endorses—there would be the result that such common sorts of singular terms as demonstratives, proper names, and definite descriptions, in ordinary use, are either thoroughly descriptional or descriptional relative only to items of direct epistemic acquaintance. This theory, though an important attempt to maintain some of the spirit of the naive view of Mill in the face of the puzzles of reference, is Fregean enough in spirit so that it too is rejected by the direct reference theory.

[23]The clearest statement of Kripke's view to be found in 1972a is at pp. 127–128, 134–135. His n. 66, p. 128, is especially important for an understanding of the view Kripke is opposing. In these passages and the surrounding text, the emphasis on the relevance of properties indicates that Kripke's arguments are aimed primarily at something like the thesis that names are nondescriptional. See also Kripke, 1979b, p. 240, and Donnellan, 1974a, pp. 227–228 of Schwartz, 1977. The alternative view that names express haecceities is put forward by Lockwood, 1971 and 1975.

whether it be the weak or strong version, does not entail a rejection of any one of the three kinds of sense mentioned above for singular terms, though it is significantly anti-Fregean. Fregean theories involve the strong thesis that singular terms are not only descriptional, but thoroughly so. Against this Donnellan, Kaplan, and Kripke show that many singular terms not only are not thoroughly descriptional; they are altogether nondescriptional. An immediate consequence is that even a great many definite descriptions, perhaps even most, fail to be thoroughly descriptional, since so many contain proper names or indexicals such as 'my', 'this', or 'that'.

The primary thesis of the theory of direct reference is significantly stronger than a simple denial of Russell's thesis that proper names and indexical singular terms, when used in ordinary contexts, are synonymous with definite descriptions.[24] Names and demonstratives not only are not synonymous with definite descriptions; they are not even similar. On the other hand, the primary thesis of the direct reference theory does not involve a denial of any of the three kinds of sense for proper names and indexical singular terms mentioned above. Kripke does not argue in *Naming and Necessity* that names do not evoke certain concepts in the minds of speakers who have learned the name. Nor does he argue there that names make no contribution, beyond their reference, to beliefs and assertions whose expression involves the name, and it is doubtful that he would want to.[25] He certainly does not want to argue that there is nothing by means of which the reference of a name is secured or semantically determined. He clearly does endorse the thesis that names lack sense if "sense" is something that is simultaneously the conceptual content, the semantical method of determining reference, and the cognitive content, all at once.

2. THE ARGUMENTS

A number or arguments have been advanced in favor of the central thesis of the theory of singular direct reference. Although the arguments are many and varied, most of them may be seen as falling under one of three main kinds: modal arguments, epistemological arguments, and semantical arguments. These arguments are usually stated for individual cases, but from them the reader can easily

---

[24]See 1911, p. 216; 1912, p. 54; 1918, pp. 200–201, 243–248 of 1956.

[25]Kripke, in 1973b, discusses the question of what we are calling the sense₃ of a name. See also 1972a, pp. 20–21.

abstract a general argument that may be applied to other proper names or indexical singular terms.

2.1. The Modal Arguments

The modal arguments are due chiefly to Kripke. Consider the name 'Shakespeare' as used to refer to the famous English dramatist.[26] Consider now the properties which someone—the speaker, the audience, someone in the general linguistic community, a Fregean semanticist, a philosopher who bears the ancestral of the *graduate student* relation to Carnap—might associate with the name as forming its sense on a particular occasion. These properties might include Shakespeare's distinguishing characteristics, or the criteria by which we identify Shakespeare, such properties as *being a famous English poet and playwright of the late 16th and early 17th centuries;* authorship of several classic plays including *Hamlet, Macbeth,* and *Romeo and Juliet;* partnership in the Globe Theatre; and so on. Note that this list may even include relational properties, as long as it does not include Shakespeare's haecceity, his property of *being this very individual.* The latter property is not the sort of property that Frege or his followers would propose as forming part of the sense of a name. The Fregean will regard any relational property occurring in this list as a *general* property, in the sense defined above.

Suppose then that the name 'Shakespeare' simply means "the person, whoever he or she may be, having these properties," or for simplicity, "the English playwright who wrote *Hamlet, Macbeth,* and *Romeo and Juliet.*" That is, suppose for the purpose of a *reductio* that the Fregean is correct and that the name is descriptional in terms of these properties. Consider now the following sentences.

> Shakespeare, if he exists, wrote *Hamlet, Macbeth,* and *Romeo and Juliet.*

> If anyone is an English playwright who is sole author of *Hamlet, Macbeth,* and *Romeo and Juliet,* then he is Shakespeare.

[26]Strictly speaking, each of the arguments applies to a proper name or indexical singular term *as it is used in a particular possible context.* This is important not only for indexicals such as 'I', 'you' or 'this', which systematically vary their reference with the context, but also for proper names such as 'Salmon', which may be the name for two or more individuals at once.

If the orthodox theory of names is correct, then by substituting for the name its longhand synonym we find that these two sentences taken together simply mean: Someone is the English playwright who wrote *Hamlet, Macbeth,* and *Romeo and Juliet* if and only if he is the English playwright who wrote *Hamlet, Macbeth,* and *Romeo and Juliet.* That is, if the descriptional theory is correct, the sentences displayed above should express *logical truths*—indeed they should be *analytic* sentences in the traditional sense—and should therefore express necessary truths, propositions true with respect to all possible worlds. But surely, the argument continues, it is not at all *necessary* that someone is Shakespeare if and only if he is an English playwright who wrote *Hamlet, Macbeth,* and *Romeo and Juliet.* In the first place, it might have come to pass that Shakespeare existed but never came to write these works. It might have to come to pass that Shakespeare elected to enter a profession in law instead of becoming a writer and dramatist. Certainly, this is a possibility. Hence, the first sentence displayed above does not express a necessary truth. There are possible circumstances with respect to which it is false. Furthermore, assuming Shakespeare had gone into law instead of drama, it could have come to pass that some Englishman other than Shakespeare, say Francis Bacon, should go on to write these plays. That is, it is not impossible that someone other than Shakespeare should write these plays.[27] Hence even the second sentence displayed above expresses only a contingent truth. It follows that the name 'Shakespeare' is not descriptional in terms of the properties mentioned.[28]

---

[27] I ignore here, because irrelevant, the intuition that some may have that the actual authorship of a work of literature is an essential characteristic of the work, so that even if Bacon had originally written a play entitled '*Hamlet*' that is word-for-word identical with the actual play of Shakespeare's, it would not be the very same play as Shakespeare's actual play, but a qualitative duplicate. This feature of the argument employed here can be avoided by changing examples. More importantly, the descriptional theorist may not rely on this intuition to block the argument without surrendering the theory. For a Fregean, the title '*Hamlet*' is a thoroughly descriptional term denoting the play solely by way of certain general properties of the play, properties which Bacon's duplicate would also have if it were written in lieu of Shakespeare's.

[28] On the "cluster" descriptional theory of Searle, the first of the two displayed sentences does not express an analytic truth. Nevertheless, a modified version of the modal argument still applies. One can replace the first sentence with the following:

> Shakespeare, if he exists, either wrote *Hamlet* or wrote *Macbeth* or wrote *Romeo and Juliet* or. . . .

(footnote continued next page)

The intuition that the two sentences displayed above are false with respect to certain possible worlds supports and is supported by a complementary intuition. The intuition is that the name 'Shakespeare' continues to denote the same person even with respect to counterfactual situations in which this individual lacks all of the distinguishing characteristics that we actually use to identify him. Since the name 'Shakespeare' continues to denote the same individual even in discourse about a counterfactual situation in which not he but some other Englishman wrote *Hamelet, Macbeth,* and *Romeo and Juliet,* the two sentences displayed above must be false in such discourse. Thus the main intuition behind the modal arguments is intimately connected with a related linguistic intuition concerning the denotation of proper names and indexical singular terms with respect to other possible worlds.

There is a weakness in the modal arguments; they show only that names and indexical singular terms are not descriptional in terms of the simple sorts of properties that come readily to mind, properties like the authorship of a certain work. This is a significant finding in itself; these are just the sorts of properties that Frege himself cites as giving the sense of a name for an individual user.[29] But faced with the

---

Since on the cluster view 'Shakespeare' means something like "the individual who did *sufficiently many* of these things," this weaker sentence should express an analytic truth even on the cluster view. But surely, the argument goes, it might have been the case that Shakespeare existed without carrying out *any* of the important achievements that are actually attributed to him. Similar modifications are needed in the epistemological and semantical arguments when applied against the cluster theory. For the sake of clarity, these niceties will be omitted from the statements of the arguments in the text. The modifications are straightforward and may be easily made by the reader. The arguments concerning the second of the two sentences apply equally against the cluster theory without modification.

The argument as formulated here may seem open to the common objection, first suggested by Dummett in 1973, pp. 112–116, that proper names are descriptional terms that ordinarily (or always) take "widest scope," i.e., that ordinarily occur outside of the scope of any modal operator when the containing sentence is perspicuously formalized. This feature of the general argument is removed, as Kripke had already noted (1972a, pp. 61–62), by formulating the argument entirely in the formal mode and speaking everywhere of the truth or falsehood with respect to various possible worlds of a nonmodal sentence, or alternatively of the truth or falsehood in a possible world of the proposition actually expressed by the nonmodal sentence, in place of using the corresponding material-mode modal operator formulations. This use of semantic ascent removes the modal operators, and thus removes any considerations of scope. See Kripke, 1972a, pp. 10–14, and Hudson and Tye, 1980.

[29]In 1892, n. 2, p. 58 of 1970; and in 1918, pp. 24–25.

modal arguments, some descriptional theorists, such as Linsky (1977, p. 84) and Plantinga (1978) have moved to fancier descriptions employing modally indexed properties, like the property of *actual* authorship of a certain work. It can hardly be objected in the style of the modal argument just considered that there are possible worlds in which Shakespeare does not *write-Hamlet-in-the-actual-world*. Shakespeare wrote *Hamlet* in the actual world, and it follows that it is necessary that Shakespeare *actually* wrote *Hamlet*. Thus the modal arguments seem ineffective against the thesis that proper names are descriptional in the Linsky way.

There are two serious problems with this move, however, problems which its initiators generally fail to acknowledge. First, as we shall see in Section 4.1, terms such as 'actual' are precisely the sorts of terms to which the theory of direct reference applies. The property of actual authorship of a certain work is not a purely qualitative property of the sort that the orthodox theory demands. Second, though the modal arguments may no longer apply to the modally indexed version of the descriptional theory, the epistemological and semantical arguments are unaffected by this recent epicycle on the orthodox theory.

2.2. The Epistemological Arguments

Consider again the two sentences

> Shakespeare, if he exists, wrote *Hamlet, Macbeth,* and *Romeo and Juliet,*

and

> If anyone is an English playwright who is sole author of *Hamlet, Macbeth,* and *Romeo and Juliet,* then he is Shakespeare.

As we know from the previous section, the orthodox theory alleges that these sentences are analytic in the traditional sense. Assuming that the orthodox theory is correct, it would follow that both of these sentences should convey information that is knowable *a priori,* i.e., knowable solely by reflection on the concepts involved and without recourse to sensory experience. If the name 'Shakespeare' were really descriptional in terms of such properties as these, it should be impossible to conceive that Shakespeare existed though he did not write any of these works, or that some one Englishman other than Shakespeare was responsible for each of these works. Imagining that

27

Shakespeare existed without these attributes should be as difficult as imagining a "married bachelor" or an "unmarried husband." Moreover, the consequence that these sentences convey *a priori* knowledge obtains even if the name 'Shakespeare' is held to be descriptional in terms of modally indexed properties. Even if the name 'Shakespeare' means something like "the individual, whoever he may be, who was *actually* an English playwright and who *actually* wrote *Hamlet, Macbeth,* and *Romeo and Juliet,*" it should still be knowable *a priori* that someone is Shakespeare if and only if he is the British playwright who wrote *Hamlet, Macbeth,* and *Romeo and Juliet.*[30] But it is not difficult to imagine circumstances in which it is discovered that, contrary to popular belief, Shakespeare did not write *Hamlet, Macbeth, Romeo and Juliet,* or any other work commonly attributed to him. Since this possibility is not automatically precluded by reflection on the concepts involved, it follows that the first sentence displayed above conveys information that is knowable only *a posteriori,* i.e., knowable only by recourse to sensory experience. One can even imagine circumstances in which it is discovered that we have been the victims of a massive hoax, and that, though Shakespeare is not responsible for any of these great works, some other Englishman, say Bacon, wrote every one of the plays and sonnets commonly attributed to Shakespeare. This means that even the second sentence displayed above is not analytic or true by definition, as alleged, but conveys genuine *a posteriori* information.

The similarity of the epistemological arguments to the modal arguments is obvious. We consider a particular proper name or indexical singular term α, as it is used in a particular possible context, and the properties $P_1, P_2, \ldots, P_n$ that might be associated with this particular use of the term α as giving its sense. If α were really descriptional in terms of these properties, then the unique possession of these properties should constitute a logically necessary and sufficient condition for being the denotation of the term. This should be true in the straightforward sense that the sentence

Someone is α if and only if he, she, or it is
the individual who Π_1 and Π_2 and ... and Π_n,

where $\Pi_1, \Pi_2, \ldots, \Pi_n$ are predicates expressing the properties $P_1, P_2, \ldots, P_n$, respectively, should be analytic, in the traditional sense, and

[30]This is true in virtue of the fact, argued for convincingly by Kaplan (1977), that $\ulcorner\phi$ if and only if it is actually the case that $\phi\urcorner$ is a truth of the logic of 'actually', and hence knowable *a priori.*

28

should therefore express a necessary and *a priori* truth. But we can imagine circumstances with respect to which even the weaker sentence

α either Π_1 or Π_2 or . . . or Π_n,

which must also be alleged to be analytic, is false, whereas

Someone other than α is the individual who Π_1 and Π_2 and . . . and Π_n

is true. Conclusion: The term α is not descriptional in terms of these properties.

2.3. The Semantical Arguments

We come now to the strongest and most persuasive of the three kinds of arguments for the primary thesis of the direct reference theory. These are the semantical arguments. Though offered in plenitude by Donnellan, Kaplan, Kripke, and Putnam, these are often the arguments most neglected by critics of the direct reference theory. One shining example is Donnellan's example concerning Thales.[31] Consider the set of properties which might be associated with the name 'Thales' as giving its sense according to the Fregean theory. Linsky, a Fregean critic of the direct reference theory, contends that the sense of a name like 'Thales' may be determined by one simple description, say 'the Greek philosopher who held that all is water'.[32] On the orthodox view, the name denotes whoever happens to satisfy this description. Suppose now that owing to some error or fraud the man referred to by writers such as Aristotle and Herodotus, from whom our use of the name 'Thales' derives, never genuinely believed that all is water. Suppose further that by a very strange coincidence there was indeed a Greek hermit-philosopher who did in fact hold this bizarre view, though he was unknown to them and bears no

---

[31]In 1972, pp. 373–375. A plethora of similar examples are given by Kripke in 1972a. A simple version of the semantical argument consists in pointing out examples of names for which there is no plausible set of properties that users of the name could be expected to rely upon in order to secure reference. See for instance Kaplan, 1973a, p. 516, n. 8.

[32]In 1977, p. 95. In cases of names of famous historical figures about whom the user of the name has little information ('Thales', 'Homer', 'St. Anne'), Linsky contends that the name is nearly synonymous with a simple definite description containing what little information the user has. The only difference in such cases between the name and the description, on Linsky's view, is that the name rigidly denotes whoever happens to satisfy the description.

historical connection to us. To which of these two philosophers would our name 'Thales' refer? This is a clear semantical question with a clear answer. The name would refer to Thales, the first of the two. Our use of the name would bear no significant connection to the second character whatsoever. It is only by way of a comical accident that he enters into the story at all.

This example is not to be confused with the corresponding modal or epistemological arguments ("Thales might not have been the Greek philosopher who held that all is water"). In the modal and epistemological arguments, the main question is what the truth-value of a sentence like 'Thales is the Greek philosopher who held that all is water', which is alleged to be true by definition, becomes when the sentence is evaluated with respect to certain imagined circumstances that are possible in either a metaphysical or an epistemic sense. The strategy in the semantical arguments is more direct. The issue here is not whom the name *actually* denotes *with respect to* the imagined circumstances; the issue is whom the name *would* denote if the circumstances described above *were to obtain.* The modal arguments are indirectly related to the question of what a particular term denotes *with respect to another possible world;* the semantical arguments are directly concerned with the nonmodal question of denotation *simpliciter.* The key phrase in the definition of a descriptional singular term is not 'denote with respect to a possible world', but 'whoever or whatever uniquely has the properties'. On any descriptional theory of names, precisely whom a name denotes depends entirely on whoever happens to have certain properties uniquely. The theory predicts that, if these circumstances were to obtain, the name would denote the hermit instead of Thales, and Linsky explicitly acknowledges that he is prepared to accept such consequences as this.[33] But here the theory is simply mistaken. The

---

[33] In 1977, p. 109. Linsky says that his sense for the name 'Thales' is determined by the description 'the Eleatic philosopher who believed that all is water', a description which, he says, "exhausts my information" (p. 95). Charles Parsons has pointed out to me that this description does not even denote Thales, since Thales was not from Elea, but from Miletus. Here then is an actual case in point. If we assume that Linsky's theory of names is correct, it will follow that, in using the name 'Thales', Linsky has probably been referring to no one, and if it should turn out that there was an Eleatic philosopher unknown to us who endorsed Thales' doctrine that all is water, Linsky's reference all along has been to this unknown Eleatic instead of Thales. Can we really accept these consequences?

existence of the hermit philosopher would be irrelevant to the denotation associated with our use of the name 'Thales'.

2.4. *Contextual Factors in Reference*

The theory that proper names and indexical singular terms are either nondescriptional or else descriptional in terms of haecceities, and even the stronger theory that these singular terms are entirely nondescriptional, should not be understood as involving the thesis that no descriptional concepts or properties, other than haecceities, are ever semantically associated with names or indexicals. Indeed all of the proponents of the direct reference theory allow that some nondescriptional terms may be "defined," or introduced into a language or idiolect, precisely by way of expressions having this sort of descriptional sense. In this special kind of definition the descriptional expression serves only to assign a denotation to the term being introduced, and does not simultaneously bequeath its sense to the new term. To use Kripke's apt phrase, the descriptional expression is used only to "fix the reference" of the nondescriptional term, and not to supply it with a Fregean sense.

This admission that there may sometimes be descriptional elements at work in fixing the designation of a term of the sort in question is generally coupled with the observation that there are almost always nondescriptional contextual elements at work as well. The semantical arguments reveal something about the nature of what we have called 'sense$_2$'. The sense$_2$ of a name, the way its reference is determined, is not a purely conceptual matter. External factors enter into it. The surrounding settings in which speakers find themselves are crucial to determining the designation of the names and other terms they use. This is true not only of the extralinguistic setting in which the referent is to be found, but also of the linguistic setting in which the term is used or was learned by the speaker, i.e., the history of the use of the name leading up to the speaker's acquisition of it. In a word, sense$_2$ is a *contextual* phenomenon. Donnellan (1972 and 1974a) and Kripke (1972a) provide accounts of proper name denotation by means of such historical chains of communication. Putnam (1973a, 1975a, and 1975b) gives a similar account for natural kind terms designating something by means of a "division of linguistic labor" and a "structured cooperation between experts and nonexperts." It is by virtue of these accounts that the theory of direct reference is often called the "causal" theory of reference. But causal factors are not the only external factors involved in determining reference—or at any rate, it is an independent philosophical thesis that all of these external factors in reference are reducible to causal phenomena (cf. Kim, 1977). It would be better to call the theory the *contextual* theory of reference—thereby including Kaplan's nondescriptional theory of indexicals, a theory that has several points in contact with the thories of reference of Donnellan, Kripke, and Putnam. By contrast, the orthodox theory of reference claims that names refer to someone or something entirely by way of associated general properties, leaving no room in its account for either the linquistic or the extralinguistic context. Thus Putnam writes: "Traditional semantic theory leaves out two contributions to the determination of reference—the contribution of society and the contribution of the real world; a better semantic theory must encompass both" (1973b, p. 711).

Linsky is correct to point out (1977, p. 110) that contextual factors such as those mentioned by the direct reference theorists have little or nothing to do with the graspable conceptual content associated with the name. The sense$_2$ of a name is not something purely conceptual, but something contextual. If a full-blown Fregean *sense* is what is wanted, such a thing as sense$_2$ simply will not do.[34]

3. RIGID DESIGNATORS

3.1. *Two Kinds of Rigid Designators: Persistence and Obstinacy*

We saw in Section 2.1 that the modal arguments for the theory of singular direct reference rely on modal intuitions that are intimately related to the pre-theoretical intuition that a particular proper name or indexical continues to denote the same individual even in discourse about certain counterfactual situations, whereas the orthodox Fregean theories come into conflict with this intuition. The direct reference theorists offer an alternative that conforms with this intuition.

One important consequence of the theory of singular direct reference is that expressions such as proper names and indexical singular

---

[34]The natures of the three kinds of "sense" given above, and their relations to one another, are further discussed briefly in Salmon, 1979a.

terms are so-called 'rigid designators'.[35] The phrase 'rigid designator' was coined by Kripke and is currently widely used, but unfortunately there are at least three distinct notions of a rigid designator that may be found in the literature.[36] The most familiar notion, perhaps, is the most general of the three: An expression is a rigid designator if it designates the same thing with respect to every possible world in which that thing exists (Kripke, 1972a, pp. 48–49). It is this usage of 'rigid designator' that shall be adhered to in the present work.

Two kinds of rigid designators, in this sense, may be distinguished. Perhaps the most frequently intended notion of a rigid designator is that of an expression which designates the same thing with respect to every possible world in which that thing exists, and which designates nothing with respect to possible worlds in which that thing does not

---

[35]Strictly speaking, of course, it is not a *logical truth* that a singular term is rigid if it is nondescriptional. One could consistently allow the denotation of a nondescriptional singular term to vary from possible world to possible world. But if nondescriptional singular terms are represented formally by syntactically unstructured individual constants, then it is natural to treat them as having a fixed denotation for all possible worlds. Carnap, for instance, treated individual constants in this way (1947, pp. 180–181). Although a number of systematic ways can be devised to vary the denotation of an individual constant from possible world to possible world, to do so seems arbitrary and artificial. As is most obvious in the clearest case of a nondescriptional singular term—the free variable whose denotation is fully and directly determined by an assignment of values to variables—there is no reason to suppose that the denotation of a nondescriptional term should change with respect to different possible worlds. The situation is quite different for syntactically and semantically structured singular terms such as definite descriptions, which naturally suggest, by way of their syntactic and semantic structure, a systematic and nonarbitrary way of varying denotation from possible world to possible world. In the case of nondescriptional singular terms, there is no such possible-world-relative process for determining denotation. Proper names do not denote by, so to speak, rummaging through the individuals in a possible world seeking anyone or anything uniquely meeting certain conditions. Hence, there remains no reason to expect the denotation to vary from one world to the next. Instead, one may think of the denotation as being fixed for all time and for all possibilities by an initial dubbing ceremony, or an assignment of values to variables, etc. Contra Linsky and Plantinga, it is not a rich semantical structure that makes for the intensional monotony of a proper name, but the absence of semantical structure altogether.

[36]Dummett (1973, p. 126), Linsky (1977, p. 51), and Putnam (1973b, p. 707) each define yet a fourth notion of rigid designator, distinct from each of the three notions given here. They call a designating expression a *rigid designator* if it designates the same thing with respect to every possible world with respect to which the expression designates anything at all. It is likely, however, that these authors do not intend to be proposing a different notion from the one intended by Kripke.

exist (Kripke, 1971, p. 146). In order to distinguish this special case from our more general notion, let us say that such expressions are *persistently rigid designators,* or simply *persistent designators.*

Another sort of rigid designator is an expression which designates the same thing with respect to every possible world, period. Let us call expressions of this sort *obstinately rigid designators,* or simply *obstinate designators.*[37] Obstinate designators may be insensitive to the question of whether their designata exist in a given possible world; they designate the same thing with respect to every possible world, whether that thing exists there or not.

Given any singular term α we may consider the semantical function which assigns to any possible world the denotation of α with respect to that possible world. Carnap (1947, pp. 181–182) called this function the *intension* of α. Using this idea we may characterize the distinction between persistence and obstinacy by noting that the semantical intension of an obstinate term is a *total* constant function on the domain of possible worlds, whereas the semantical intension of a persistent term is a constant function which is undefined for possible worlds in which its constant value does not exist, and hence may be a *partial* function on the domain of possible worlds.

By definition, persistent designators and obstinate designators are rigid designators in the general sense. Kripke calls an expression a *strongly rigid designator* if it is a rigid designator of a necessary existent, that is, if it rigidly designates something that exists in every possible world. A designator is strongly rigid if and only if it is both persistent and obstinate. Mathematical descriptions, such as 'the even prime integer', may be examples of strongly rigid designators. But no persistent designator of a contingent entity can be an obstinate designator of that same contingent entity.

Definite descriptions such as 'the even prime integer' and '$(\imath x)\ [([x + 2 = 5] \wedge p) \vee ([2x = 6] \wedge \sim p)]$' illustrate that even descriptional designators may in some cases turn out to be rigid. Kripke calls such expressions rigid *de facto,* as to be distinguished

---

[37]Kaplan seems to anticipate this notion where he writes: "we should restrict our attention to a smaller class of names; names which are so intimately connected with what they name that they could not but name it. I shall say that such a name *necessarily denotes* its object . . ." (1969, p. 222).

Kaplan (1977, n. 5) suggests that the phenomenon which we call *obstinacy* is the intended notion, and that the other two definitions are confused misdescriptions of this intended notion. See the preface of the book edition of Kripke, 1972a, p. 21n.

34

from rigid *de jure,* or rigid by semantic stipulation.[38] By the very definition of a descriptional singular term, all rigid descriptional singular terms must be persistent. As we noted earlier, it is assumed throughout the present work that all definite descriptions are descriptional. In formal terms, we adopt the practice of restricting the domain over which individual variables range with respect to a given possible world w to the existent individuals of w. We also adopt the practice of treating definite descriptions that are improper with respect to a given possible world w as nondenoting with respect to w. This has the effect that singular terms formed from the variable-binding definite descriptions operator, $\imath$, can denote something with respect to a given possible world only if that thing exists in the given possible world. Thus, this formal treatment of definite descriptions has the effect that all rigid definite descriptions must be persistent. Even relationally descriptional singular terms, if rigid, must be persistent. If, for instance, a singular term α obstinately designates a contingent individual i, then even the rigid designator $\ulcorner(\imath x)\ (x = \alpha)\urcorner$ fails to denote anything with respect to the possible worlds in which the individual i does not exist. Similarly, if a definite description $\ulcorner(\imath x)\phi(x)\urcorner$ denotes a contingent individual i, then even the rigid designator

$$(\imath x)A\phi(x),$$

i.e., the unique individual who is, in *actuality,* such that ϕ, where 'A' is the sentential actuality operator, only persistently designates i. It is often convenient in modal contexts to be able to replace a nonobstinate singular term with a co-referential obstinate term, but on our treatment the definite descriptions-operator, even bolstered with the actuality operator, is not adequate for his purpose. Kaplan (1970) has invented an indexical operator, '*dthat*', which transforms any given singular term α into a rigid designator that, in a given context of utterance, obstinately designates whatever α designates with respect to that context. Thus, whereas the sentence

It is necessary that: the author of *Hamlet* is rational

makes the *de dicto* assertion that the writing of *Hamlet* could only have been achieved by a rational being, the sentence

---

[38]Kripke, 1972a, preface, p. 21n. Kripke's notion of rigidity *de facto* corresponds to our notion of descriptional rigidity, and his notion of rigidity *de jure* corresponds to our notion of nondescriptionality (modulo the qualifications of footnote 35 above).

> It is necessary that: *dthat*(the author of *Hamlet*) is rational

makes a *de re* assertion about the actual author of *Hamlet*. The latter sentence asserts a necessary property of Shakespeare, of *that very individual,* to wit, that he is such that it would have been impossible for him to have been irrational. We shall make use of this operator in several places throughout this book.

3.2. *Proper Names, Nondescriptionality, and Obstinacy*

Issues concerning the differences between persistent and obstinate designators are given their sharpest focus in the work of Kaplan. Kaplan has argued compellingly (1977) that nondescriptional singular terms are obstinately rigid designators, and that indexicals and proper names are nondescriptional. Earlier (1973a, appendix X, pp. 503–505) he had already argued that proper names are obstinate designators.

The case that nondescriptional designators are obstinate is supported by the clearest example of nondescriptionality, free occurrences of individual variables. Kaplan aptly criticizes the prejudice that the denotation of a singular term must be an element of the domain over which bound occurrences of individual variables range. As we have already seen, the denotation with respect to a given possible world of a free occurrence of an individual variable under an assignment of values to variables is determined nondescriptionally by the assignment of values to variables.[39] Any feature of the given

---

[39]The reason for this involves certain niceties of ordinary Tarski-style semantics. In order to evaluate a closed modal sentence such as

> Necessarily, something is such that possibly, it has ϕ,

we must first evaluate the closed sentence

> Something is such that possibly, it has ϕ,

with respect to every possible world w. In order to do this we must carry the existent objects of w over into other possible worlds accessible to w—whether that object exists there or not—and determine whether or not the object satisfies the open expression

> _____ has ϕ

with respect to the new possible world. In general, the assignment of values to variables under which an open expression is to be semantically evaluated is determined as part of the process of semantic evaluation of a closed containing expression. For the purpose of evaluating the second closed sentence above with respect to w, the question of whether a given object has ϕ in a given possible world is raised only in connection with those objects that exist in w. An object existing in w is singled out for semantic possible world, including the question of whether the assigned value exists in that world, is strictly irrelevant. The value of an individual variable under an assignment of values to variables remains constant regardless of the choice of possible world with respect to which the variable is evaluated. Just as the value of a free variable with respect to a given possible world need not be in the domain over which bound variables range with respect to that possible world, the "existent" objects of that world, so generally the denotation of any nondescriptional designator with respect to a given possible world need not be among the existing objects of that world. Nondescriptional designators do not look to the qualitative aspects of a given possible world in determining a designatum, and there is no reason why they should look to the "quantitative" or ontological aspects either. In light of these considerations, we may conclude with Kaplan that nondescriptional singular terms are obstinately rigid.

Kaplan's case that proper names are obstinate employs the now widely recognized close analogy between the formal semantics for quantified tensed languages and modal languages. If we evaluate the sentence

Nathan Salmon is dead,

we shall find that it is false with respect to the year 1980 but becomes true with respect to any time after my death. Does the proper name 'Nathan Salmon' denote anyone with respect to, say, the 22nd century? It is assumed that I cease to exist when I die. On the usual theories of the truth-value of a simple subject-predicate sentence containing a nondenoting subject term, we should not expect the sentence displayed above to be true with respect to a future time if the name 'Nathan Salmon' denotes no one with respect to that time. But it is more natural, then, to say that the name 'Nathan Salmon' does indeed denote someone with respect to the 22nd century, namely me, Nathan Salmon. I am alive today, but I will someday be

---

evaluation with respect to possible worlds other than *w*. In Kripke-style semantics for quantified modal languages, variables serve as the devices which place a fix on objects from one world for evaluation with respect to other worlds. Variables, at least, are obstinate designators. See Kripke, 1963.

The account given here of the semantics for a modal language differs substantially from the counterpart theory set out by David Lewis (1968). For our present purpose counterpart semantical theories are to be regarded as nonstandard. One version of counterpart theory will be discussed and criticized briefly in Section 28.2. See Appendix I, footnote 16.

dead. The name 'Nathan Salmon' denotes someone who exists today but who will no longer exist in the 22nd century. It is precisely because the person denoted by 'Nathan Salmon' with respect to the 22nd century will be dead by that time that the sentence is true with respect to that time.

The same point can be made in connection with sentences which contain the name of a person and which are to be evaluated with respect to some time prior to that person's birth. Consider for instance the truth-conditions of a sentence like

John Locke anticipated Saul Kripke.[40]

In this case it is most natural to say that the proper name 'Saul Kripke' denotes the present-day philosopher Saul Kripke with respect to the year 1689 despite the fact that in 1689 he did not yet exist. This is not to say that the name 'Saul Kripke' was used in 1689 as a name for the present-day philosopher. The latter is surely a false historical claim. The notion of *denotation with respect to a time* is not an historical notion; it is a semantical notion. In 1689, the name 'Saul Kripke' was probably not in use, and it certainly was not used as a name of the present-day philosopher. The name is presently used to denote that philosopher, and it is presently used to denote him even in discourse about events that took place in 1689, long before his birth. In fact, the name is presently used to denote him with respect to every time, past, present, and future. Exactly similar considerations lead to the conclusion that indexical singular terms such as 'I', 'you', and 'she', if used successfully in a particular context (i.e., if used with a reference), denote the same thing with respect to every time.

By analogy, just as a proper name or an indexical singular term denotes its present referent with respect to past and future times, a proper name or indexical singular term, assuming it is rigid at all, also denotes its actual referent with respect to every possible world, including those worlds in which the actual referent does not exist. This is not to make an essentialist claim about the name itself, e.g., that the name 'Saul Kripke' is such that it *must* be used as a name of the actual philosopher, even if he had never existed. The latter claim is patently false. If there were no language speakers in existence, and Kripke did not exist, then the name 'Saul Kripke' would not be used as a name at all. Even if there were speakers of English, it is difficult

[40]See Mackie, 1974, where this claim is made.

to imagine how these speakers would come to use the name 'Saul Kripke' as a name for Kripke, as distinct from all the other merely possible individuals, if he had never existed in any form.[41] We ually use the name as a name of an actual person, and we use the name to refer to him even in discourse about counterfactual situations in which he may not exist (or may not go by that name), as in the sentence:

It might have come to pass that Kripke was never born.

According to the theory of singular direct reference, proper names and indexical singular terms are either nondescriptional or descriptional in terms of the haecceity of the term's denotation, the property of *being this very individual.* Singular terms that are thus descriptional in terms of haecceities are persistent. We have seen the argument that nondescriptional singular terms are obstinate. (See footnote 35 above.) Thus it is a consequence of the theory of singular direct reference that proper names and indexical singular terms are

---

[41]For more on this pragmatic difficulty in naming merely possible individuals, see Kaplan, 1973a, pp. 505–508. Here (pp. 517, n. 19) Kaplan toys with the view that in certain rare cases a merely possible object can be uniquely specified, and hence named—namely, whenever the parts that would constitute the object actually do exist and are specifiable. Thus, for instance, we may consider the person who *would have* developed from the union of *this* sperm and *that* egg, had they been united, and name this individual 'Noman'. Both Kaplan and Kripke, in lecture and in conversation, have taken this position. (This view presupposes principles that allow for the identification of individuals made from the same matter, or of the same constituent parts, in different possible worlds. Such principles are discussed in Appendix I below.) Tempting though it is, there is an apparent difficulty with this view. Taken at face value, it apparently implies, by existential generalization (in the metalanguage), that there are, i.e., there exist, objects that do not exist. Hence, the position threatens to be contradictory. This difficulty might be avoided by reinterpreting the claim that " 'Noman' denotes the merely possible individual who would have resulted if sperm S had fertilized egg E " as the counterfactual claim that "if S had fertilized E, then it would have been the case that: some individual x results and 'Noman' actually denotes x," or something similar. The latter claim is baffling, but it avoids explicit ontological commitment to a merely possible individual. It asserts only that *there might have been* a person resulting from the fertilization of E by S, and apparently avoids asserting that *there is in fact* a possible individual, denoted by 'Noman', who does not exist but might have existed. Take special notice. The claim is not merely that there might have been someone denoted by 'Noman'. That is a trivial claim which fails to capture the intent. The claim is that there might have been someone who does not actually exist, but *actually is* denoted by 'Noman'. It is mysterious, though, how it can be that while there is no one actually denoted by 'Noman', there still *might have* existed someone who not only would have been, but *actually is,* denoted by 'Noman'.

either persistently or obstinately rigid. In either case, they are rigid designators, in the general sense used here.

We have also seen Kaplan's argument by systematic analogy to temporal semantics that proper names and indexical singular terms, if rigid at all, are obstinately rigid. A descriptional singular term that rigidly designates a contingently existing object must be persistent and cannot be obstinate. Proper names and indexical singular terms can obviously be used to refer to contingent objects. Thus Kaplan's argument by analogy, which is separate and supplementary to the initial arguments for the theory of singular direct reference, leads directly to the strong version of the theory according to which proper names and indexical singular terms are entirely nondescriptional.

3.3. A Criterion for Obstinacy

If α is an obstinately rigid singular term, we can express the fact that α is obstinate in the object language by a modal sentence with the logical form:

(1) $(\exists y)\square[\alpha = y]$.

If β is any singular term co-referential with α (with respect to the actual world), we can further express in the object language *what α obstinately denotes* using β. One way of doing this makes use of the familiar Russellian device of scope and "quantification in":

(2) $(\exists y)(y = \beta \wedge \square[\alpha = y])$.

Another way to express in the object language the fact that α obstinately denotes the referent of β makes use of Kaplan's indexical operator, '*dthat*':[42]

(3) $\square[\alpha = dthat(\beta)]$.

---

[42]One difference between either (1) or (2) and (3) might be that (3) allows for the prospect of an obstinate designator for a merely possible entity that does not actually exist, whereas (1) and (2) do not. Still, (1) and (2) provide sufficient conditions for the obstinacy of α. Sentences (1) and (2) can be prefixed with the possibility operator to accomodate the more general notion of obstinacy. For present purposes, the special situation of reference to the merely possible may be safely ignored.

It is important to note that as we shall be using the phrase, any instance of (1), (2), or (3) involves what we call a *commitment to essentialism with respect to an haecceity*. Since these may be taken as object language assertions to the effect that the singular term α is rigid, and since it is part of the theory of direct reference that certain singular terms are rigid, it will follow that the theory of direct reference involves a commitment to a special form of essentialism. This will be made clearer below in Sections 7 and 8.

Both (2) and (3) employ the necessitation of an identity sentence in which one term is α and the other an obstinately rigid designator. Sentences with the logical form of either (2) or (3) may be used in the object language as stipulative "definitions" (in a loose sense of 'definition') that fix the reference of α as an obstinately rigid designator. Indeed, if we assume that the object language allows for the well-formedness either of sentences of the form of (2) or of sentences of the form of (3), then since a singular term α obstinately denotes what a singular term β denotes if and only if a sentence of the form of either (2) or (3) is true, the truth of a sentence of the form of either (2) or (3) may be taken as a *criterion* for α being an obstinately rigid singular term that denotes an individual i, where β is a singular term that denotes the individual i.[43] Of course, if one is interested only in fixing the reference of α without making explicit the further stipulation that α shall be obstinate, a simple identity sentence of the form

(4) $\qquad \alpha = \beta$

suffices. The sentence form (4) in conjunction with (1), the assertion that α is obstinate, is equivalent to (2).

---

[43]β need not be distinct from α. The truth of a sentence of the form $\ulcorner \Box [\alpha = dthat(\alpha)] \urcorner$ may be taken as a criterion for α being rigid, but taken as "definition" of α it is circular.

TWO · *The Theory Extended to General Terms*

4. A REFORMULATION OF THE THEORY

4.1. Descriptional General Terms

Although only singular terms have been discussed so far, the theory of direct reference is not only a theory of singular reference. It is also applicable to certain general terms, such as certain single-word natural kind common nouns ('water', 'tiger', etc.), and the theory may even be extended to certain single-word adjectives and verbs.[1] A general term, such as the noun 'tiger', does not purport to denote a single individual.[2] General terms are essentially predicative. Grammatically, a general term (in the singular) cannot ordinarily serve as the subject of a sentence, and one is prohibited from existentially generalizing on occurrences of the term in sentences. In the sentence

Tony is a tiger

---

[1]Donnellan, Kripke, and Putnam all apply their arguments to natural kind terms. Kripke extends his account to terms for natural phenomena such as 'heat' (1971, pp. 158–160, and 1972a, pp. 131–137). Putnam extends his account to physical magnitude terms such as 'energy' (1973a, pp. 198–204 of Putnam 1975d), and to artifact terms such as 'pencil' (1975a, pp. 242–244). In addition, Kripke suggests that his account may be extended to certain natural phenomenon adjectives such as 'hot', 'loud', and 'red' (1972a, p. 134; see also p. 128, n. 66), while Putnam suggests that his account extends to certain adjectives such as 'red', to certain natural kind verbs such as 'grow', and to "the great majority of all nouns" (1975a, pp. 240, 242, 244). See also Chapter One, footnote 14 above.

[2]As we shall see below, Putnam may be understood as treating the mass noun 'water' as a general term that applies to any and all individual samples of water, as if the term were an abbreviation for some common noun phrase such as 'sample of water'. We shall follow Putnam's implicit treatment of mass nouns as general terms in our exposition of the direct reference theory of the designation of general terms. We remain neutral, however, regarding the question of whether mass nouns are singular terms denoting abstract universals (often chemical substances), or general terms applying to individual instances. (Indeed, mass nouns often seem schizophrenic, sometimes performing the function of a singular term, and sometimes that of a general term.) For background on the controversy over the syntactic and semantic status of mass nouns, see Burge, 1972; Parsons, 1970; and Quine, 1960, pp. 90–100.

42

the subject term 'Tony' is a singular term that purports to denote a single individual, and the speaker is committed, by his or her own words, to the existence of this individual. There do not seem to be any other ontological commitments contained in this sentence, as there are in the sentence

Tony is a member of the species *Tiger*.

The latter sentence contains an additional singular term that purports to denote a certain *kind* of animal, a certain abstract entity or *universal*. The sentence allows existential generalization on both occurrences of singular terms. A nominalist with respect to species may confidently assert the former sentence, but not the latter.

Our definition of a descriptional singular term suggests a similar definition for general terms. Let us call a general term τ *descriptional in the Carnap way* if there is associated with τ (as part of its sense$_{1'}$) a set of properties such that the *extension* of τ (the class of things to which τ applies) with respect to a possible world and a time is determined by semantics alone to be the class of things, whoever or whatever they are, which exist in that possible world at that time and which have all of these properties in that world at that time. Note that this definition for general terms differs from the earlier definition for singular terms only in that it mentions extension where the earlier definition mentions denotation. By altering this definition in the obvious way, one may similarly redefine the notions of *descriptional in the Linsky way, descriptional in the Searle way*, and so on, to cover general terms as well as singular terms. The notion of general descriptionality is then defined, as before, as the disjunction of all these notions. A descriptional general term is a term that applies by way of properties. It is a term which expresses a way of conceiving something or some kind of thing (as its sense$_{1'}$), and for which the extension, with respect to a possible world and a time, is secured indirectly by means of this "sense." The paradigm of a descriptional general term is a common noun *phrase*, such as 'ferocious, four-legged, tawny-coated, black-striped, cat-like creature'. Such common noun phrases are the general term analogue to definite descriptions, but, as in the case of singular terms, common noun phrases are not the only possible sorts of descriptional general terms. General "cluster terms," if indeed there are any (as argued by Putnam, 1966), are also descriptional.

As in the case of singular terms, the central and primary thesis of a strong version of the direct reference theory of general terms can be simply stated thus: Certain single-word common nouns which are alleged by the orthodox Fregean theory to be descriptional are in fact nondescriptional. Just as it is natural for the orthodox theorist of singular reference to adopt an analogous theory of *sense* for general terms, so it is natural that propounders of the theory of singular direct reference sketched in the previous chapter should endorse a corresponding thesis for general terms. If some (indeed a great many) singular terms manage to refer directly to some independently determined individual, without seeking whoever or whatever has certain properties, in order to allow the speaker to say (ask, etc.) something directly about *it*, then why shouldn't some common nouns also manage to *apply* to things directly, without using properties? As we shall soon see, this deceptively simple and obvious philosophy of semantics leads just as naturally, almost inexorably, into unexpected, and often surprising, philosophical theses.

Singular and general terms are not the only sorts of expressions with respect to which one may sensibly apply the terms 'descriptional' and 'nondescriptional'. Depending on the sort of language in question, such expressions as quantifiers and sentential operators may be descriptional, if for instance the sense of the expression determines by way of a sort of conceptual "description" the domain of quantification or the parameters relevant for semantic evaluation. One may sensibly ask whether the quantifier 'everyone' "describes" its domain of quantification, say, as the class of *persons*, or whether it nondescriptionally indicates its domain by way of direct semantical rules. Does the sentential actuality operator 'actually' describe the actual world, say as the only possible world that has the (nonrelational) ontological status of *being actual* ("in the actual world it is the case that")? Or does it directly and nondescriptionally indicate the actual world for semantic evaluation? Although the present work is concerned mainly with singular and general terms, the reader should bear in mind that the distinction between descriptional and nondescriptional expressions is pervasive, and that the theory of direct reference is similarly wide in its scope of application.

4.2. Common Nouns as Proper Names

The prospect that some common nouns may be nondescriptional suggests an imposing analogy to the case of proper names and singular reference. If a nondescriptional general term applies to some things but not others, then there must be *something* that the individuals in its extension have in common, by virtue of which the

44

term applies to them but not anything else, even though the term is nondescriptional. The objects in its extension must be *of the same kind*, and the term must be a nondescriptional label for things *of that kind*. Another way of putting what seems to be the same point is that a nondescriptional general term must be a label for a certain *kind* of thing. In fact, it is characteristic of the direct reference theory of general terms to speak of certain single-word common nouns almost as if they were proper names that refer to certain *kinds* of things. Natural kind terms, such as 'tiger' and 'water', are said to "designate" natural kinds, in much the same way that a proper name is said to "designate" its bearer. Thus in a manner similar to Carnap's use of the term, proper names and certain common nouns alike are classified as "designators."[3]

A thoroughgoing attempt to treat common nouns as names for kinds naturally suggests certain straightforward consequences. If a single-word common noun such as 'tiger' is thought of as analogous to a proper name *designating* the species *Tiger*, then there does not seem to be any reason why a common noun phrase such as 'female fox' should not in the same way be thought of as analogous to a singular term phrase, or to a singular definite description, *designating* a certain kind of animal by way of its properties. Once we count common noun phrases as expressions that designate kinds of things, we ought to be willing to generate kinds as liberally as language generates common noun phrases. This much is not immediately objectionable. We are often forced to single out certain kinds of individuals by way of cumbersome locutions, e.g., 'white Anglo-Saxon Protestant', although repeated usage generally results in the introduction of single-word abbreviations. This proposal to treat common nouns as names and to treat noun phrases as descriptions is even plausible. Natural kinds do, like people, play a central role in our lives, and it stands to reason that language in its evolution would see fit to reserve special names for these kinds of things while providing less specific linguistic devices, such as indexicals and descriptions, for reference to other things.

Consider now the common noun phrase 'member of a species that serves as mascot for Princeton University'.[4] What does it designate?

---

[3]See Carnap, 1947, p. 6; Kripke, 1972a, p. 24.

[4]Strictly speaking, Princeton University chose *the tiger* as its mascot, not the species *Tiger*. Sellars (1963) calls such entities as *the tiger, the whale,* etc. distributive individuals. For present purposes, the distinction between a distributive animal and its corresponding species is best ignored.

The obvious answer seems to be that it designates the "kind", or category, *Member of a Species that Serves as Mascot for Princeton University*. This is a certain kind of animal. Unlike a biological species or genus, it is not a natural kind. Of course, since the species *Tiger* is the only species that serves as mascot for Princeton University, tigers and only tigers are animals of this nonnatural kind. That is, the noun 'tiger' and the phrase 'member of a species that serves as mascot for Princeton University' have exactly the same semantical extension. Let us call the class of instances of an abstract universal (such as a kind or category) *k* the *metaphysical extension of k*. We say of common nouns and common noun phrases that they *designate* a certain *kind*. The *class* of entities of that kind is at once the *semantical* extension of the expression and the *metaphysical* extension of the kind.

The species *Tiger* and the nonnatural kind *Member of a Species that Serves as Mascot for Princeton University* have exactly the same metaphysical extension. But this fact is not sufficient to make the two kinds numerically identical. It is only a contingent fact that they coincide in metaphysical extension. From a broad metaphysical point of view, the coincidence in extension is merely a coincidence. Princeton might have chosen the raccoon as its mascot instead of the tiger. If it had, raccoons would be animals of the latter category, and tigers would not. The contingency of the connection between the term 'tiger' and the nonnatural kind or category *Member of a Species that Serves as Mascot for Princeton University* is a marked contrast with the relationship that obtains between 'tiger' and its alleged designatum, the species *Felis tigris*. The term 'tiger' applies to an animal only *by virtue of* the animal's being one of a certain natural kind. Formally, 'tiger' applies, with respect to any possible world and time, to all things that are members of that natural kind in the given world at the given time, and only to those things. As in the case of singular terms, given any general term τ we may consider the semantical function that assigns to any possible world the semantical extension of τ with respect to that world. Following Carnap let us call this function the *semantical intension* of τ. Given any abstract universal *k*, we may also consider the function that assigns to any possible world the class of instances of *k* in that world. Let us call this function the *metaphysical intension of k*. Then we may say that the semantical intension of the term 'tiger' is precisely the same function as the metaphysical intension of the species *Felis tigris*. Despite a common metaphysical extension, the species *Felis tigris* differs in metaphysical intension from the nonnatural kind *Member of a Species that Serves as Mascot for Princeton University*. The latter, but not the former, might have included all raccoons, and only raccoons, among its members. Therefore, the two kinds are numerically distinct.[5]

It apparently follows from this that if common nouns and common noun phrases designate kinds, then co-designative common nouns and common noun phrases must be not only co-extensional but also co-intensional. This seems to be a natural consequence of the proposal to treat common nouns as designators of kinds, for it seems that the semantical intension of a common noun phrase must coincide with what we have called the metaphysical intension of the kind designated by the noun phrase. The term 'tiger' and the phrase 'member of a species that serves as mascot for Princeton University'

[5]The argument here unobviously assumes an obvious truth of metaphysics, namely, that in any two possible worlds w_1 and w_2, the kind in w_1 that is *Member of a Species that Serves as Mascot for Princeton University* is the very same entity as the kind in w_2 that is *Member of a Species that Serves as Mascot for Princeton University* (and likewise, the species *Tiger* in w_1 is the very same entity as the species *Tiger* in w_2). This is a metaphysical assumption because it asserts that the entity that is the kind *Member of a Species that Serves as Mascot for Princeton University* is such that it could not be a kind of a different sort, say a natural kind or the kind *Animal in the San Diego Zoo*. It must, by necessity, be a kind that picks out its metaphysical extension by its being a class of members of a species having a certain contingent property. Otherwise, the very entity that, in the actual world, is the kind *Member of a Species that Serves as Mascot for Princeton University* might instead have picked out its metaphysical extension by its being the class of animals in the San Diego Zoo, i.e., it might instead have been the kind *Animal in the San Diego Zoo*. To use the vernacular, the assumption is one of *essentialism* concerning kinds.

It is fair to say that this trivial form of essentialism is already presupposed in the very foundations of the theory of direct reference for general terms. But, as we shall see in Sections 8 and 9, some of the essentialist doctrines that direct reference theorists attempt to extract from their theories of reference embody a much stronger form of essentialism.

The tacit assumption of this trivial form of essentialism concerning kinds is not special to the theory of direct reference. An analogous assumption of essentialism concerning properties was also presupposed in our discussion of the orthodox theory of singular reference, and is a tacit presupposition in virtually all philosophical discussion relating to properties and modality. Thus, for example, in supposing a rough equivalence between the sentences 'Shakespeare is such that it would be possible for him never to have written *Hamlet*' and 'Shakespeare is such that it would be possible for him to have lacked the property of *writing Hamlet*', one tacitly presupposes that the property of *writing Hamlet* is an entity that must be an authorship-of-*Hamlet* property, and could not in another possible world w be, say, the property (*in w!*) of *writing Macbeth*. This observation foreshadows much that is yet to come. It serves to show just how rampant and unnoticed our essentialist presuppositions tend to be.

clearly differ in semantical intension. Apparently, then, they must also differ in designation.

4.3 A Point of Disanalogy

We have argued that an apparent consequence of the proposal to treat common nouns as designators of kinds is that co-designative common nouns are co-intensional. But this apparent consequence has still further consequences, some of which seem to threaten any systematic and thoroughgoing attempt to treat the relationship between a common noun and its associated kind as analogous to denotation among proper names and singular definite descriptions. There are at least two basic facts about singular denotation which it might be expected that a theoretical analogy for the case of common nouns would respect. One is that logically equivalent singular terms—singular terms α and β such that $\ulcorner \alpha = \beta \urcorner$ is logically true—denote the same thing. Indeed, this is a semantic theorem about singular terms. Corresponding to this theorem, one might make the assumption that logically equivalent common nouns designate the same thing. More precisely, one might assume that a pair of common nouns ν and ν'—whether single-word nouns or noun phrases—designate the same thing whenever the sentence $\ulcorner$Something is ν if and only if it is a $\nu'\urcorner$ is logically true. Note that this sentence expresses in the object language the metalinguistic fact that ν and ν' have the same semantical *extension*. If it is logically true, we may ordinarily conclude that ν and ν' have the same semantical *intension*. Thus the term 'tiger' on this assumption designates the same thing as any of its "logical equivalents," such as 'self-identical tiger' and 'tiger which is either striped or not striped'. If 'tiger' designates the species *Tiger*, then on this assumption so does 'self-identical tiger', and so does 'tiger which is either striped or not striped'. This assumption, though perhaps somewhat strained, poses no pressing difficulty for the proposal to treat the relationship between a common noun and its associated kind as analogous to denotation.

A second basic fact about singular denotation is that, as Frege noted, the denotation of a definite description containing one or more component singular terms as a proper part is ordinarily a function of the (customary) denotation of the component singular terms, in the sense that the denotation of the containing description is ordinarily preserved under all substitutions of co-referential component singular terms. This second fact about singular denotation can be specified

48

more fully if we borrow a notion from Quine. Let us say that an occurrence of a singular term α within a containing expression ϕ is *purely referential* if the semantical rules which jointly specify the applicability conditions of ϕ make essential reference to the denotation of α in that occurrence, but do not essentially involve any other aspect of α in that occurrence, such as its sense, or α itself qua syntactic entity.[6] In plainer English, a purely referential occurrence of a singular term, within a containing expression, is one whose semantic function in the application of the containing expression is simply to denote the term's denotation. Then it is a basic semantic fact that in complex constructions not involving aberrant devices such as quotation marks, etc., and particularly in most noun phrases, whether definite descriptions or common noun phrases, any component singular terms occurring as a proper part do so referentially. In the case of definite descriptions we may prove the following interchange principle as a theorem:

> If τ_α is a definite description and τ_β is just like τ_α except that it contains a purely referential occurrence of a singular term β where τ_α contains a purely referential occurrence of a singular term α that designates the same thing as β, then τ_β designates the same thing as τ_α.

Let us call this 'the Interchange Principle for Definite Descriptions'.

Corresponding to the Interchange Principle for Definite Descriptions, one might hope as Frege did, in the interests of analogy, to maintain a parallel Interchange Principle for Common Noun Phrases, using the same notion of a *purely referential occurrence*:

> If τ_α is a common noun phrase and τ_β is just like τ_α except that it contains a purely referential occurrence of a singular term β where τ_α contains a purely referential occurrence of

---

[6]The term α may be an open singular term, with free variables that become bound in ϕ. In particular, α may itself be a variable. In such cases, the phrase 'the denotation of α' is understood as meaning the denotation of α under an assignment of values to variables. The definition given here does not fully accord with the letter of Quine's criterion (as given, e.g., in 1953a, p. 139f), though I believe that it accords with his Fregean intent. Quine states his criterion only for occurrences within a sentence ϕ, and requires only that the truth-value of ϕ be preserved under co-referential substitutions for the occurrence, though not, as we have, that the preservation of truth-value be a direct result of the role of the occurrence in the semantical rules specifying the truth-conditions of ϕ. Thus, as Quine notes, by his criterion 'Shakespeare' occurs referentially in ' 'Shakespeare' denotes a playwright'. By our criterion, it does not.

a singular term α that designates the same thing as β, then τ_β designates the same thing as τ_α.

This principle, however, in conjunction with the previous assumption paralleling the first semantic theorem about singular terms, sharply clashes with the proposal to treat common nouns as designating kinds of things rather than classes of things, as the following argument makes plain.[7]

For any common noun ν, we may define its *semantic characteristic function* f_ν as that function which assigns the number 1 to any individual x (and possible world w and time t) to which ν applies (with respect to w and t), and the number 0 to any other individual (and world and time). Accordingly, let us define a measure, which we shall call the *degree of tigerness* of an individual x (in a world w at a time t), to be 1 if x is a tiger (in w at t), and 0 otherwise. Similarly, we define the *degree of Princeton-mascotness* of an individual x (in w at t) to be 1 if x is a member of a species that serves as mascot for Princeton University (in w at t), and 0 otherwise. It happens that in the actual present, for any x, x's degree of tigerness is always the same number as x's degree of Princeton-mascotness, though one can easily describe possible circumstances in which an individual's degree of tigerness differs from its degree of Princeton-mascotness.

We also note that it is always possible to transform any open sentence in one free variable into a corresponding common noun phrase which applies (with respect to any possible world w and time t) to all those individuals that satisfy the open sentence (with respect to w and t), and only to those individuals. In English, this may usually be accomplished, somewhat awkwardly, by prefixing the open sentence with the phrase 'thing which is such that' and

---

[7]The argument employed here is derived from similar arguments presented on Frege's behalf by Church (1943, pp. 299–301), Davidson (1967, pp. 305–306), and Gödel (1944, pp. 128–129). Its essentials trace back to Frege himself. The arguments of Church, Davidson, and Gödel apply to sentences, whereas our argument is applied to common nouns. Church, Davidson, and Gödel use their arguments to show that if sentences are to be taken as having denotation, then they are plausibly taken as denoting their truth-values. Quine gives a similar argument (on the last page of 1953a, and in 1953c, p. 161) to show that any non-truth-functional sentential operator that allows for interchange *salva veritate* of logical equivalents must be opaque. We shall take our argument to show that the direct reference view of the designation of common nouns suggests a rejection of the principle that the designation of a common noun phrase is a function of the designation (denotation) of component singular terms occurring referentially.

substituting the pronoun 'it' for every free occurrence of the variable. Thus from the open sentence 'x is striped and eats meat' we obtain the closed common noun phrase 'thing which is such that it is striped and eats meat'. If we allow ourselves a slight formal indulgence—though this is by no means essential to the argument—we may retain the formal variable and use our prefix as a variable-binding operator, to obtain the semi-formal common noun phrase 'thing x which is such that x is striped and eats meat'. This procedure may involve a small departure from idiomatic English, but in many cases the gain in perspicuity more than compensates.

Now consider the following sequence of common nouns:

(*i*)   tiger
(*ii*) thing x which is such that the degree of tigerness of x is 1
(*iii*) thing x which is such that the degree of Princeton-mascotness of x is 1
(*iv*) member of a species which serves as mascot for Princeton University.

Noun (*i*) is trivially equivalent to (*ii*), in the sense defined above, for it follows directly from the definition of the degree of tigerness of an individual that something is a tiger if and only if its degree of tigerness is 1. Similarly, (*iii*) is trivially equivalent to (*iv*). It follows by our first assumption above, then, that (*i*) and (*ii*) are co-designative common nouns, and similarly that (*iii*) and (*iv*) are co-designative common nouns. Now (*iii*) is just like (*ii*) except that it contains a referential occurrence of the singular term 'the degree of Princeton-mascotness of x' where (*ii*) contains a purely referential occurrence of the singular term 'the degree of tigerness of x'. These singular terms are open definite descriptions, with 'x' occurring as a free variable which becomes bound within the context of (*ii*) or (*iii*). As we noted above, for any individual i taken as value of the variable 'x', the descriptions 'the degree of Princeton-mascotness of x' and 'the degree of tigerness of x' designate the same number. If i is a tiger, they both designate 1; otherwise they both designate 0. It follows by the Interchange Principle for Common Noun Phrases that (*iii*) and (*iv*) are co-designative common nouns. Hence, by the transitivity of the co-designative relation, it follows that 'tiger' designates the same thing as 'member of a species that serves as mascot for Princeton University'. But we have argued in the previous section that the species *Tiger* and the nonnatural kind or category

Member of a Species that Serves as Mascot for Princeton University are numerically distinct kinds or categories.

The general argument given above can be extended to any pair of common nouns *v* and *v'* that only happen to apply to exactly the same things with respect to the actual world and the present time. The two assumptions, paralleling two semantic theorems about singular terms, directly yield the consequence that *v* and *v'* designate the same thing. This result would strongly suggest that, insofar as the two assumptions are plausible principles concerning a notion of designation for common nouns, common nouns designate not their associated kind but their associated extension. That is, the assumptions strongly suggest the Fregean position that common nouns designate not kinds or categories, but classes.

If one wants to say, as the direct reference theorists do, that the term 'tiger' designates the species *Tiger* but not the class of actual tigers and not the category *Member of a Species that Serves as Mascot for Princeton University,* then at least one of the two assumptions of this argument that all co-extensional common noun phrases designate the same thing must be rejected. In fact, it is clear that the Interchange Principle is causing most of the trouble. Shakespeare is England's greatest playwright, but if common nouns designate kinds, then the phrases 'neighbor of Shakespeare' and 'neighbor of England's greatest playwright' designate different kinds of people, and it is easy to imagine circumstances in which there are individuals who are of one kind but not of the other.

A rejection of this Interchange Principle for Common Noun Phrases constitutes a noteworthy point of disanalogy between the notions of designation for common nouns and for singular denotation involved in the theory of direct reference. Although it is helpful in expounding the direct reference theory of general terms to think of certain common nouns as proper names that denote kinds, one must keep in mind that the exact nature of the similarity between common nouns and proper names has not yet been thoroughly explored in the literature of the theory of direct reference.

4.4. Designation

Our discussion in Part II of philosophical issues arising from the direct reference theory of general terms does not require that the theory specify the exact nature of the similarity between single-word common nouns and proper names. In particular, the criticisms that will be made in Part II do not depend on the way in which the direct reference theorists apply their notion of designation to common nouns. In order to grant the direct reference theorists the strongest case possible in support of some of their claims, however, it is convenient at this point simply to stipulate a meaning for 'designate' which conforms with the current use of the term. We have already seen that an apparent necessary condition for a common noun v to designate a kind k is that the semantical intension (function from possible worlds to extensions) of v coincide with the metaphysical intension of k. It is not implausible that this should also be regarded as a sufficient condition. Indeed, the key feature of natural kind common nouns that suggests the idea that they are names of kinds is just that these terms apply to an individual *only by virtue of* that individual's being one of a certain kind. In conformity with the original Carnapian intentions behind the current use of the term, we shall use 'designation' as a neutral term both for the denoting relation between singular terms and individuals, and for the relation that holds between general terms and appropriate abstract universals when the semantical intension of the first and metaphysical intension of the second coincide.[8] We shall say that a singular term α *designates* an individual i with respect to a possible world w and a time t if α denotes i with respect to w and t. We shall also say that a general term τ *designates* a universal k of the appropriate type (with respect to a world w and a time t) if the semantical extension of τ with respect to any possible world w' and any time t' is the metaphysical extension of k in w' at t'.[9] Both general and singular terms are purported *designators*, in this sense, provided that semanticists are willing to countenance such abstract universals as *phenomena* and *kinds* of things for common nouns, *properties* of things for adjectives, *states* and *action* types for verbs, and the like.

This definition accords well with the findings of the previous section concerning the Interchange Principle for Common Noun Phrases. Since we are using the term 'designate' in such a way that

[8]Cf. Carnap, 1947, p. 161f.

[9]We do not assume here that kinds or categories having the same metaphysical intension are identical, nor do we assume the opposite. Our proposal is simply that a common noun v may be said to designate *any* universal k (of the appropriate sort) whose metaphysical intension coincides with the semantical intension of v. If there is more than one universal (of the appropriate sort) that coincides in intension with v, then v will designate each of them. Thus, our definition may yield a notion of "multiple designation" for common nouns. On the other hand, it is not implausible that kinds having the same metaphysical intension are identical, so that the metaphysical intension of a kind uniquely determines the kind in question.

53

the common noun 'tiger' designates the species *Tiger* but does not designate the class of actual tigers or any other universal having a different metaphysical intension from the species *Tiger*, the argument given in the previous section may be taken as a *reductio ad absurdum* of the Interchange Principle. This demonstrates an important difference between the designation of common noun phrases and that of singular definite descriptions. Unlike the definite descriptions operator—'the' in the singular—the common-noun-forming operator 'thing which is such that' is a sort of intensional operator, at least in the sense that the *designation* of a common noun phrase is not a function simply of the *designations* of its component singular terms. The *intensions* of component singular terms are relevant to the determination of the designation of a common noun phrase, as is illustrated by the contrast between 'neighbor of Shakespeare' and 'neighbor of England's greatest playwright'. Still, singular terms occurring in common noun phrases typically occur referentially, in the sense defined earlier. Thus the common-noun-forming operator 'thing which is such that' is also an extensional operator, at least in the sense that the extension of an ordinary common noun phrase is a function simply of the *extensions* (denotations) of its component singular terms.

4.5. *Relationally Descriptional Designators*

With these preliminary matters resolved in the manner proposed here, the definitions given in Section 1.3 can now be more or less duplicated for general terms. Following the definition of a property involving direct reference to an individual, let us say that a property *involves direct reference to* a *kind* of thing if in giving a standard gerund specification of the property one must employ a nondescriptional term, either singular or general, that designates the kind.[10] The property of *seeing a ferocious, four-legged, tawny-coated, black-striped, cat-like creature* involves reference to the kind *Ferocious Four-legged Tawny-coated Black-striped Cat-like Creature*, but it does not involve direct reference to that kind of creature, since the common noun phrase 'ferocious, four-legged, tawny-coated, black-striped, cat-like creature' is descriptional. (Continuing in this vein, we may say that a modally indexed property such as that of *actually neighboring Shakespeare* involves direct reference to the actual

---

[10]This is not intended as a precise definition. See Chapter One, footnote 17.

54

world, provided that the actuality operator 'actually' is nondescriptional.)

Modifying the earlier notion of a general or purely qualitative property, let us call properties that do not involve any direct reference, whether to an individual or to a kind (or to a possible world), *general* or *purely qualitative*. General properties are "pure" conceptual entities. They do not involve nonintensional entities as constituents in any way.

Let v be a nondescriptional common noun and let k be the kind designated by v. Then the property denoted by $\ulcorner being\ a\ v \urcorner$ involves direct reference to k. It is in some sense logically (or kind-theoretically, on analogy to set-theoretically) equivalent to the property of being of kind k, i.e., the intrinsically relational property represented by the ordered couple $\langle k$, the kind-membership relation$\rangle$, necessarily possessed by all things of kind k, and only by things of kind k. If the term 'tiger' is nondescriptional, for instance, then the property of *being a tiger* is equivalent, in the sense used here, to the property represented by $\langle$the species *Felis tigris*, the kind-membership relation$\rangle$. Indeed, the former property and the latter property may even be one and the same, so that *being a tiger* is a sort of concealed relational property. Just as it is helpful to think of a nondescriptional common noun v as a proper name that directly denotes its designatum k, so it is helpful to think of the property denoted by $\ulcorner being\ a\ v \urcorner$ as the intrinsically relational property represented by $\langle k$, the kind-membership relation$\rangle$. Accordingly, expanding on our initial definitions for singular terms, we shall now say that a descriptional expression, whether a singular term or a general term (or a quantifier or sentential operator), is *relational* or *relationally descriptional* if some of the properties expressed involve direct reference to something, whether to an individual or to a kind of thing (or to a possible world), and we shall say that it is *thoroughly descriptional* otherwise. We shall continue to say that a relationally descriptional expression is *descriptional relative to* the thing or things to which its expressed properties involve direct reference.

4.6. Orthodox Theories and the Theory of Direct Reference

The orthodox theory of general terms, as held in various forms by Frege and modern Fregeans such as Carnap, Church, Dummett, and Linsky, holds that all general terms are thoroughly descriptional. For the Fregean, the sense of a term like 'tiger' is analyzable into properties like *being four-legged*, *being striped*, *being cat-like in*

55

appearance, and so on, each of which is held to be either further analyzable into more primitive general properties or itself a primitive general property. At no stage in the analysis will the Fregean admit a property involving direct reference.

As in the case of singular terms, a more precise statement of the direct reference theory of general terms is that certain general terms alleged by the orthodox theory to be thoroughly descriptional, in particular single-word natural kind common nouns, are in fact entirely nondescriptional—unless they are descriptional only in the trivial sense of being descriptional relative to the kind k designated by the term, in terms of the property of *being something of kind k*. Thus, for instance, the direct reference theory denies that the term 'tiger' is shorthand for some descriptive phrase, such as 'ferocious, four-legged, tawny-coated, black-striped, cat-like creature', but holds instead that the term is entirely nondescriptional, or else descriptional only in terms of a special property involving direct reference to the species *Tiger*, the property of *being something of this very kind*. The strong and more usual version of the direct reference theory holds that 'tiger' is altogether nondescriptional, period.

The remarks made above in Section 1.4 concerning the relation between the direct reference theory of singular reference and the Fregean notion of *sense* apply *mutatis mutandis* to the direct reference theory of general terms. The theory of direct reference does not deny the existence of any of the three kinds of "sense" mentioned above in Section 1.1 for proper names, indexicals, or natural kind terms. It would be silly to deny that these sorts of terms evoke certain concepts in the minds of their users (sense$_1$), or that they secure their designations in some manner (sense$_2$), or that they contribute to beliefs that are formulated using them (sense$_3$). What the direct reference theory denies is the Fregean assumption that the same thing is responsible for all three, that the mental concept evoked by a term is what secures the reference and is also what forms a part of the user's beliefs and desires.

4.7. The Traditional Theory of Cognition and Understanding

An important feature of the orthodox theory that our words are thoroughly descriptional is its connection with a certain point of view in epistemology and the philosophy of mind concerning belief, thought, and the understanding of language. We have already noted that the Fregean sense of an expression is supposed to be, among other things, the conceptual content of the expression, its sense₁. The senses of simple expressions, such as predicates or singular terms, are attributes or concepts of individuals—the conceptual building blocks of the senses of sentences. Frege called the senses of sentences 'thoughts' (*Gedanke*). He stressed that the sense of an expression is not private, but public property. A sense exists independently of its being grasped by anyone, and the same sense may be grasped by different people, and by the same person at different times. In this respect, sense is objective. But Frege also insisted that one gains access to the sense of an expression only by a special mental apprehension. He clearly indicates (1918) that he regards the "grasping" or "apprehending" of a sense as, at least in part, a mental process, in some ways analogous to visual perception. Thus, for instance, he says, "A particular mental capacity, the power of thought, must correspond to the apprehension of thought [the sense of a sentence]. In thinking we do not produce thoughts but we apprehend them" (1918, Strawson ed., p. 35). Later he says, "Although the thought does not belong to the contents of the thinker's [private] consciousness yet something in his consciousness must be aimed at the thought" (p. 35), suggesting that the grasping of a sense always essentially involves a directed mental experience. In the final paragraph Frege says that the grasping or apprehending of the sense of a sentence "is a process in the inner world of a thinker. . . . When a thought is apprehended, it . . . brings about changes in the inner world of the apprehender" (p. 38).

The Fregean notion of the sense of a sentence—its thought content—like the Fregean sense of a term, has aspects of sense₃ as well as of sense₁. The sense of the sentence 'Shakespeare is a playwright' is what a person believes, thinks, asserts, etc., when he or she believes, thinks, or asserts that Shakespeare is a playwright. Fregean thoughts are bits of information, and the sorts of things that are the objects of belief, assertion, and propositional attitudes generally. Thus the sense of a sentence, its thought, is at once the purely conceptual content before the mind and also the object of belief, thought, and understanding.

Putnam (1975a, pp. 218–222) points out that this orthodox Fregean theory of sense nicely complements a traditional view concerning language understanding and thought. On this view, the state of a speaker in understanding an expression is regarded as

57

wholly internal, involving nothing in addition to the speaker but what may be present in, or directly accessible to, his or her mind. Similarly, the state of a subject thinking a certain thought or having a certain occurrent belief is regarded as wholly internal. Such "psychological states," as Putnam calls them, involve only a subject and the contents of his or her consciousness, which include certain public conceptual entities. A person's being in such a psychological state entails the existence of the person and perhaps of some things that are conceptual in nature, but nothing essentially or fundamentally external to the subject is involved. On the orthodox Fregean theory, the objects of thought consist solely of general properties that do not involve direct reference, and hence do not include nonintensional entities as constituents. Pure intensional entities are precisely the sort of thing allowed by this internalistic view of language understanding and propositional attitudes. The orthodox theory does more than support an internalistic philosophy of language understanding and cognition; with its identification of sense$_3$ with sense$_1$, it strongly suggests one. Grasping a sense, and thinking a thought, are seen as activities or states that are completely determined by the general properties before the mind of the subject. In order to decide what thought a person is apprehending, it would be sufficient to investigate only what is in the person's mind. We would not have to concern ourselves with such external phenomena as the speaker's linguistic community as a whole, or the circumstances surrounding the speaker's acquisition of an expression.[11]

By contrast, the theory of direct reference paves the way for a rejection of this traditional view of understanding and cognition. This point will emerge when we reconsider the semantical arguments for the direct reference theory.

[11]The same may be said of Russell's theory of logically genuine proper names. (See Chapter One, footnote 22.) Loosely speaking, a Russellian theory of meaning and reference allows that meanings may consist of intrinsically relational properties, but only intrinsically relational properties that involve direct reference to items of direct and intimate epistemic acquaintance. The apparatus of this theory, though slightly richer than that of the orthodox Fregean theory, is still limited to the mentally accessible. It constructs its meanings solely from materials permitted by the traditional mentalistic view of cognition: the knowing subject, his or her private subjective experiences, purely qualitative properties, and in a recursive manner, properties involving direct reference to things already allowed.

Putnam does not consider this Russellian theory, but the inter-subjective psychological states of the orthodox Fregean theory.

58

5. THE ARGUMENTS RECONSIDERED

5.1. *The General Form of the Arguments*

Each of the three kinds of arguments given above in Section 2—modal, epistemological, and semantical—are easily modified to apply to certain single-word common nouns such as 'tiger' or 'water'. These new arguments show that such terms as these cannot be descriptional, except in the trivial sense of being descriptional in terms of the special property of *being an instance of kind k*, where *k* is the kind designated by the term.

We begin by considering a typical natural kind term like 'tiger', and those properties that the orthodox theory would associate with the term as forming its sense. These properties might include the distinguishing characteristics of tigers, properties like those of *being a four-legged animal, being cat-like in appearance, having a tawny yellow coat with black traversing stripes, being a meat-eater*, and so on. Notice that we do not include among these properties the special intrinsically relational property of *being an animal of this very kind k*, where *k* is the species *Tiger*. This special property involving direct reference to the species of tigers is not the sort of property that the orthodox theory can or would allow as forming part of the sense of 'tiger'.

If the term 'tiger' is, as the orthodox theorist maintains, descriptional in terms of the properties cited above, then the sentence

> Something is a tiger if and only if it is a four-legged, meat-eating, cat-like animal with a tawny yellow coat and black traversing stripes

should be analytic, in the traditional sense, and should therefore express a truth that is both necessary and knowable *a priori*. To say that the sentence expresses a necessary truth is to say that, in discourse about counterfactual situations, the term 'tiger' must apply to just those things, whatever they are, that have all of the features mentioned. There can be no possible world in which tigers, properly so called, lack these features, and in any possible world anything that has all of these features is *ipso facto*, and by definition, a *tiger*, whatever else it is. To say that the sentence expresses a truth that is knowable *a priori*, or that it conveys *a priori* information, is to say that, by mere reflection on the concepts involved and without any reliance on information gathered by means of sensory experience, one can know that nothing having these features fails to be a tiger, and there are no tigers that lack these features. Indeed the supposition that tigers lack these features, or that certain nontigers have them, should make as little sense as the supposition of a "married bachelor" or an "unmarried wife." If the term 'tiger' is descriptional in the manner prescribed by the orthodox theory, then the term correctly applies to all those things, whatever they may happen to be, that have the distinguishing characteristics that we use to identify tigers, and only those things. But, the argument continues, surely we can imagine, as a genuine possibility, the surprising discovery of a rare and exotic species of felines which look exactly like tigers, but which are genetically different enough from tigers so that interbreeding between the two species is biologically impossible. It is possible, that is, in both a metaphysical and an epistemic sense, that there be another species of tiger look-alikes that have all of the properties cited above, though they are not tigers. Conversely, we can just as easily imagine that, owing to some sort of mass hallucination and certain deceptive appearances, the things that we have been calling *tigers* turn out not to have any of the properties cited above. We can imagine, for instance, that tigers turn out not to be organisms at all, but cleverly disguised robots,[12] that what we took to be black stripes were really sequences of blue dots, and so on. It is conceivable, that is, that tigers may lack the properties cited by the orthodox theorist as being analytically tied to the term 'tiger'. These considerations indicate that the sentence displayed above cannot be analytic. It expresses a proposition that is neither a necessary truth nor a truth knowable *a priori*. This is the main thrust of the modal and epistemological arguments against the descriptionality thesis.[13]

In order to make a convincing semantical argument, imagine that, though we do not know it, there happens to be on a distant planet in a far corner of the universe an exotic species of animals that look

---

[12]The example of tigers turning out to be robots is derived from an example of Putnam's (1962).

[13]In arguing against the "cluster" descriptional theory of natural kind terms, the displayed sentence must be replaced by the following two sentences:

> Any tiger is an animal that is either four-legged, meat-eating, cat-like in appearance, tawny-coated, or black-striped.

> Any four-legged, meat-eating, cat-like animal with a tawny yellow coat and black traversing stripes is a tiger.

See Chapter One, footnote 28.

exactly like tigers, though they are biologically quite distinct from the species found on earth. Now ask yourself: When we use the word 'tiger', are we referring to the members of this distant and alien species, with which we have never had any contact, simply by virtue of the coincidental fact that they happen to resemble the local animals that we do intend to refer to? Clearly not. Our term 'tiger' is a label that applies only to animals of a certain familiar kind. It does not apply to everything whatsoever that might happen to have the general features that we associate with tigers. In short, the term 'tiger' is not descriptional in terms of the properties alleged by the orthodox theory.

The structure of the argument for the nondescriptionality of general terms is the same as that for singular terms. We consider a particular term τ of the sort in question. If τ were descriptional in terms of the properties which one might associate with τ as forming its sense, then certain systematic metaphysical, epistemological, and semantical consequences would have to obtain. Intuitively these consequences do not obtain; therefore τ is not descriptional in terms of these properties.

5.2. An Obvious Objection

Perhaps, it may be argued, the arguments considered so far work only because we have chosen the wrong properties. There seems to be an obvious property which, taken by itself, apparently satisfies all of the constraints imposed by the modal, epistemological, and semantical arguments for constituting the sense of the term 'tiger'. This is the property of *being a tiger*. For it is indeed analytic that all and only tigers have this property, and it is equally obvious that the term 'tiger' correctly applies to all and only those things that have this property. Similarly for the case of singular terms, the orthodox theorist may argue that the name 'Shakespeare' is descriptional solely in terms of a single property, a property whose standard gerund specification is *'being identical with Shakespeare'* or more simply *'being Shakespeare'*. None of the arguments considered so far can be made to show that the name 'Shakespeare' does not connote the property of *being Shakespeare*.

Of course, an orthodox theorist disposed to make such argument must maintain that the property of *being Shakespeare* is not Shakespeare's nonqualitative haecceity, but a special general qualitative property, one that cannot be fully specified in terms of more

61

primitive general properties. But an orthodox theorist might be expected to take just this position.

That the arguments considered thus far do not apply to properties like that of *being a tiger*, however, is a point that is explicitly recognized by the direct reference theorists. Putnam writes:

> In the traditional view, the meaning of, say 'lemon', is given by specifying a conjunction of *properties*. For each of these properties, the statement 'lemons have the property P' is an analytic truth; and if P_1, P_2, ..., P_n are all the properties in the conjunction, then 'anything with all of the properties P_1, ..., P_n is a lemon' is likewise an anlytic truth.
>
> In one sense, this is trivially correct. If we are allowed to invent unanalyzable properties *ad hoc*, then we can find a single property—not even a conjunction—the possession of which is a necessary and sufficient condition for being a lemon, or being gold, or whatever. Namely, we just postulate *the property of being a lemon*, or *the property of being gold*, or whatever may be needed. If we require that the properties P_1, P_2, ..., P_n *not* be of this *ad hoc* character, however, then the situation is very different. Indeed, with any natural understanding of the term 'property', it is just *false* that to say that something belongs to a natural kind is just to ascribe to it a conjunction of properties (1970, p. 140 of 1975d).

Similarly, in outlining his views about proper names and natural kind terms, Kripke says:

> It is interesting to compare my views to those of Mill. Mill counts both predicates like 'cow', definite descriptions, and proper names as names. He says of 'singular' names that they are connotative if they are definite descriptions but non-connotative if they are proper names. On the other hand, Mill says that *all* 'general' names are connotative; such a predicate as 'human being' is defined as the conjunction of certain properties which give necessary and sufficient conditions for humanity—relationality, animality, and certain physical features. The modern logical tradition, as represented by Frege and Russell, seems to hold that Mill was wrong about singular names, but right about general names. ... My own view, on the other hand, regards Mill as more-or-less right about 'singular' names, but wrong about 'general' names. *Perhaps* some 'general' names ('foolish', 'fat', 'yellow')

express properties. In a significant sense, such general names as 'cow' and 'tiger' do not, *unless being a cow counts trivially as a property*. Certainly 'cow' and 'tiger' are not short for the conjunction of properties a dictionary would take to define them, as Mill thought (1972a, pp. 127–128, emphasis added).

Both Putnam and Kripke are prepared to allow that a natural kind term v may be said to be descriptional in terms of the alleged property denoted by $\ulcorner$*being a* $v\urcorner$, although neither seems daunted by this concession. Indeed, both seem to be suspicious of whether such alleged properties ought to be counted as genuine properties.

This sort of skepticism regarding such properties as those of *being a lemon* and *being a cow* may seem a little strange. Indeed, it may even seem an *ad hoc* attempt to save the theory of direct reference. Surely, a requirement that every genuine property be completely and exhaustively "analyzable" into several definite components is excessive, at least in the absence of some substantial argumentation that such analysis can always be carried out further. Sensible qualities, for instance, notoriously defy such "analysis." Neither Putnam nor Kripke seem to give any cogent reason for countenancing some properties as playing an important role in the theory of meaning while dismissing such obvious properties as those of *being a lemon* and *being a tiger* as *ad hoc* or trivial.

The dismissal of these latter properties calls for an explanation. Even if no reason for dismissing them is explicit, such a reason may be extracted from the goals and methods of Kripke and Putnam. Consider again the term 'tiger'. For the purpose of interpretation we may take Kripke and Putnam to hold, at least as a first approximation, that the term is entirely nondescriptional. Suppose it is. Then the property denoted by '*being a tiger*', if there is such a property, involves direct reference to the species *Tiger* and is necessarily equivalent, in some sense, to the intrinsically relational property of *being an animal of this very kind*, said with direct reference to the species *Tiger*. We represent this property as the ordered couple consisting of the species *Tiger* and the kind-membership relation. If one who initially held that 'tiger' is entirely nondescriptional were to concede that 'tiger' may be said to be descriptional in terms of this property, this concession would not represent a very serious retreat. The new claim is that 'tiger' is either nondescriptional or (if one endorses the existence of properties involving direct reference) perhaps trivially descriptional, but only in terms of this anti-Fregean property.[14] Indeed, one reason for the disjunctive character of the theory of direct reference is that the arguments show only that certain expressions are either nondescriptional or descriptional relative to their designata. Strictly speaking, a separate and supplementary argument is needed if one is to show that expressions of the sort in question are not even descriptional relative to their designata. In the case of singular terms, such an argument was given above in Section 3.2. As we shall soon see, however, this argument does not extend to the case of general terms. If one countenances intrinsically relational properties, it is difficult indeed to argue that the term 'tiger' does not express the property that we represent by ⟨the species *Tiger*, the kind-membership relation⟩, the property of *being an animal of that very kind*.

One reason for skepticism concerning such alleged properties as that of *being a tiger* stems from the dubious status of intrinsically relational properties in the theory of meaning. Relational properties which include their relata as constituents may seem philosophically curious, and one would be justified in questioning whether such complexes ought to be counted among genuine properties.[15] Introducing intrinsically relational properties into the theory of meaning does indeed seem an *ad hoc* attempt to save some remnant of the theory that all terms are descriptional. Once intrinsically relational properties are admitted, there is nothing to block the positing of such properties as that of *being a member of kind k*, where *k* is a natural kind. It would be a trivial matter that *being a member of k*, where *k* is the species *Tiger*, is to be counted as a property. Moreover, this is a move to save the bath water after losing the baby. Intrinsically relational properties stand in direct opposition to everything that the orthodox theory stands for. The claim that the term 'tiger' is descriptional in terms of the property of *being an animal of this very kind k* is only a small step away from the claim that 'tiger' is altogether nondescriptional. Whether 'tiger' is nondescriptional or descriptional in terms of this intrinsically relational property, the

---

[14]In fact, the remarks of Kripke and Putnam quoted above may be cited as primary evidence of the disjunctive character of their theories of reference.

[15]One might object here that kinds are intensional entities very much like attributes, so that the property represented by ⟨the species *Tiger*, the kind-membership relation⟩ is a pure intensional entity, in which only intensional entities occur as constituents. This objection is misplaced. What makes the property anti-Fregean is not the *nature* of its constituents, but the *way* in which they occur. This is discussed and resolved by Kaplan (1977, n. 9).

property denoted by '*being a tiger*' is, or is in some sense logically equivalent to, this same intrinsically relational property.

On the other hand, if 'tiger' is descriptional but not in terms of an intrinsically relational property, then the property denoted by '*being a tiger*' is not intrinsically relational, and the theoretical assertion that 'tiger' is descriptional in terms of the property of *being a tiger* directly conflicts with the theories of Kripke and Putnam concerning natural kind terms. Since the arguments for the theory of direct reference cannot rule out the possibility that 'tiger' expresses the property of *being a tiger*, the important issue is whether the property denoted by '*being a tiger*' involves direct reference to the species *Tiger* or not. If the property of *being a tiger* is a general property that does not involve direct reference to the species *Tiger*, then the orthodox theory is reaffirmed, and the direct reference theory neatly refuted, by the simple observation that 'tiger' may be said to express the property of *being a tiger*.

5.3. A Reply: Putnam's Twin Earth Argument

Since none of the arguments considered thus far can rule out the possibility that the term 'tiger' is descriptional in terms of the property of *being a tiger*, what the direct reference theorist needs is an argument to show that, if there is a property denoted by '*being a tiger*', then it is not a general property but one that involves direct reference. Such an argument can be extracted from Putnam's special version of one of the semantical arguments, his imaginitive Twin Earth argument. The Twin Earth argument demonstrates that the general properties normally associated with a natural kind term do not constitute a logically sufficient condition for application.[16] The argument takes advantage of the connection discussed in Section 4.7 between orthodox Fregean theories of meaning and the internalistic account of language understanding and cognition. As we have seen, according to the orthodox account, the sense of a term is a special sort of intensional entity. It is a concept composed solely of items grasped by the mind. Grasping the sense of a term and having an occurrent belief are supposed to be pure "psychological states," in

[16]Putnam's argument is presented in 1973b, pp. 700–704, and in 1975a, pp. 223–227. (Putnam presents the argument for the case of the substance term 'water', though we shall consider the analogous argument for the case of 'tiger'.) Putnam's argument that the properties normally associated with a natural kind term do not constitute a logically *necessary* condition for application is presented in 1970, pp. 141–143 of Putnam, 1975d.

the sense described above. Subjects grasping distinct senses or having distinct occurrent beliefs must be in distinct psychological states.[17] Thus the psychological state of grasping the sense of particular term τ, or believing a proposition expressed by a sentence containing τ, must uniquely determine the sense in question, and one may determine which properties are included in a given concept or sense by investigating which properties are included in the psychological state of a subject in grasping the sense or in believing a proposition involving the concept. The set or cluster of properties included in a sense or concept, in turn must uniquely determine an extension with respect to any possible world and time. Thus, on the orthodox view, the psychological state of a subject in grasping the sense of a term τ, or in believing a proposition involving the concept expressed by τ, must uniquely determine the semantical intension of τ.

For our present purpose it is important to note that, even if one ultimately rejects the orthodox theory of meaning and reference by holding that there are some terms which are nondescriptional, it should still hold true that, for those terms whose senses *do* consist solely of general properties, grasping the sense of the term is a wholly internal, psychological state. Even if the psychological state of a subject in understanding a term τ, or believing a proposition expressed by a sentence containing τ, may sometimes underdetermine the semantical intension of τ, it should still be true that for a thoroughly descriptional term τ, the psychological state of grasping the sense of τ or believing a proposition expressed by a sentence containing τ must uniquely determine the descriptional sense, and hence the semantical intension, of τ. In particular, if the term 'tiger' is thoroughly descriptional, then the general property or properties included in the psychological state of someone who is grasping the sense of 'tiger', or having an occurrent belief that a tiger is about to attack, must uniquely determine the extension of 'tiger' with respect to any possible world. The possession of the properties included in the relevant psychological state should constitute at least a sufficient condition for the correct application of 'tiger'.

Consider now the following imaginary set of circumstances. There is a distant planet exactly like Earth in every respect except that there are no tigers on this planet. Following Putnam let us call this imaginary planet 'Twin Earth'. On Twin Earth, in place of tigers

---

[17]See Putnam, 1975a, pp. 221–222, for an argument that on the orthodox view, the psychological state of a speaker uniquely determines the grasped sense.

there is a species of felines whose members, though superficially indistinguishable from tigers, are genetically different enough from tigers so that interbreeding between the two species is biologically impossible. Let us call this alien species 'k'. We may even suppose that the species *Tiger* and the species k both evolved from ancestors of the same species, some members of which were transported to Twin Earth by intelligent aliens during pre-historic times. We also suppose that English is spoken on both planets, except that, as the syntactic sound and shape 'tiger' is used on the alien planet, it designates the species k rather than the species *Tiger*. The term 'tiger' functions on Earth just as it actually does, designating the species *Tiger*. Aside from this difference, Twin Earth is presently as much like Earth as it could be. We even suppose that for every speaker on Earth there is an exact counterpart, or doppelgänger, on Twin Earth whose mental biography is qualitatively the same as that of the given Earth speaker. Speaking qualitatively, we may suppose that the same course of nonrelational mental associations, events, and images runs through the minds of any given Earth subject and his or her alien counterpart.

Now consider a typical English speaker of Earth and his or her alien counterpart in grasping the native meaning of the expression 'tiger', or in thinking to himself or herself, "There is a tiger coming after me!" It is virtually true by hypothesis that, despite their different settings, the two speakers are in precisely the same wholly internal, "psychological state." Indeed, as Kaplan has pointed out, at the precise moment in question, their very *brains* could be interchanged though neither would be the wiser. In our earlier terminology, both subjects attach precisely the same senses$_1$ to the word 'tiger'; the qualitative properties and mental concepts evoked in them are precisely the same. Yet the extensions, and hence the intensions, are different. On Earth, the word 'tiger' applies only to tigers. On Twin Earth, their word 'tiger' applies only to animals of kind k. As we would say, the *meanings* of the terms are different. The vocable 'tiger', as it is used on the alien planet, does not mean what it does when used on Earth. The difference in meaning is not accompanied, and hence not accounted for, by a difference in sense$_1$. Rather, the difference in meaning is accounted for by the different external contexts surrounding the speakers, by the different linguistic and extralinguistic settings in which the speakers are found. As Putnam points out, this is one respect in which natural kind terms are similar to indexical expressions. Extension, and in fact intension, is determined at least partly contextually, and not solely by internally associated general properties.

The similarity between Putnam's Twin Earth argument and the other semantical arguments considered earlier in Sections 2.3 and 5.1 is evident. Instead of talking about the properties associated with a term, Putnam talks outright about sense$_1$, the psychological concept, but the thrust of the argument is the same. Variations of the argument demonstrate that the sense$_1$ that a speaker attaches to a proper name, indexical, or natural kind term—the purely conceptual content or purely qualitative properties—can always underdetermine the denotation or extension.[18] The sense$_2$ of a term, by definition, is something that uniquely determines the denotation. Hence there is nothing that can be identified as the sense$_1$ and the sense$_2$ of a proper name, indexical, or natural kind term simultaneously, though this is precisely what is required by any full-blown Fregean notion of *sense*.[19]

The Twin Earth argument does seem to provide a special bonus. It solves the crucial question, raised in the previous section, of whether properties like that of *being a tiger* or *being Shakespeare* are purely qualitative or involve direct reference. Science fiction thought experiments of the sort offered by Putnam show that proper names, indexicals, and natural kind terms are not descriptional solely in terms of properties that might be included in a wholly internal psychological state. General properties may be included in someone's psychological state, whereas properties that involve direct reference to external things of a certain kind, or to a certain kind of thing, cannot be part of a psychological state. Therefore, even if 'tiger' is descriptional in terms of the property of *being a tiger*, the property of

[18]Cf. Wiggenstein's observations:

"At that word we both thought of him." Let us assume that each of us said the same words to himself—and how can it mean MORE than that?—But wouldn't even those words be only a *germ*? They must surely belong to a language and to a context, in order really to be the expression of the thought *of* that man.

If God had looked into our minds he would not have been able to see there whom we were speaking of (1953, p. 217).

[19]It is characteristic of the propounders of the theory of direct reference to steer clear of sense$_3$ altogether, aiming their arguments toward the nondescriptionality of proper names, indexicals, or natural kind terms, and toward the consequent failure of any straightforward sense$_1$-sense$_2$ identification for such terms. It was an initial interest in sense$_3$ that provided the impetus for Frege's theory of *sense*, with its three-way identification. The puzzling nature of sense$_3$ is discussed briefly in Salmon, 1979a. See also Kripke, 1979b.

being a tiger cannot be a general property involving no direct reference. Precisely similar arguments may be given for other sorts of general terms, as well as for proper names and indexical singular terms.

It is interesting to note that in this respect Putnam's Twin Earth argument is more powerful than the other arguments considered earlier. Putnam invokes the notion of the sense₁ of a term—the "psychological state" in understanding the term or having an occurrent belief—where Kripke and others invoke the notion of "properties associated with a term." The former notion is, in effect, automatically restricted to general properties, properties that do not involve direct reference. By relying on our intuition as to whether two individuals are in the same psychological state, Putnam's version of the initial argument enables us to decide whether a certain specified property such as that of *being a tiger* is intrinsically relational. The arguments given by the other direct reference theorists must simply presuppose that the property of *being a tiger*, if it exists, involves direct reference to the species *Tiger*.[20]

6. RIGID DESIGNATORS RECONSIDERED

6.1. *General Term Designation and Rigid Designation*

In Section 3 we considered the notion of a rigid designator as applied to singular terms only. Donnellan, Kaplan, Kripke, and Putnam have all explicitly labeled general natural kind terms as "rigid designators" of natural kinds.[21] Putnam (1975a, pp. 240, 242–244) has also

---

[20]Kripke's notion of the *qualitative epistemic situation* of a subject is very close to Putnam's notion of a *psychological state*, but Kripke uses his notion for an entirely different purpose: to explain away the apparent contingency of certain necessary identity statements, e.g., that Hesperus is identical with Phosphorus, or that heat is mean kinetic molecular energy. (See Section 7.2.) He does this by observing that, though it is necessary that Hesperus and Phosphorus are identical, there might indeed have been two distinct heavenly bodies with respect to which we would have been in precisely the same qualitative epistemic situation that we were actually in with respect to Hesperus and Phosphorus before the discovery that they were one. That is to say, the senses₁ or psychological concepts that were associated with the names 'Hesperus' and 'Phosphorus' were such that it was indeed possible, in a metaphysical sense, that there be two distinct planets fitting the two concepts. Kripke does not directly use his notion of a qualitative epistemic situation as part of the initial argument that 'Hesperus' and 'Phosphorus' are nondescriptional.

[21]See for instance Donnellan, 1973a, p. 712; Kaplan, 1973a, p. 518, n. 31; Kripke, 1972a, p. 139; and Putnam, 1975a, pp. 231–232.

said that general artifact terms and some verbs and adjectives are rigid designators, and Kripke (1971, p. 160; 1972a, pp. 134, 148–149) that general terms for natural phenomena and their corresponding adjectives are rigid designators. One might suppose that the case of these general terms is entirely analogous to the case of proper names. It might be supposed, for instance, that the rigidity of a natural kind term is a consequence of nondescriptionality (or of a special kind of relational descriptionality), as it is with a proper name. This is not correct.

By our original definition of 'rigid designator', it is a conceptual truth that any general term that designates anything at all rigidly designates that thing. It makes no difference whether the general term is nondescriptional, relationally descriptional, or thoroughly descriptional. The reason for this is that, in defining our notion of a general term τ designating a universal k, we required not only that the semantical extension of τ coincide with the metaphysical extension of k, but that the corresponding *intensions* coincide as well. Let us call this proposed definition for general term designation *Proposal A*. This notion corresponds roughly to Carnap's notion of "L-designation" (1947, pp. 161–167). We might have been more lenient in our definition by requiring only coincidence in extension, a requirement that would correspond roughly to Carnap's more general notion of "designation." Let us call this *Proposal B*. Proposal B would render it a substantive question whether a given general term τ rigidly "designates" k, given that τ "designates" k. We have already seen that the question of whether a given singular term rigidly designates its referent is a substantive one. In the case of most descriptional singular terms the answer is that it does not. This is but one respect in which the more lenient notion for general terms given by Proposal B is more analogous to singular denotation than is coincidence in intension.[22] To say that it is a substantive question whether a general term τ coincides in intension with a universal k given that they coincide in extension is to say that there are, or could be, cases of a general term τ having as its semantical extension the very class that is the metaphysical extension of a universal k, yet departing from k with respect to other possible worlds. We have already seen one possible instance of this with the term 'tiger' and the

---

[22]There is another respect in which the more lenient Proposal B yields a notion of designation for general terms more closely analogous to singular denotation. Proposal B preserves the Interchange Principle for Common Noun Phrases given in Section 4.3.

categories *Ferocious Four-legged Tawny-coated Black-striped Cat-like Creature* and *Member of a Species that Serves as Mascot for Princeton University*. Another instance may be the term 'tiger' and its semantical extension itself, the class of actual tigers—if we view classes as special universals whose metaphysical extensions are themselves, and whose metaphysical intensions are constant functions from possible worlds to the class itself.[23] The species *Tiger* may coincide in metaphysical extension with all of these universals, but it does not coincide in metaphysical intension with any of them. Indeed, for most universals k, there are a multitude of universals that have the same metaphysical extension as k but different metaphysical intensions. Thus, given that a general term τ coincides in extension with a certain universal k, there will be a number of other universals that coincide in extension with τ but differ in metaphysical intension from k. The semantical intension of τ cannot coincide with the metaphysical intensions of all of these universals at once. There will be possible worlds with respect to which the semantical extension of τ differs from the metaphysical extension of some universal in that world despite a common extension in the actual world. The important point is that this is true whether τ is descriptional or nondescriptional. Even if we had chosen Proposal B with its more lenient requirement of coincidence in extension for our notion of "designation" for general terms, we would still have to abandon the claim in the case of general terms that nondescriptional designation implies rigid "designation." The term 'tiger' "designates," in this weak sense, the class of actual tigers. But even if the term 'tiger' is nondescriptional, it does not rigidly "designate" this class.

In adopting Proposal A and requiring coincidence in intension for our notion of designation between general terms and universals, we place a severe restriction on the sorts of entities that can be designated by a general term. In most cases, the semantical extension of a general term, for instance, cannot be its designatum, since the semantical extension of most general terms varies with respect to different possible worlds. We must look instead to properties, kinds, categories, states, and the like. With this restricted notion of designation for general terms, the distinction between *designation* and *rigid*

---

[23]Fine (1977a) and Kaplan (1969, p. 224) argue that classes or sets exist only in those possible worlds in which all the members exist, so that the singleton class {Quine}, which contains Quine as its only element, fails to exist in any possible world in which Quine himself fails to exist. If they are correct, the metaphysical intension of a class may be a constant *partial* function on the domain of possible worlds.

designation disappears. Every general term that designates at all, whether descriptionally or nondescriptionally, is a rigid designator. This accords with the notion of designation for general terms employed by the direct reference theorists. Thus Kaplan writes:

> Designators like the 'red' in 'Your eye is red' and the 'penguin' in 'Peter is a penguin', which would not ordinarily be regarded as proper names, may yet be rigid if regarded as designating the appropriate entities. If 'red' designates the property of being red, it is probably rigid. It it designates the class of red things, it is certainly not rigid. In my own esoteric doctrines, 'red' rigidly designates a third entity, the color red. Similarly, 'penguin' rigidly designates the species penguin (almost all single words other than particles seem to me to be rigid designators) (1973a, p. 518, n. 31).

Similarly, Donnellan writes:

> When 'tiger' is taken as a concrete name, it does not rigidly designate what it then denotes, individual tigers; it is only when it is taken as an abstract name denoting tigerhood or the species, tiger, that it becomes a rigid designator.
> This same distinction can be made, however, for all varieties of common nouns. Taken as a concrete name, for example, 'bachelor' denotes a number of individual men and is not a rigid designator. But if we look at the abstract name, 'bachelorhood', it seems that it rigidly designates a certain state, a state which is the same in all possible worlds (1973a, p. 712).

In Section 3.1 we contrasted two kinds of rigid singular terms: persistent designators and obstinate designators. No such distinction exists in the case of general terms. By our definitions, all general terms are obstinately rigid. As we have seen, one reason that a rigid designator might be obstinate is that its designatum is a necessary existent. This is the situation in which persistence and obstinacy collapse. Many philosophers have maintained that abstract entities, or at least such abstract entities as kinds and states—the sorts of entities designated by general terms—exist in all possible worlds if they exist at all. (But see footnote 23.) Donnellan (1973b and 1974b), for instance, suggests that natural kinds like biological species and chemical substances exist in all possible worlds, including those worlds in which the kind in question has no instances or examples. If this view is correct, then all general terms may be *strongly rigid*, in the sense presented in Section 3.1, and hence obstinate. It is not clear, however, that this view is correct. Presumably, the species *Tiger* exists in any possible world in which there are tigers. But consider a possible world in which there never were, and never will be, any tigers. It is tempting to say that in such a world the species *Tiger* simply never evolves into being, and therefore does not exist. Similarly it is tempting to say that any possible world in which there are no samples of water is a world in which the substance water itself simply does not exist. The important point is that even if some kinds are contingent entities, by our definition of 'rigid designator', there is still no distinction to be drawn between persistent and obstinate general terms. For if we assume that species, substances, and so on, are genuinely existing entities, it is presumably the case that in any possible world in which there are tigers, the species *Tiger* exists, and in any possible world in which there is some water, the substance water exists. Thus it is also the case that in any possible world in which the species *Tiger* does not exist, there are no tigers, so that the metaphysical extension of the species in such a world—the class of its members—is simply the empty class. But the semantical extension of the term 'tiger' with respect to any possible world in which there are no tigers is also the empty class. Hence the semantical extension of the term 'tiger' coincides with the metaphysical extension of the species *Tiger* even with respect to possible worlds in which the species does not exist. A similar situation obtains in the case of the term 'water' and the substance water, and so on. Hence all general terms are not only rigid, but obstinate.[24]

6.2. A Criterion for General Term Designation

In Section 3.3 we found various ways of expressing in the object language the fact that a given singular term α is an obstinate designator, and what α obstinately designates. It is desirable to be able to do something analogous for general terms in a first-order

---

[24]The possibility should be mentioned that a general term like 'tiger' may be assigned no extension at all—not even the empty extension—with respect to those possible worlds in which the species *Tiger* does not exist, so that the semantical intension of 'tiger' may be a partial function on the domain of possible worlds, rather than always a total function. (Of course, if the species *Tiger* is a necessary existent, then the semantical intension of the term 'tiger' is a total function in either case.) If some or all general terms function in this way rather than in the way described in the text, then it would seem that at least some general terms are persistent rather than obstinate.

modal object language. Since common nouns are not singular terms, one cannot use the identity predicate '=' in a first-order object language in a manner analogous to (2) or (3) in order to express what a given common noun designates. By our definition, a general term τ designates k if and only if the semantical extension of τ with respect to any possible world w is precisely the class of instances of k in w. Given this definition, in order to fix the reference of a common noun, ν, it is sufficient to fix the semantical intension of ν in such a way that it coincides with the metaphysical intension of the intended designatum of ν. This is easily done using the necessitation of a universally quantified biconditional in place of the necessitation of an identity, along with a rigid designator of the intended designatum. We shall need some formal way of transforming an arbitrary common noun or common noun phrase into its corresponding predicate. That is, if ν is an arbitrary count noun such as 'tiger' we need a formalization of the predicate $\ulcorner$is a $\nu\urcorner$, and if ν is a mass noun such as 'water' we need a formalization of the predicate $\ulcorner$is a bit of $\nu\urcorner$. If ν is any common noun or common noun phrase, we shall append ν as a subscript to the Greek letter 'Π', and use the result $\ulcorner\Pi_\nu\urcorner$ as our formalization of its corresponding predicate. Then if β is any singular term that denotes with respect to the actual world the kind designated by a common noun ν, we can express in the object language what ν designates by

(5) $\qquad (\exists y)\,[y = \beta \wedge \Box(x)(\Pi_\nu(x) \leftrightarrow x \in y)]$

or by

(6) $\qquad \Box(x)[\Pi_\nu(x) \leftrightarrow x \in dthat(\beta)],$

where '$\in$' is used as the predicate for the relation that holds between an individual and a universal of which the individual is an instance. For example, we can express the fact that the noun 'tiger' designates the species *Felis tigris* using, but not mentioning, the term 'tiger' with the sentence

> It is necessarily the case that: something is a tiger if and only if it is a member of *dthat(Felis tigris)*.

Schema (5) is the analogue of (2), and (6) the analogue of (3). Either may be used to fix the designation of ν. Indeed, if we assume that the object language allows for the well-formedness either of sentences of the form of (5) or of sentences of the form of (6), then since a common noun ν (rigidly) designates what a singular term β denotes if and only if a sentence of the form of either (5) or (6) is true, the truth of a sentence of the form of either (5) or (6) may be taken as a *criterion* for ν being a (rigid) designator of an appropriate universal k, where β is a singular term denoting the universal k. (As we shall see in Section 15.1, Putnam's theory of natural kind terms apparently relies on just this criterion.)

It should also be noted that one cannot use the merely material universally quantified biconditional

(7) $(x)[\Pi_\nu(x) \leftrightarrow x \in \beta]$

in place of the necessitation of a universally quantified biconditional in order to fix the designation of ν. Schema (7) fixes only the semantical extension of ν with respect to the actual world, and does not fix a semantical intension. With (7) there is no guarantee that the semantical extension of ν will coincide with respect to every possible world with the metaphysical extension of the referent of β, and hence no guarantee that ν and β share the same designation.

THREE · *Reference and the Necessary* A Posteriori

7. SOME CONSEQUENCES OF THE THEORY

7.1. Traditional Assimilations

It has been commonly held that any state of affairs that can be known to obtain only by *a posteriori* means must be metaphysically contingent, and that any fact that is metaphysically necessary can be known *a priori*.[1] The reasoning behind this thesis is simple and intuitively appealing. Empirical investigation is investigation into particular features of the world, whereas any state of affairs that is necessary cannot depend on the peculiar features of any possible world, since it obtains in every possible world regardless of that world's individual characteristics. If one has to resort to empirical means in order to determine whether or not a given state of affairs obtains, the state of affairs in question must in some way involve, or depend on, the particular features of one's circumstances. Otherwise, empirical investigation should be unnecessary. Thus, any empirical state of affairs must be contingent.

The traditional view held not only that any necessary state of affairs can be known to obtain *a priori,* but also the converse thesis that any contingent state of affairs is *a posteriori*. The reasoning behind the latter thesis consists primarily in the observation that one must empirically investigate the actual world in order to determine whether or not a given possible but unnecessary state of affairs actually obtains. Thus metaphysical and epistemic modalities were traditionally assimilated; metaphysical necessity was identified with *a priority,* and metaphysical contingency with *a posteriority.*

Following the contemporary usage, we shall say that a sentence or statement is *necessary* whenever it describes a necessary state of affairs, and similarly for the other modal adjectives. A sentence is necessary, of course, if and only if it is true with respect to every

[1]The view was generally held by the logical positivists from the 1920's through the 1950's, and retains widespread popularity today.

possible world. We shall also say that a true sentence or statement is *a priori* whenever its cognitive informative content, its sense₃, is such that one could come upon that bit of knowledge entirely by means of reflection on the concepts involved, without recourse to sensory experience, and we shall say that it is *a posteriori* if one can gain its contained information (or that of its negation) only by way of sensory experience. Then on the traditional view described above, a sentence or statement is metaphysically necessary if and only if *a priori,* and metaphysically contingent if and only if *a posteriori.*

7.2. *Necessary* A Posteriori *Indentities*

We have already seen that one of the consequences of the theory of direct reference is that certain sorts of commonly used terms are rigid designators. A further and perhaps more interesting alleged consequence is the existence of nontrivial examples of truths that are metaphysically necessary but nevertheless *a posteriori* and conceptually contingent. In this way the theory of direct reference proposes counterexamples to the traditional identification of the metaphysically necessary with the *a priori* and of the metaphysically contingent with the *a posteriori.*

Kaplan (1977) and Kripke (1972a, pp. 54–56) have also claimed as consequences of their theories the existence of nontrivial examples of truths that are contingent but *a priori.* One example adduced by Kripke is the statement 'Given that stick *S* exists, it is now exactly one meter long', as understood by a speaker in the context of his or her having fixed the reference of the term 'meter' as a name for the unit of length that is the present actual length of stick *S.* Kaplan cites as examples of the contingent *a priori* certain contingent sentences that crucially involve indexical expressions in such a way that linguistic knowledge of the meaning or rules governing the usage of these expressions is sufficient to guarantee that the sentence is true regardless of the context in which it is used, e.g., 'I am here now'. If Kaplan and Kripke are correct, the theory of direct reference belies not only the thesis that all necessary truths are *a priori* but also the converse thesis that all *a priori* truths are necessary. It is a matter of some controversy, however, whether the examples adduced by Kaplan and Kripke express genuinely *a priori* knowledge. Donnellan (1979), for instance, questions whether there are any interesting examples of contingent *a priori* truths other than Cartesian self-confirmatory truths of the *Cogito* variety.[2] Still, there is widespread agreement among the direct reference theorists that certain statements involving proper names, indexicals, or natural kind terms are, as a consequence of the theory, metaphysically necessary yet *a posteriori*.

The clearest examples of necessary yet apparently *a posteriori* truths are certain sorts of true identity statements. Such statements as

Hesperus = Phosphorus,
Cicero is identical with Tully,
I am Nathan Salmon,
Mark Twain is the same individual as Samuel Clemens,

and

She is Carol Burnett,

when used in a context which makes them true, are typical examples. In each case, the identity statement is constructed from two distinct singular terms, each of which is either a proper name or an indexical.

Each of these identity statements seems to convey *a posteriori* information. Consider for instance the statement that Hesperus is Phosphorus. Let us assume that we, the audience, acquired the name 'Phosphorus' as a name of the planet Venus by ostension to Venus at dawn or by learning, or stipulating, that the term names the last heavenly body visible at dawn in a certain part of the sky from a certain point on earth, "the Morning Star." And let us assume that we similarly acquired the name 'Hesperus' as a name of Venus by ostension to Venus at dusk or by learning, or stipulating, that it names the first heavenly body visible at dusk in a certain part of the sky from a certain point on earth, "the Evening Star." Let us further assume that there was nothing present in the circumstances of our acquisition of the two names that gave the slightest indication that they both name the same thing. Given all that we learn in acquiring

[2]See also Plantinga, 1974, pp. 8–9, n. 1. For further criticism of Kripke's view concerning the contingent *a priori* see Casullo, 1977, pp. 154–159; Evans, 1979; Kaplan, 1969, pp. 228–229; Odegard, 1976; and Schiffer, 1979, pp. 61–62. (As far as this writer can determine, the same criticism is raised by both Casullo and Odegard.) In support of Kripke, see Kaplan on the 'Newman-1' example: 1970; 1973a, pp. 499, 500, 516, n. 7; and 1977. A trivial example of a contingent *a priori* truth is any sentence of the form $\ulcorner p$ if and only if it is actually the case that $p \urcorner$, where p is contingent. See Chapter One, footnote 30.

the two names, we can easily imagine, and may even believe, that Hesperus and Phosphorus are two distinct heavenly bodies. Since the names were acquired on different occasions under quite different circumstances, we apparently cannot discover that Hesperus is the same heavenly body as Phosphorus except by empirical means. A similar situation obtains with each of the other identity statements in the list. (But see Kripke, 1979b, pp. 269, 281 n. 44.)

On the theory of direct reference, these identity statements, even if *a posteriori* and conceptually contingent, must be metaphysically necessary if true at all. To see this, let us first assume the strong version of the theory according to which proper names and indexical expressions are entirely nondescriptional and hence obstinately rigid. On this version of the theory, both of the terms contained in any of the identity statements are obstinate. The names 'Hesperus' and 'Phosphorus', for instance, designate that object which is the planet Venus, and they designate this planet with respect to every possible world, whether the planet exists there or not. By ordinary modal semantics, an identity sentence is true with respect to a possible world w if and only if the denotations of the two contained terms are the same with respect to w. Given that the identity sentence 'Hesperus = Phosphorus' is true, the names 'Hesperus' and 'Phosphorus' denote the same thing with respect to the actual world. Since the two names are supposed to be obstinate, it follows that they share the same denotation with respect to every possible world. Hence, the identity sentence 'Hesperus = Phosphorus' is true with respect to every possible world, i.e., necessary.

If we assume instead a weaker version of the direct reference theory according to which proper names and indexical expressions are descriptional relative to their designata, and hence only persistently rigid, there is instead the result that an identity sentence like 'Hesperus is identical with Phosphorus' is true with respect to every possible world in which the planet Venus exists, and not true (either false or without truth-value) with respect to those worlds in which Venus fails to exist. Although this identity sentence is not quite necessary, since it is not true with respect to every possible world, the conditional identity statement 'If Hesperus exists, then it is identical with Phosphorus' is true with respect to every possible world and hence necessary. And the conditional itself appears to be *a posteriori* like its consequent. Thus even on weaker versions of the direct reference theory, certain sorts of apparently *a posteriori* identity claims turn out to be necessary.

79

7.3. The General Phenomenon

Donnellan (1973b and 1974b) has pointed out that the necessity of *a posteriori* identity statements constructed between two proper names results directly from the fact that the two terms rigidly designate the same thing, and that this feature extends to other kinds of statements as well. Consider for instance any antecedently known necessary truth that involves two or more occurrences of the same proper name or indexical singular term, say 'If Hesperus is a planet, then Hesperus is a planet'. Now substitute an occurrence of a distinct but co-designative proper name or indexical singular term for some but not all occurrences of the term in question, e.g., 'If Phosphorus is a planet, then Hesperus is a planet'. We thereby obtain a new necessary truth, but one that appears to be *a posteriori*. That this statement is necessary is also a consequence of the fact that the names 'Hesperus' and 'Phosphorus' rigidly designate the same thing.

We know that 'Hesperus' and 'Phosphorus' rigidly designate the same thing from two sources. First, we know that 'Hesperus' and 'Phosphorus' denote one and the same thing; this represents an empirical discovery of astronomy. Second, we know that the expressions 'Hesperus' and 'Phosphorus', being proper names, are rigid designators; this represents a thesis of the theory of singular direct reference.

The important thing to notice is that the result that each of these apparently *a posteriori* statements is necessary is derived directly from the theory of reference together only with the empirical and uncontroversial claim that the relevant identity statement is true, some elementary modal semantics, and logic. No special metaphysical theory involving modality is invoked other than what is already contained in the theory of direct reference.

8. OTHER ALLEGED NECESSARY *A POSTERIORI* TRUTHS

8.1. The Examples

Not all of the necessary *a posteriori* examples adduced by the direct reference theorists result from substituting an occurrence of a proper name or indexical singular term for some but not all occurrences of a co-designative proper name or indexical singular term in an antecedently known necessary truth. Of special interest are those which do not. Alleged examples of this latter kind include certain generalizations subsuming one natural kind under another and certain identities involving some substance. One example given by Donnellan, Kripke, and Putnam is the sentence 'Water is H_2O'. This sentence is different in character from the identity statements involving individuals given above in that, while the term 'H_2O' designates the substance water—or perhaps more accurately *pure* water—it seems to be descriptional relative not to (pure) water but to the component substances hydrogen and oxygen ("the compound whose chemical composition is two parts hydrogen and one part oxygen"). The statement involving water is thus less like 'Hesperus is Phosphorus' and more like 'Hesperus is the second planet from the sun'. (But see Chapter Two, footnote 2.) Other examples include 'Gold is the element with atomic number 79' (Kripke), 'Tigers are carnivorous' (Donnellan), 'Tigers are mammals' (Donnellan, Kripke), and 'Cats are animals' (Donnellan, Kripke, Putnam). Kripke has also suggested that certain truths which involve singular reference to an individual but which do not result from substitution, as with the examples from the previous section, may also be necessary and *a posteriori*. His examples include 'Richard M. Nixon is not an inanimate object' (1972a, p. 46), 'Elizabeth Tudor the Second originated from the gametes G_1 and G_2', where 'G_1' and 'G_2' rigidly denote the gametes from which Queen Elizabeth actually sprang (1972a, pp. 112–113), 'This very table was not originally constructed from matter entirely distinct from H', and 'This is a table', said with reference to a particular table that was originally made from a hunk of wood rigidly denoted by 'H' (1972a, pp. 113–115; see also 1971, pp. 151–153).

The two examples of Kripke's involving Queen Elizabeth and the wooden table fairly obviously convey *a posteriori* information. It is less obvious that Kripke's example involving Nixon and the examples involving natural kinds are *a posteriori*. One might suppose for instance that it is part of the very sense of the name 'Richard Nixon', when used to refer to the former president, that its bearer is human and not an inanimate object. Similarly, one might suppose that *being a carnivorous mammal* and *being an animal* form part of the senses of such terms as 'tiger' and 'cat'. If this were correct, then the statements in question would be *analytic* in the traditional sense, and hence *a priori*. But it is the major tenet of the theory of direct reference that such terms as 'Richard Nixon' and 'tiger' do not express any such properties as part of their sense. Donnellan, Kripke, and Putnam all explicitly deny that their examples express *analytic* truths in any sense resembling the traditional one. It is difficult to see

81

how the statements in question can be *a priori* if they are not "true solely by virtue of sense." Yet the theory of direct reference maintains that these statements are true not solely by virtue of sense. To this extent, it is a consequence of the theory that these examples are *a posteriori*.

8.2. Trivial Essentialism

We have already seen one respect in which these examples are philosophically significant. If they are genuine examples of necessary *a posteriori* truths, then a traditional connection between necessity and *a priority* has been broken. Another respect in which these examples take on a special philosophical significance is their connection to certain metaphysical doctrines of *essentialism,* the view that certain properties of things are properties that these things could not fail to have, except by not existing.

A sentence containing a rigid designator τ is necessary if and only if the designatum of τ has a certain property *essentially*. The sentence 'The even prime integer is mystical' for example is necessary if and only if the number two is such that it could not fail to be mystical. As we have seen, it is a consequence of the theory of direct reference that the names 'Hesperus' and 'Phosphorus' are rigid designators, and hence that the identity sentence 'Hesperus is identical with Phosphorus', if true, is necessary, or at least true with respect to every possible world in which the planet Venus exists. Given that 'Hesperus' rigidly denotes the planet Venus, the identity sentence 'Hesperus is identical with Phosphorus' is necessary in this sense if and only if Venus is such that it could not fail to have the property of *being identical with Phosphorus*. Hence, using only some elementary modal semantics and the established fact that Hesperus is Phosphorus, we are able to derive from the theory of direct reference the result that the planet Venus has a certain essential property, namely the property of *being Phosphorus*. Similarly, given that 'Hesperus' rigidly denotes the planet Venus, the sentence 'If Phosphorus is a planet, then Hesperus is a planet' is necessary if and only if Hesperus, i.e., Venus, is such that it would be impossible for it not to have the property of *being a planet if Phosphorus is*. It is thus a genuine consequence of the theory of direct reference that there exist necessary yet apparently *a posteriori* statements that ascribe essential properties to objects. What this apparently shows is that the theory of direct reference has consequences that are relevant not only to philosophical semantics proper but also, at least to some extent, to *metaphysics.* The theory of direct reference—a theory primarily having to do with the single most basic semantic aspect of language, the reference of single words—has also at least some *essentialist* import.[3] It entails that if Hesperus in fact has the property of *being Phosphorus,* then Hesperus is such that it would be impossible for it not to have the property of *being Phosphorus* and hence also the property of *being a planet if Phosphorus is.* Given the philosophically uncontroversial fact that Hesperus is in fact identical with Phosphorus, we may derive the result that Hesperus has as essential properties the features of *being identical with Phosphorus* and of *being a planet if Phosphorus is.*

This derived result, however, if it is a brand of essentialism at all, is a brand of essentialism of the most trivial and innocuous kind. It is not the deeply metaphysical sort of essentialism that has come under

---

[3]There is considerable vagueness in the notion of an assertion (statement, sentence, proposition, etc.) "having nontrivial essentialist import." A number of philosophers have proposed criteria for saying when an assertion has essentialist import, but these proposals are usually stricter than what we have in mind here. We wish to acknowledge the apparent commitment to some special form of essentialism in an assertion such as:

> If Socrates is human, then Socrates is such that he could not have been nonhuman.

This assertion falls just short of *logically entailing* that someone is such that he could not have been nonhuman. It requires the further empirical and uncontroversial premise that Socrates is indeed human. With this in mind, the following criteria are hereby proposed: We shall say that an assertion *A involves a commitment to essentialism with respect to* the property P whenever assertion A supplemented only by further premises that are themselves trivial, purely empirically verifiable, or otherwise philosophically uncontroversial (modal) logically entails some statement of the form $\ulcorner(\exists x)\Box[Exists(x) \rightarrow \phi(x)]\urcorner$, where $\ulcorner\phi(x)\urcorner$ "expresses" (or *designates*) the property P. (Some qualification is needed if existence is to count as a property, yet not always an essential property.) We shall also say that an assertion *A has essentialist import* or is *essentialist* whenever, for some property P or other, A involves a commitment to essentialism with respect to P. Finally, we shall say that an assertion *A has nontrivial essentialist import,* or is nontrivially essentialist, whenever for some property P, A involves a commitment to essentialism with respect to P, and the entailed sentence $\ulcorner(\exists x)\Box[Exists(x) \rightarrow \phi(x)]\urcorner$, where $\ulcorner\phi(x)\urcorner$ expresses (or designates) P, is not trivially true (i.e., either not true, or true but not trivially so).

Of course, the vagueness and context-relativity of the relevant notion of *triviality* enters into each of these definitions, and consequently the defined notions are left somewhat vague and context-relative. (A simple assertion may be nontrivially essen-

(footnote continued on next page)

so much criticism.[4] Under our scheme of representing intrinsically relational properties by sequences, the property of *being identical with Phosphorus* is represented by the ordered couple ⟨Phosphorus, the *identity* relation⟩, that is ⟨Venus, identity⟩. In the terminology of Section 1.3, it is the haecceity of the planet Venus, the property of *being that very thing*. The assertion that Venus has this property essentially, or any property entailed by this property, is little more than a boring truism, and can hardly begin to stir the emotions of foes of Aristotelian essentialism. It is perhaps none too surprising that this minimal sort of essentialism may be derived from the philosophy of language together with an uncontroversial fact.

8.3. Nontrivial Essentialism Concerning Natural Kinds

The situation is slightly different with the examples involving substances and natural kinds. Given that natural kind terms like 'water' and 'tiger' rigidly designate natural kinds, sentences like 'Water is H₂O' and 'Tigers are mammals' are necessary if and only if the liquid (pure) water is such that it would be *impossible* for it not to be composed of two parts hydrogen and one part oxygen, and the species *Tiger* is such that it *must* consist of mammals and nothing

---

tialist relative to some contexts, and not so relative to others.) It is hoped, nevertheless, that these definitions are at least a first step toward clarification of the notions we have in mind. It should be noted that it is apparently a consequence of these definitions that *every* assertion whatsoever has *some* essentialist import. This is in virtue of the fact that, for any predicate 'F', the sentence $\ulcorner(\exists x)\Box[Exists(x) \rightarrow (F(x) \lor \sim F(x))]\urcorner$ is a truth of (most systems of modal) logic, and hence logically entailed by every statement. (We are ignoring here the question of whether a statement with existential import can be a genuine logical truth; in any case, the assertion that something is either F or not-F is perfectly trivial, if anything is.) In addition, in the $S5$ and *Brouwersche* systems, any atomic subject-predicate statement $\ulcorner\Pi(\alpha)\urcorner$ entails $\ulcorner\Box\Diamond\Pi(\alpha)\urcorner$, and hence many assertions involve, by these systems, a commitment to essentialism with respect to a certain *modal* property, namely that of *being possibly such-and-such*. (This fact about these definitions was pointed out to me by Kaplan.) On the other hand, involvement in a commitment to essentialism with respect to such properties as these, *per se*, yields only trivial essentialist import. The assertion mentioned above concerning Socrates has *nontrivial* essentialist import since it involves a special commitment to essentialism with respect to *not being nonhuman*, a form of essentialism that is a matter of considerable philosophical controversy.

In conformity with established practice, we shall often say that a premise, statement, etc. "has essentialist import," or is "essentialist," where we mean that it has *nontrivial* essentialist import, and that a premise is "nonessentialist," or "essentialism-free," where we mean that it has no nontrivial essentialist import.

[4]Quine is the best known and most outspoken critic of essentialism. See 1953a, pp. 154–158; 1953c, pp. 173–174; 1960, pp. 199–200; and 1962, p. 182.

else.[5] Similarly, given that the term 'gold' rigidly designates the precious metal gold, the sentence 'Gold is an element with atomic number 79' is necessary if and only if the metal gold is such that it *must* be an element with exactly 79 protons in the nuclei of its component atoms.

These examples strongly suggest certain general principles of essentialism concerning natural kinds. The examples involving water and gold suggest that the chemical composition of a compound is an essential feature of that compound, and that the atomic number of an element is an essential feature of that element. The examples involving tigers and cats suggest that the taxonomically higher biological kinds of which a species is a subkind are essential features of that species, e.g., that the kind which is the species *Tiger* is such that it cannot but be a subkind of the order *Carnivora,* the class *Mammalia,* and the *Animal Kingdom.* This sort of essentialism concerning natural kinds has considerably more metaphysical bite than the completely trivial sort of essentialism concerning the identity of individuals which maintains that the planet Venus has its haecceity essentially, and it is easier to see how this essentialism concerning natural kinds might offend one's metaphysical doctrines and beliefs. It might be argued, for instance, that the taxonomic

---

[5]Although 'Tigers are mammals' expresses a necessary truth, we cannot conclude from this fact that individual tigers are such that they *could not* fail to be mammals—even granting that the term 'tiger' is a rigid designator. For it may be consistently held that what is in fact a tiger might not have been a tiger but, say, a robot, and hence not a mammal. That is, from

$$\Box(x)[Tiger(x) \rightarrow Mammal(x)]$$

(i.e., necessarily, tigers are mammals) together with

$$\Box(x)[Tiger(x) \leftrightarrow x \in dthat(Felis\ tigris)]$$

(i.e., 'tiger' rigidly designates the species *Felis tigris*), we may conclude

$$\Box(x)[x \in dthat(Felis\ tigris) \rightarrow Mammal(x)]$$

(i.e., *having exclusively mammals as members* is an essential property of *Felis tigris*), but we may not conclude

$$(x)[Tiger(x) \rightarrow \Box Mammal(x)]$$

(i.e., tigers are essentially mammals) without the additional premise

$$(x)[Tiger(x) \rightarrow \Box Tiger(x)]$$

(i.e., tigers are essentially tigers). Teller (1975) calls this the *problem of covariance of properties.*

structure of the biological world might have been such that the very kind which is in fact the species *Tiger,* although it is actually a *natural* kind, was instead an *artificial* kind, created in Dr. Moreau's laboratory, so that its members would not classify as mammals. Regardless of whether such a position is ultimately correct, it is at least *prima facie* tenable. If the theory of direct reference, together with some uncontroversial empirical facts, genuinely conflicts with this anti-essentialist position, the theory takes on considerable metaphysical significance in addition to significance for philosophical semantics proper.

Still one may doubt whether very much metaphysical significance can be attached to essentialism concerning natural kinds. It may be argued that natural kinds, being theoretical universals, are in some sense ultimately "creatures of the mind," and that unlike concrete physical things, theoretical constructs may take on certain essential properties as part of the process of their invention by the scientific mind.[6] In this way one's metaphysical doctrines may leave room for essentialism concerning abstract entities while excluding anything but the most trivial sort of essentialism concerning concrete individuals such as people and physical objects.[7]

8.4. *Nontrivial Essentialism Concerning Individuals*

Nontrivial essentialism concerning individuals is Aristotelian essentialism *par excellence,* and it is this form of essentialism that

[6]Chemical elements and compounds should not be identified with concrete physical things. For if the substance water were reified as, say, the Lésniewskian or Goodmanian scattered whole consisting at a time t of all H_2O molecules existing at time t and only those molecules, then it seems that we could not allow what is obviously true, namely that there might have been different samples of what is in fact the substance water than there actually are, and indeed that there might have been an entirely different set of water samples, *completely disjoint* with the set of actual water samples. Similar considerations count against identifying biological species with aggregates of animals or plants. We may be willing to accord to aggregates of individuals the same lax necessary conditions for identity across possible worlds that govern the potentiality of other physical objects (such as the bodies of living organisms) that might have had (at any given time t) different physical constitutions than those which they actually have (at time t). Even so, we still seem prohibited from allowing that a scattered whole might have (originally) consisted of *completely* different "parts." This intuition will be discussed further in Chapter Seven and Appendix I.

[7]Kaplan (1969, pp. 224–225) expressed such metaphysical beliefs. Donnellan (1974b) also shows a willingness to accept essentialism concerning certain universals while remaining somewhat skeptical with regard to nontrivial essentialism concerning people and tables.

opponents most vigorously dispute. It is in this context that Kripke's examples involving Nixon, Queen Elizabeth, and the wooden table (see Section 8.1) take on a special philosophical significance. For given that the names 'Richard M. Nixon' and 'Elizabeth Tudor' and the demonstrative 'this' are rigid, Kripke's examples express necessary truths if and only if it is an essential feature of Nixon that he is animate, and an essential feature of Queen Elizabeth that she sprang from the very gametes from which she actually sprang, and an essential feature of the table referred to by the speaker that it is a table originally made from a particular hunk of wood, or at least from no entirely distinct matter. This is precisely the substantive sort of essentialism that is the subject of so much philosophical controversy.

If the theory of direct reference together only with empirically verified or otherwise philosophically uncontroversial facts has the consequence that any of these examples indeed express necessary truths, then the theory has considerable and rather surprising implications. Philosophical questions concerning nontrivial essential properties (are there any, and if so, what are they?) are time-honored and notoriously difficult.[8] If solutions to these questions can be obtained from this relatively simple theory about the reference of single words, then the theory should be regarded either with awe or with skepticism. For if the theory genuinely yields such consequences, it has substantial ramifications, not only for philosophical semantics proper (rigid designators, necessary *a posteriori* truth, etc.), but also for classical philosophical problems that are squarely metaphysical.

9. A CRUCIAL QUESTION

The important philosophical question and the central question to be addressed in Part II of the present work is this: Is the situation with these examples involving natural kinds, and with Kripke's examples involving people and tables, like that of necessary identities between rigid designators? Specifically, is the claim that these examples express necessary truths derived in some way from the theory of direct reference without an appeal to some controversial metaphysical theory entirely independent of the theory of reference, or do

---

[8]For an illuminating discussion of the debate between essentialists and anti-essentialists, and of the difficulties inherent in arguing either side, see Cartwright, 1968.

these claims ultimately rely on some special independent metaphysical theory in addition to the theory of reference? In claiming that these examples express necessary truths, are direct reference theorists like Putnam revealing the nontrivial essentialist import of their theories of reference, or is the nontrivial essentialism that they espouse completely seperable from their theories of reference? (See footnote 3.) In short, are any of these nontrivial forms of essentialism concerning natural kinds and individuals, in any significant sense, further consequences of the theory of direct reference?

We do not want to require, of course, that the claim that there are necessary *a posteriori* truths which ascribe nontrivial essential properties to natural kinds or to individuals be derived *solely* from the theory of direct reference. Even the claim that the statement 'Hesperus = Phosphorus' is necessary depends on something in addition to the theory of direct reference for proper names. The theory of direct reference taken by itself only tells us that this identity statement is necessary *provided that it is true.* In order to derive the necessary identity of Hesperus and Phosphorus from the theory of direct reference, we must appeal to a certain independent fact, namely that Hesperus is in fact identical with Phosphorus. The thesis that Hesperus has the essential property of *being Phosphorus* is thus a consequence only of the theory of direct reference supplemented by the perfectly innocuous and uncontroversial fact that Hesperus is Phosphorus. Similarly, we are not asking here whether the necessity of the examples mentioned above concerning natural kinds or individuals can be derived *solely* from the theory of reference. It is enough if these essentialist theses can be derived from the theory of direct reference supplemented by other factual premises, e.g., that water is in fact H_2O, provided that these further premises are themselves purely empirically verifiable, or otherwise philosophically uncontroversial. In particular, the premises must not beg the question by presupposing a nontrivial metaphysical theory of essentialism.[9] We have already seen that, given certain empirical premises

[9]What sort of supplementary premise is ruled out as "question-begging"? Any nontrivially essentialist premise, in the sense partly clarified in footnote 3, but that is not all. 'Hesperus is Phosphorus', 'Water is H_2O', and 'Tigers are mammals' are all perfectly admissible supplementary premises. Their necessitations, on the other hand, are plainly question-begging. Yet it is not that the necessitations are essentialist *per se;* an orthodox Fregean theorist might maintain the necessitation of any one of these sentences on the grounds that the sentence itself is analytic (true solely by virtue of Fregean sense). It is only on the anti-Fregean assumption that the terms 'Hesperus', 'water', and 'tiger' are rigid designators of Hesperus, the substance water, and the

completely free of any essentialist import, the theory of direct reference entails certain trivial forms of essentialism, e.g., that Hesperus is such that it could not fail to have the property of *being identical with Phosphorus*. It may be said, therefore, that the theory of direct reference has at least some essentialist import, even if it is only a trivial essentialism that asserts of some object that it is such that it *must* have the property of *being this very thing*. Our primary purpose in Part II, however, will be to assess the extent to which the case can be made that nontrivial forms of essentialism concerning natural kinds or individuals are similarly derivable from the theory of direct reference without begging the important philosophical question of essentialism.[10]

---

species *Tiger,* respectively, that the necessitations are essentialist assertions about Hesperus, water, and the species *Tiger,* respectively. For the direct reference theorist, who cannot have the Fregean's nonessentialist reason for maintaining the necessitations, the necessitations are essentialist assertions, nothing more and nothing less. Following the notions partly clarified in footnote 3, let us say that an assertion A is (*nontrivially*) *essentialist in the context of* a theory T if it is a consequence of T that assertion A is (nontrivially) essentialist, in the sense that assertion A supplemented by premises that are trivial, purely empirically verifiable, or otherwise philosophically uncontroversial, and supplemented further by the theory T, yields a (nontrivial) consequence of the form $\ulcorner(\exists x)\Box[Exists(x) \rightarrow \phi(x)]\urcorner$. (The notion of an assertion's being nontrivially essentialist *simpliciter* is the special case of nontrivial essentialist import in the context of every theory, or alternatively, in the context of the null theory, i.e., logic alone. We may similarly define the notion of an assertion *involving a commitment in the context of* a theory T to essentialism *with respect to* a particular property P. Notice that by this definition, any assertion whatsoever is nontrivially essentialist in the context of a nontrivially essentialist theory.) Then any supplementary premise which is essentialist in the context of the theory of direct reference (or involves a commitment in the context of the theory of direct reference to nontrivial essentialism concerning natural kinds or individuals) and which is not itself trivial, purely empirically verifiable, or otherwise philosophically uncontroversial, nor shown to be a consequence of the theory of direct reference, is to be ruled out as question-begging.

[10]There is an interesting class of examples of essentialism concerning certain abstract entities, viz., numbers, that are derivable as consequences of the direct reference theory of numerals, supplemented by the traditional and relatively uncontroversial view that any true proposition of pure mathematics is necessarily true. For example, it is a theorem of arithmetic that 0 is an even integer; hence it is a necessary truth that 0 is even. Given the further premise that '0' is an obstinate designator, $(\exists x)\Box[0 = x]$, it follows that the number 0 is such that it could not fail to be even. (The premise that '0' is obstinate is needed for the inference. If for instance '0' were synonymous with a nonrigid definite description, e.g., 'Russell's favorite even number', the essentialist thesis would not follow.) The premise that '0' is obstinate follows directly from the direct reference theory of numerals (in the sense clarified in Chapter
(footnote continued on next page)

The question may be put thus:

> Given only whatever logical devices one may need (e.g., higher-order logic, set theory, $S5$ modal logic, etc.) and given further whatever non-question-begging, purely empirically verifiable, or otherwise philosophically uncontroversial facts one may need (e.g., that water is in fact H_2O), is it possible to derive a substantive and nontrivial form of essentialism concerning natural kinds or individuals (like organisms or artifacts) from the philosophy of language, i.e., from syntax, the theory of reference, and modal semantics?

Donnellan (1973b and 1974b), Kripke (1972a, p. 114, n. 56), and Putnam (1973b, pp. 708–709) have all said things which suggest that the answer is 'yes', that surprising though it may be, their theory about the most basic semantic aspect of language has much to say about the nature of things of certain kinds, or of certain kinds of

---

One, footnote 35). A descriptional theory of numerals such as Frege's, can also accommodate the metamathematical fact that '0' is obstinate, but only by embracing the view that the properties expressed by '0' are essential to 0. Thus it might be said that the theory of direct reference yields a certain nontrivial (though relatively uncontroversial) version of essentialism concerning abstract mathematical entities. The warrantedness of this claim depends on the extent to which the thesis that all mathematical theorems are necessary truths is not to be regarded as begging the question of mathematical essentialism. The thesis is independent of the theory of direct reference and involves a commitment to mathematical essentialism in the context of the direct reference theory of numerals. See the preceding footnote. (The thesis is not essentialist *per se*. An extreme anti-essentialist could maintain the thesis, e.g., by holding the Fregean descriptional theory of numerals and maintaining the further Fregean thesis that all mathematical theorems are analytic. Frege held both of these theses, though this is no reason to suppose that he was opposed to mathematical essentialism. Mathematical essentialism is quite independent of the two Fregean theses.) Thus the claim that the direct reference theory of numerals yields mathematical essentialism as a "consequence," in our sense, depends on the extent to which the thesis that, e.g., it is necessary that 0 is even, can be regarded as trivial or philosophically uncontroversial.

It has sometimes been maintained that essentialism concerning classes (or sets) and their membership is derivable using standard modal reasoning from the axioms of class theory. A fairly explicit instance is given by David Wiggins (1980):

> A proof that, for all finite classes α, if α has x as a member then α necessarily has x as a member can be framed by employing the pairing axiom and the axiom of extensionality, plus the same meagre resources of modality as [are] employed in the proof of the necessity of identity (p. 113, n. 18).
>
> ... Once it is conceded that [a set $\{x,y\}$] is necessarily a set, the principles of set theory bring it about (*qua* definitive of what sets are and of how they are

things, about what they could not be and what they must be.[11] It shall be argued in Part II below, however, that the correct answer to our question is 'no'. We shall do so by attempting to reconstruct the

---

individuated) that the actual membership of the pair is its only possible membership (p. 114).

(See also Sharvy, 1968. For criticism of Sharvy see Parks, 1972, Van Cleve, 1978, and Salmon, 1979c, appendix II.) Wiggins does not provide the alleged proof, nor does he specify exactly what meager modal resources are needed. Whatever Wiggins's intent, it is not true that this form of essentialism concerning (finite) classes can be derived from the axioms of set theory using $S5$—though nothing more than (one formulation of) $S5$ is needed to derive the necessity of identity. There is a crucial difference between the axioms of class theory and the usual postulates of arithmetic. The usual postulates of arithmetic involve primitive individual constants, at least the one numeral '0', whereas the axioms of class theory involve no closed singular terms but class abstracts (e.g., '$\hat{x}[F(x)]$', '$\{x,y\}$', etc.) and these are descriptional. (A class abstract $\ulcorner \hat{x}[\phi(x)] \urcorner$ may be regarded as an abbreviation for a definite description $\ulcorner (\imath y)(Class(y) \wedge (x)[x \in y \leftrightarrow \phi(x)]) \urcorner$.) The axioms of class theory simply characterize a certain type of structure on the universe of classes, a structure that can be satisfied in a given model by isomorphic but numerically different or, so to speak, "shuffled" universes of entities from one possible world to the next (even keeping the ur-elements constant), without doing violence to the necessitations of the axioms. The necessitations of the axioms require only that in each possible world there be a null class, a pair class $\{x,y\}$ for every x and y, only one class for any given membership, etc. They do not require that each of these classes be the very same entity from one world to the next. (This is not to say that a model which varies the memberships of the classes from world to world reflects the modal reality of classes, for surely it does not. It is only to point out that such a model may satisfy the necessitations of the axioms, so that a further essentialist axiom is needed to preclude these anti-essentialist models in a modal set theory, as Kit Fine provides in 1978b.)

[11] The degree of explicitness on this point varies among the three philosophers mentioned. Putnam and Donnellan speak primarily of deriving the result, using the theory of direct reference, that certain *a posteriori* or conceptually contingent truths involving a natural kind term (e.g., that water is H_2O) are metaphysically necessary. Putnam explicitly labels this a "consequence" of his theory of natural kind terms. He makes no mention of the fact that, on the direct reference theory, this result is equivalent to a nontrivial form of essentialism concerning natural kinds. Given that Putnam's explicit claim is correct, it follows that the answer to our question must be in the affirmative. Donnellan, whose primary concern in 1973b and 1974b is to elaborate and develop Putnam's program for deriving the necessity of certain *a posteriori* truths concerning natural kinds from the theory of direct reference, speaks of the program also as one to derive certain forms of essentialism. Kripke speaks of providing a certain form of essentialism concerning the origins of concrete artifacts with "something like proof, using the principle of the necessity of identity for particulars" (as discussed in Section 7.2 above), together with a seemingly innocuous premise, one which appears (or more accurately, appeared to me) from his presentation to be essentialism-free. The premise which Kripke had in mind, however, is essentialist, and he has informed me that his "proof" was probably not intended as yielding an affirmative answer to

(footnote continued on next page)

strongest possible case for the affirmative claim, and then revealing its shortcomings.[12]

Let us be clear about this. We do not want to challenge the theory of direct reference. Indeed, we have argued in the preceding two chapters in its favor. As far as the purposes of Part II are concerned, however, it does not matter whether we accept, reject, or withhold judgment concerning the theory of direct reference. Nor do we want to challenge any essentialist doctrines. What we want to question is simply whether the theory yields as consequences certain nontrivial essentialist doctrines concerning natural kinds or concrete individuals, and what is important for this purpose is that we have some *characterization* of the theory of direct reference. Throughout the remainder of the present work, the theory will be taken to be as characterized in the preceding chapters.

The most elaborate attempt to substantiate the claim that nontrivial forms of essentialism are derivable from the theory of direct reference is to be found in Putnam's presentation of his theory of natural kind terms and in Donnellan's elucidations of Putnam's "mechanism," as he calls it, for "generating" necessary *a posteriori* truths concerning natural kinds. In the next chapter, the closing chapter of Part I, we undertake a detailed study of Putnam's theory of natural kind terms.

---

our question. Still, there is a widespread view among philosophers that the theory of direct reference, as propounded in Kripke's *Naming and Necessity* and elsewhere, has the consequence that certain *a posteriori* truths, like 'Water is H_2O' and the others listed in Section 8.1, are necessary, and hence that certain forms of essentialism concerning natural kinds and individuals are true. (One version of this view even finds its way into the liner notes to the 1980 book edition of *Naming and Necessity*.) My primary purpose in Part II will be to dispel that view.

[12]Specifically, we shall show that certain attempts to derive nontrivial essentialist consequences from the theory of reference fail because they beg the question of essentialism by presupposing a tacit essentialist premise, one that is independent of the theory of reference. Thus, the metaphysically loaded consequences derive their essentialist import not from the theory of reference but from independent metaphysical presuppositions. The work of Kripke and Putnam in the philosophy of language, and in particular their alleged attempts to derive nontrivial essentialism from the theory of reference, is criticized by D. H. Mellor (1977). Among Mellor's criticisms is the charge that the attempts to derive essentialism fail precisely because they "gratuitously assume the essentialist conclusion." Despite a similar theme, the relationship between Mellor's criticism and the criticism to be presented in Part II of the present work is tenuous. Mellor's main critical arguments are very different from those that we shall give below, and seem to be based on quite different conceptions of essentialism, the theory of direct reference, and the attempt to derive the one from the other.

FOUR · *Putnam's Theory of*
Natural Kind Terms

10. PUTNAM'S THESES

We have already seen Putnam's version of the semantical argument that the general properties normally associated with a natural kind term do not constitute a logically sufficient condition for application. The "psychological state" of someone grasping a certain concept uniquely determines the set or cluster of general properties included in that concept. This is virtually true by the definition of 'general property'. If natural kind terms are descriptional, whether relationally or not, then the concept, or sense, expressed by a natural kind term must uniquely determine the semantical intension, and hence also the semantical extension, of that term. Simple thought experiments involving doppelgängers show that the internal psychological state of someone in understanding a natural kind term such as 'tiger' or 'water', or in having an occurrent belief expressed by a sentence containing the term, underdetermines the extension of the term. One's mental concept of a tiger is simply too loose, loose enough to befit imaginary species of nontigers. Nonqualitative aspects of the context or external setting are generally relevant to the determination of the semantical intension and extension of the natural kind terms we use. Therefore, natural kind terms are not descriptional solely in terms of general properties that may be included in a wholly internal psychological state. As Putnam puts it, their " 'meanings' just ain't in the head!" (1973b, p. 704). Putnam also points out that similar thought experiments may be conducted to show that indexical terms are context-sensitive and not descriptional solely in terms of qualitative properties:

> Words like 'now', 'this', 'here' have long been recognized to be *indexical,* or *token-reflexive*—i.e., to have an extension which varies from context to context or token to token. For these words, no one has ever suggested the traditional theory that "[thoroughly descriptive sense] determines extension." To take our Twin Earth example: if I have a *Doppelganger* on Twin Earth, then when I think "I have a headache," *he* thinks "I have a headache." But the extension of the particular token of 'I' in his verbalized

thought is himself (or his unit class, to be precise), while the extension of the token of 'I' in *my* verbalized thought is *me* (or my unit class, to be precise). So the same word, 'I', has two different extensions in two different idiolects; but it does not follow that the [purely qualitative] concept I have of myself is in any way different from the [purely qualitative] concept my Doppelganger has of himself (1973b, pp. 709–710).

Thus Putnam's account of natural kind terms begins with the following two theses:

(T1)   The semantical extension, and hence the semantical inten-
        sion (function from possible worlds to extensions), of a
        natural kind term is not uniquely determined solely by the
        wholly internal "psychological state" of a speaker in under-
        standing the term, or in having an occurrent belief
        expressed by a sentence containing the term. In this respect
        natural kind terms resemble indexical terms (1973b, pp.
        700–702, 709–710).

(T2)   Hence, natural kind terms are not descriptional solely in
        terms of general properties that may be included in a
        wholly internal psychological state.[1]

Before proceeding with the rest of the theory, Putnam considers a possible challenge to (T1) and (T2). It may be objected that if, as Putnam argues, one's psychological state in understanding the term 'tiger' or in thinking "There is a tiger coming after me!" is nonspe-cific enough to include animals of a species k distinct but superfi-cially indistinguishable from the species *Felis tigris,* then there is no reason to suppose that the term 'tiger', for such a speaker, applies only to members of *Felis tigris.* If the sense$_1$ or mental concept that one attaches to the term 'tiger' is really so loose as not to exclude animals of a different species k, then perhaps the term 'tiger', at least for such a speaker, expresses some gross superficial characteristics of tigers, perhaps *being a feline, having black stripes, having a tawny coat,* and so on, and therefore designates not the species *Felis tigris* but some general category which, as it happens, subsumes both *Felis tigris* and k. Similarly, one might argue that if one's psychological concept of "water" is so loose as to include not only liquid samples of H_2O (with impurities) but also liquid samples of chemical substances

[1]Thesis (T2) is left tacit in Putnam's writings, but this conclusion is clearly implicit in thesis (T1).

94

distinct but superficially indistinguishable from H_2O—Putnam's imaginary liquid compound XYZ—then perhaps the term 'water' for such a speaker is descriptive in terms of such characteristics as *being a colorless liquid, being odorless, being thirst quenching,* and so on. The term 'water' would then designate not H_2O but a more general category, something like the category *Colorless Odorless Thirst-quenching Liquid,* a category that may include samples of chemical substances other than H_2O. Why should we suppose otherwise? Of course, today nearly everyone knows that a liquid sample is a sample of water if and only if it is basically composed of H_2O, mixed with varying amounts of impurities, and hence the modern concept of water would probably exclude samples of Putnam's imaginary liquid compound XYZ, or "fool's water." But since the popular concept of water that prevailed in olden times could not have excluded samples of XYZ, why should we suppose that the term 'water', as used back then, would not properly apply to samples of XYZ?

This sort of doubt concerning theses (T1) and (T2) cannot be laid to rest simply by reproducing the initial arguments for the theory of direct reference. It is true that if 'water' is descriptive in terms of the properties of *being colorless, odorless, thirst quenching,* and so on, then the term 'water' must apply to any substance that happens to have these properties. Moreover, it must be *a priori* and metaphysically necessary that water is a liquid that has these characteristics, and that any liquid that has these characteristics is water. The initial arguments for the direct reference theory consist in denying the consequents of these conditionals and drawing a *modus tollens* inference. But the present demur is over the question of whether we should not be performing *modus ponens* instead of *modus tollens.* Perhaps we should just accept it that, as the term 'water' was used in olden times, any colorless, odorless, thirst-quenching liquid would be *water,* properly so-called, even if its chemical composition is XYZ and not H_2O.

Putnam attempts to allay this doubt by presenting an alternative picture.[2] He writes:

> Suppose I point to a glass of water and say "this liquid is called water." My "ostensive definition" of water has the following empirical presupposition: that the body of liquid I am pointing to bears a certain sameness relation (say, *x is the same liquid as y,* or

[2]Putnam's response to the present objection is elaborated in 1975a, pp. 235–241.

x is the same$_L$ as y) to most of the stuff I and other speakers in my linguistic community have on other occasions called "water." If this presupposition is false because, say, I am—unknown to me—pointing to a glass of gin and not a glass of water, then I do not intend my ostensive definition to be accepted. Thus the ostensive definition conveys what might be called a "defeasible" necessary and sufficient condition: the necessary and sufficient condition for being water is bearing the relation *same$_L$* to the stuff in the glass; but this is the necessary and sufficient condition only if the empirical presupposition is satisfied. If it is not satisfied, then one of a series of, so to speak, "fallback" conditions becomes activated.

The key point is that the relation *same$_L$* is a *theoretical* relation: whether something is or is not the same liquid as *this* may take an indeterminate amount of scientific investigation to determine. Thus, the fact that an English speaker in 1750 might have called XYZ "water," whereas he or his successors would not have called XYZ water in 1800 or 1850 does not mean that the "meaning" of 'water' changed for the average speaker in the interval. In 1750 or in 1850 or in 1950 one might have pointed to, say, the liquid in Lake Michigan as an example of "water." What changed was that in 1750 we would have mistakenly thought that XYZ bore the relation *same$_L$* to the liquid in Lake Michigan, whereas in 1800 or 1850 we would have known that it did not (1973b, pp. 702–703).

The point of this passage is that a term like 'water' may be "defined," in the sense that its meaning may be entirely conveyed (Putnam's "definitions" are "meaning explanations," not abbreviations or other means of introducing new bits of language), in such a way that the audience acquires a psychological "concept" that is to be associated with the term, but nothing in addition to this concept that might be used without the aid of any further information to settle the question of whether a given sample that happens to fit the concept is something to which the term applies. If 'water' is "ostensively defined" in this way, the audience may judge from the paradigm sample involved in the definition that water is supposed to be a colorless, odorless, thirst-quenching liquid, and the audience thereby acquires a concept of water; but confronted with a fresh liquid sample, the audience may not be in a position to know whether this sample bears the *same$_L$* relation to the sample demonstrated in the ostensive definition. Putnam illustrates this point in the case of an ostensive definition, but elsewhere he also allows that the term 'water' may be defined "operationally," using a list of supposed identifying characteristics of water—what Putnam calls the *stereotype* associated with the term 'water'—in place of a paradigm sample, with the same result that the audience cannot always know from the definition alone when a given sample is a sample of water.[3]

The remainder of Putnam's theory of natural kind terms is given by the following six theses, extracted from 1975a, pp. 229–234.[4]

(T3)   One may "explain the meaning" of a natural kind term such as 'water' in an ostensive definition that has the intended logical force of the following:

> For every possible world w, and every individual x in w, x is water in w if and only if x in w is the same liquid as *this* (or *those*) in the actual world,

where the demonstrative 'this' rigidly denotes a sample of water in the actual world (pp. 229–232).

(T4)   One may also "explain the meaning" of a natural kind term such as 'water' in a so-called operational definition, using a description of water in terms of its supposed identifying characteristics (the "stereotype" of water), in place of indexical reference to a paradigmatic sample of water (pp. 229–230).

(T5)   Natural kind terms such as 'water' are rigid designators of natural kinds, as a consequence of (T3) (p. 231).

(T6)   Natural kind terms such as 'water' "have an unnoticed indexical component," one which is brought out in (T3) (p. 234).

(T7)   (T1) is true of natural kind terms for the same reason that it is true of any other indexical terms (p. 234).

---

[3]That the "stereotype," or set of properties associated with a natural kind term in the appropriate way, exhausts the conceptual content of the meaning of the term, and yet may fail as either a logically necessary or sufficient condition for application, is a recurrent theme in Putnam's writings on the theory of meaning and reference. See for instance 1970, especially pp. 148–152. See Chapter One, footnote 7 above.

[4]We omit from this bare reconstruction further significant theses concerning the so-called *division of linguistic labor* and Putnam's sociolinguistic hypothesis. See 1973b or 1975a, especially pp. 227–229. This part of Putnam's theory is an important supplement to thesis (T2), but not central to the concerns of Part II below. We are interested primarily in those aspects of Putnam's theory that have, in his words, "startling consequences for the theory of necessary truth." See the Introduction, footnote 6, above.

(T8)   Natural kind terms that differ in semantical extension *ipso facto* differ in "meaning." The meaning of a natural kind term such as 'water' alone uniquely determines its extension (with respect to a possible world) without further dependence on context (p. 234).

Putnam explicitly claims that this theory yields the consequence that the statement 'Water is H_2O', though conceptually contingent, is necessary. He writes:

> What Kripke was the first to observe is that this theory of the meaning (or "use," or whatever) of the word 'water' (and other natural-kind terms as well) has startling consequences for the theory of necessary truth. . . .
>
> Suppose . . . that I discover the microstructure of water—that water is H_2O. At this point I will be able to say that the stuff on Twin Earth that I earlier *mistook* for water isn't really water. In the same way, if you describe, not another planet in the actual universe, but another possible universe in which there is stuff with the chemical formula XYZ which passes the "operational test" for *water,* we shall have to say that that stuff isn't water but merely XYZ. You will not have described a possible world in which "water is XYZ," but merely a possible world in which there are lakes of XYZ, people drink XYZ (and not water), or whatever. In fact, once we have discovered the nature of water, nothing counts as a possible world in which water doesn't have that nature. Once we have discovered that water (in the actual world) is H_2O, *nothing counts as a possible world in which water isn't H_2O.*
>
> On the other hand, we can perfectly well imagine having experiences that would convince us (and that would make it rational to believe that) water *isn't H_2O.* In that sense, it is conceivable that water isn't H_2O. It is conceivable but it isn't possible! Conceivability is no proof of possibility.
>
> . . . a statement can be (metaphysically) necessary and [conceptually] contingent. Human intuition has no privileged access to metaphysical necessity (1973b, pp. 708–709; also in 1975a, pp. 232–233).

Thus Putnam maintains as a further thesis the following:

(T9)   The theory put forth in theses (T1) through (T8) has "startling consequences for the theory of necessary truth," to wit, the existence of (nontrivial) examples of metaphysically necessary but conceptually contingent truths, for example, that water is H_2O.

Our task in the remainder of this chapter is to clarify and develop the first eight theses of Putnam's theory of natural kind terms. In Part II we shall attempt to gauge the extent to which they may lend support to the additional thesis (T9). Theses (T1) and (T2) have already been discussed at some length. Let us move now to theses (T3) through (T8).

11. INITIAL EXEGETICAL REMARKS

11.1. The 'is' of Instantiation

Some simple points of clarification must be made at the outset. The verb 'is' occurring in the predicate 'is water', as it is used by Putnam, is an 'is' of predication, not the 'is' of identity. The predicate may be thought of as short for 'is a sample of water'. The "ostensive definition" of water given in (T3) may be rewritten thus:

> For every possible world *w*, and every individual *x in w*, x is a sample of water in *w* if and only if *x* in *w* *is a sample of* the same liquid that *this* in the actual world *is a sample of.*

The reader must take care to bear in mind a sharp distinction between a substance and its samples. Water is a liquid substance—a natural kind—and a glass of water contains a sample of that kind. Water is the liquid that every sample of water is a sample *of*. The *same liquid* relation is an equivalence relation between liquid samples, not the relation between a liquid substance and any of its samples or the identity relation restricted to liquid substances. It is the relation that holds between two liquid samples when they are both samples of the same substance,[5] or as we shall say, when they are *consubstantial*. Presumably, if the natural kind term in question were a species term such as 'tiger' instead of a substance term, in place of the *same liquid* relation one would use the *same animal* relation, i.e., the relation that holds between two animals when they are *conspecific,* or animals of the same species.

[5]This is slightly inaccurate. We shall see below that Putnam's *same$_L$* relation is an equivalence relation between what we shall call "possible world-slices" of liquid samples.

11.2. A Gross Misinterpretation

Another relatively obvious and simple point of clarification concerns thesis (T6). Putnam is not claiming here that 'water' is an abbreviation for some indexical phrase such as 'the same liquid as *this* in the actual world', or 'the liquid substance that *this* is a sample of'. Taken as an account of the semantical properties of a term like 'water', such a claim is patently false, and explicitly denied in thesis (T8). If the term 'water' were an abbreviation for some partially indexical description such as 'the liquid substance that *this* is a sample of', then whenever it is used while pointing to a glass of tomato juice, it should designate the substance tomato juice. But 'water', as a term of English, does not designate tomato juice in any context. As a term of English, 'water' always designates the substance water irrespective of extraneous contextual factors such as accompanying demonstrations. It is important to recognize that the designation of a natural kind term does not vary with the context of utterance.[6] This much is

[6]A few natural kind terms may be thought of as exceptions to the rule that natural kind terms are completely *univocal* or *context-insentitive*. One such word, according to Putnam, is 'jade', which is supposed to be applicable to samples of jadeite and nephrite alike. There is some plausibility to the claim that the term 'jade' designates jadeite with respect to some contexts, and nephrite with respect to others. On the other hand, if there is this sort of equivocation in the term, it may be plausibly attributed to simple semantic ambiguity (as with the vocable 'bank') rather than to genuine indexicality (as with the word 'you'). Other examples may be certain disease names, perhaps 'cancer'. Still another example may be the term 'elephant', which applies to animals of two different species, and in fact two different *genera,* the African elephant and the Indian elephant. Here again, it is not implausible to attribute the equivocation (if there is any) to ordinary semantic ambiguity rather than to a built-in systematic dependence on particular contextual factors like those that constitute Kaplan's purified notion of a "context" (1977): an individual in the role of agent; another, perhaps, in the role of addressee; a time; a location; perhaps accompanying demonstrations; and so on. Putnam (1975a, p. 241) discusses the special problem posed by terms like 'jade'. On his view, 'jade' is entirely univocal, applying (with respect to any possible world w) to anything having (in w) the (actual) superficial identifying characteristics of jadeite or nephrite. Putnam's account treats the term 'jade' as if it were descriptional in terms of the usual identifying characteristics of jade, thus univocally designating a certain nonnatural kind or category, perhaps the kind *Hard Translucent Stone that is Green or White in Color.* That is, on Putnam's view, the term 'jade' applies with respect to any possible world w to anything x that superficially resembles in w actual jade, as it *actually* is, whether or not x is a sample of either jadeite or nephrite in w. Another possible view is that a term such as 'jade' univocally designates the *kind-union* (on an anology to class-union) of the two substances in question, i.e., the kind *Jadeite or Nephrite.* Similarly, the term 'elephant' may be taken to designate the kind *African Elephant or Indian Elephant,* or more accurately, the kind-union of all those actual species, both present and extinct, that constitute the

explicitly recognized in thesis (T8). When Putnam claims that one may "explain the meaning" of the term 'water' by way of a partially indexical description, he explicitly requires that the description be *used* with an accompanying demonstration of a sample of water. It is precisely this requirement that makes the ostensive definition *defeasible*. So-called ostensive definitions need not literally involve ostension, e.g., pointing, but they must involve genuine *reference* of some sort, in this case reference to a sample of water. Providing an abbreviation for a complex indexical expression in isolation from any context of utterance is not the same thing as giving an ostensive definition. The two speech acts are not even similar.

11.3. A Subtle Misinterpretation

One might interpret Putnam as claiming instead that the sense of the term 'water' is the sense taken on by the partially indexical phrase 'the same liquid as *this* in the actual world' *when it is used in a particular context* with reference to a particular sample of water, so that 'water' is descriptional relative to that sample. This interpretation would explain several of the central theses. If 'water' is synonymous with the complex phrase 'the same liquid as *this* in the actual world', as it is used in a particular context, then it may be said that it is *analytic,* and hence true in every possible world, that something is a sample of water if and only if it is a sample of the same liquid as "this" in the actual world. (Compare (T3).) The occurrence of the demonstrative '*this*' is an indexical component of the complex phrase, one that remains hidden in its alleged synonym, 'water'. (Compare (T6).) When the demonstrative is used in the relevant context to refer to a liquid sample, both the speaker and the audience may associate certain general properties with that use of the term, perhaps the properties of *being a liquid sample, being colorless,* and so on, but the reference of the demonstrative is at least partly determined contextually, by the setting in which the term was used,

---

family *Elephantidae*. (Of course, the term may also be plausibly taken as designating the family *Elephantidae* itself. We are leaving open here the question as to whether this family is identical with the kind-union of all of the *actual* species that it subsumes.) By contrast with Putnam's view, this alternative view entails that the term 'jade' cannot apply to something *x* with respect to a possible world *w* unless *x* is either jadeite or nephrite in *w*, even if *x* superficially resembles in *w* actual jade. There remains a question on this view as to whether a term such as 'jade' must always designate a genuine natural kind. The kind-union *Jadeite or Nephrite* is not one of the kinds of substance ordinarily treated in a chemical theory of minerals. On the other hand, the family *Elephantidae* is unquestionably a natural kind.

and not solely by way of psychologically associated general properties. The designation of the containing phrase 'the same liquid as *this*
in the actual world' depends on the reference of the demonstrative
'*this*'. Since the latter designates a particular sample of water, the
complex phrase designates the substance water. Hence there is also a
contextual element in the determination of the designation of the
containing phrase. Because of a hidden indexical component, the
designation of the term 'water' is not uniquely determined solely by
way of general properties that might be included in a wholly internal
"psychological state." (Compare (T7).) If the demonstrative '*this*'
were used to refer to a sample of tomato juice, then it would itself
take on a different sense, and so would the complex containing
phrase. The phrase would designate tomato juice instead of water.
Thus if the demonstrative were used to refer to a sample of tomato
juice, the containing phrase would no longer be synonymous with the
term 'water'. (Compare (T8).)

The theory imputed to Putnam on the interpretation sketched
above is an implausible theory about the meaning of natural kind
terms. In the first place, it is vulnerable to some version of the initial
arguments for the theory of direct reference. Whatever sample (or
samples) of water were used in the ostensive definition of water, it
seems obvious that we could imagine discovering that *these* samples
were not really water at all but gin. But we would not be able to
imagine that these samples were not samples of "water" if 'water'
simply *meant* 'whatever liquid substance *these* are samples of'. The
supposition that these are not samples of "water" would be like the
supposition of a "married bachelor."

More than this, it is obvious that water can be "ostensively
defined" in Putnam's sense, and its "meaning" thereby "explained,"
by pointing out virtually any fairly typical samples of water whatsoever. The description 'the liquid substance that *these* are samples
of' would do just as well to explain the meaning of 'water' no matter
which fairly typical samples of water are referred to. If an indexical
term takes on different senses when used in different contexts, then
surely we should say that a demonstrative takes on different senses
when it is used to refer to numerically distinct entities, even if those
entities happen to be qualitatively identical twins. When a speaker on
Earth and his Twin Earth doppelgänger both utter the sentence 'I
have a headache', the sense of the utterance differs in the two cases.[7]

---

[7] The point illustrated by this example of Putnam's is put forcefully in Kaplan,
1977.

Similarly, the description 'the liquid substance that these are samples of' takes on one sense when said with reference to certain samples of water, and quite another sense when said in another context with reference to other samples of water. Yet either sense would do as well as the other to explain the meaning of 'water'. Since the synonymy relation is transitive and symmetric, 'water' cannot be simultaneously synonymous with both of these uses of the description in question. Yet it would be plainly arbitrary to choose one of these two senses over the other as *the* sense of 'water'.

To point out that a theory is implausible does not in itself show that some particular philosopher should not be interpreted as holding that theory. Some of Putnam's central theses do indeed seem to suggest that he holds that 'water' is synonymous with 'the same liquid as *this* in the actual world', when said with reference to a particular sample of water in the actual world. Even so, the interpretation in question cannot be a correct interpretation. One reason for this is Putnam's contention in (T4) that the "meaning" of the term 'water' may be "explained" equally well by way of an operational definition instead of an ostensive definition, using a description of water in terms of its "stereotypical" properties in place of indexical reference to a paradigmatic sample. He explicitly denies (1975a, pp. 230, 232) that either the ostensive definition or the operational definition is an "analytical specification" of the meaning of 'water'. (See footnote 3.) It is precisely in connection with the ostensive definition of water that Putnam "heartily endorses" (1975a, pp. 234–235) the following clear and unambiguous quote from Kripke:

> Let us suppose that we do fix the reference of a name by a description. Even if we do so, we do not then make the name *synonymous* with the description, but instead we use the name *rigidly* to refer to the object so named, even in talking about counterfactual situations where the thing named would not satisfy the description in question. Now, this is what I think in fact is true for those cases of naming where the reference is fixed by description. And by this I do not just mean what Searle says: "It's not a single description, but rather a cluster, a family of properties which fixes the reference." I mean that properties in this sense are not used *at all* (Kripke, 1971, p. 157).

In another passage (1975a, p. 265) Putnam is fairly explicit when he writes:". . . if we are right, 'water' is neither synonymous with a description nor with a fuzzy set of descriptions. . . ."

103

This textual evidence strongly suggests that the partially indexical description used in the ostensive definition of water is not intended by Putnam to indicate the sense of 'water'. It is intended only to indicate the designation. Theses (T2) may thus be strengthened. The evidence seems to show that Putnam holds the strong version of the theory of direct reference according to which natural kind terms are entirely nondescriptional.[8]

The idea that natural kind terms such as 'tiger' and 'water' are nondescriptional terms that are generally taught or introduced by ostension to paradigmatic samples is an idea that also figures prominently in Kripke's account of natural kind terms. In pointing out similarities between Putnam's views and his own, Kripke says:

> The original concept of cat is: *that kind of thing,* where the kind can be identified by paradigmatic instances. It is not something picked out by any qualitative dictionary definition . . . (1972a, p. 122).
>
> For species, as for proper names, the way the reference of a term is fixed should not be regarded as a synonym for the term. In the case of proper names, the reference can be fixed in various ways. In an initial baptism it is typically fixed by an ostension or a description. . . . The same observations hold for such a general term as 'gold'. If we imagine a hypothetical (admittedly somewhat artificial) baptism of the substance, we must imagine it picked out as by some such 'definition' as, 'Gold is the substance instantiated by the items over there, or at any rate, by almost all of them'. . . . I believe that in general, terms for natural kinds (e.g., animal, vegetable, and chemical kinds) get their reference fixed in this way; the substance is defined as the kind instantiated by (almost all of) a given sample (pp. 135–136).

11.4. A Difficulty in Interpretation

We have already made the point that the designation of a natural kind term does not vary from one context of utterance to another. Taken as terms of English, 'water' designates liquid H_2O (with varying amounts of impurities) in every context, and 'tiger' designates the species *Felis tigris* in every context. As we have been using the term, an *indexical* expression is one whose semantical intension

---

[8]This is not to say that natural kind terms, for Putnam, have no "meaning." On the contrary, his primary purpose in 1975a is to clarify a notion of "meaning" for natural kind terms, as well as for other sorts of terms.

varies in a systematic way with the context of utterance. Since the intension of a general term determines, and is determined by, the term's designation, an indexical general term may be defined as one whose designation varies systematically with the context. More generally, an indexical expression may be defined as one whose extension with respect to some fixed possible world (and some fixed time if the expression is tensed) varies from context to context. Putnam seems to indicate that his use of the term accords with ours when he writes: "Words like 'now', 'this', 'here' have long been recognized to be *indexical* or *token-reflexive*—i.e. to have an extension which varied from context to context or token to token" (1973b, p. 709). Indexical expressions are context-sensitive; natural kind terms are context-insensitive. Putnam gives every indication that he fully recognizes this fact about natural kind terms in putting forth his thesis (T8). In a later passage he even suggests that if an expression such as 'tiger' were used by an alien English-speaking population in such a way that in their community it designated a different but superficially similar species, then their term 'tiger' would not be the same word as ours used in a different context with a different extension, and not even the same word with a different meaning, *but a different word altogether:*

> Speakers on Twin Earth who have the same linguistic habits as we do, count as having acquired the word 'tiger' only if the extension of 'tiger' in their idiolect is the set of tigers. . . . (If Twin Earth organisms have a silicon chemistry, for example, then their 'tigers' aren't really tigers, even if they look like tigers, although the linguistic habits of the lay Twin Earth speaker exactly correspond to those of Earth speakers.) . . . In this case we have decided to say that Twin Earth speakers have not acquired our word 'tiger' (although they have acquired another word with the same spelling and pronunciation) (1975a, pp. 247–248).

This presents a difficult problem of interpretation. Putnam suggests that he is using the term 'indexical' in such a way that indexicals are, by definition, context-sensitive. He also recognizes the fact that natural kind terms are context-insensitive. How then are we to understand theses (T6) and (T7) so that they may be reconciled with (T8)? In what sense are natural kind terms, for Putnam, indexical?

The answer is, in part, that on Putnam's theory, indexicality, in the truest sense of the word, plays a crucial role in "explaining the meaning," and thereby in fixing the designation, of a natural kind

105

The Theory of Direct Reference

term. As we shall see later, this is true even of the operational definition as well as the ostensive definition of a natural kind term. Natural kind terms are not themselves context-sensitive, but context plays an important role in explaining the meaning of natural kind terms, and this is in part what is meant by (T6). It is the role of indexicality in determining the designation of a term that Putnam stresses when he writes that ". . . extension is, in part, determined *indexically*. The extension of our terms depends upon the actual nature of the particular things that serve as paradigms, and this actual nature is not, in general, fully known to the speaker" (1973b, p. 711). It is also this role of indexicality in fixing the designation of a term which Putnam is referring to when he speaks of "the indexical component of meaning—the fact that our terms refer to things which are similar, in certain ways, to things that we designate *rigidly,* to *these* things, to the stuff we call 'water', or whatever, *here* . . ." (1975a, p. 265).

Since indexicality plays a significant role in "explaining the meaning" of a natural kind term, one must rely in part on contextual factors to fix the designation of the term. One cannot rely solely on the general or purely qualitative properties that one might associate with a natural kind term on the basis of its definition, whether that definition is ostensive or operational. Because of the nondescriptional component in the definition of a natural kind term, these general properties will not usually be sufficient, and this is partly what is meant in (T6). It is precisely the relevance of the nonlinguistic setting in which we find ourselves that Putnam wants to emphasize when, in criticizing orthodox Fregean theories of meaning and reference, he writes: "Ignoring what we have called the *indexicality* of most words is ignoring the contribution of the environment" (1975a, p. 271).

12. First Formulations

12.1 An Initial Formalization

The role played by indexicality in fixing the designation of a natural kind term surfaces when we attempt to make formally precise the logical form of the ostensive definition of 'water' mentioned in (T3). Getting clear about the logical form of this definition is also important to our understanding of thesis (T5), for (T5) is most naturally construed as the thesis that natural kind terms such as 'water' are rigid designators of natural kinds *as a formal conse-quence of their ostensive definitions.*

In what follows we shall use a standard logical notation. The lower-case characters 'w', 'w_1', 'w_2', etc. will be used as variables that range only over possible worlds. The character '$W_@$' will serve as an individual constant denoting the actual world.[9] The lower-case letters 'x', 'y', and 'z', with or without primes, are individual variables, ranging over the entire domain of individuals. Thus our symbolic language is a two-sorted language. We shall adopt the practice of subscripting predicates with possible world variables or with '$W_@$' to indicate that the predication is asserted to hold in a certain possible world. Recall also that if ν is a common noun, then $\ulcorner \Pi_\nu \urcorner$ is our formalization of the corresponding predicate $\ulcorner$is a $\nu\urcorner$ or $\ulcorner$is a bit of $\nu\urcorner$. When the distinction between a noun and its corresponding predicate is unimportant, we shall sometimes use the capitalization of the noun directly as a predicate rather than affixing the noun as a subscript on 'Π'.

The following passage is crucial to understanding the intended logical force behind Putnam's suggested ostensive definition of water, as given in his thesis (T3):

Let me introduce the notion of a *cross-world relation*. A two-term relation R will be called *cross-world* when it is understood in such a way that its extension is a set of ordered pairs of individuals *not all in the same possible world.* For example, it is easy to understand the relation *same height as* as a cross-world relation: just understand it so that, e.g., if x is an individual in a world W_1 who is 5 feet tall (in W_1) and y is an individual in W_2 who is 5 feet tall (in W_2), then the ordered pair x,y belongs to the extension of *same height as.* (Since an individual may have different heights in different possible worlds in which that same individual exists, strictly speaking, it is not the ordered pair x,y that constitutes an

---

[9]In saying that '$W_@$' is an individual constant denoting the actual world, the question remains open whether it functions in the same way as a proper name such as 'Charley', or as an indexical singular term that denotes, when uttered in a context c, the possible world of the context c, analogous to the indexical phrase '*this* possible world', or 'the *actual* world' (in one sense; see Section 4.1). In Section 14.4 we shall be concerned with translating expressions involving '$W_@$' into expressions that employ the sentential actuality operator in its place. Since the actuality operator we shall use is an indexical operator, which "designates" with respect to any context c the possible world of c, it is best if we stipulate at this point that '$W_@$' is to be an indexical singular term that denotes with respect to any context c the possible world of c.

107

element of the extension of *same height as,* but rather the ordered pair *x-in-world-W₁, y-in-world-W₂.*)

Similarly, we can understand the relation *same$_L$* (same liquid as) as a cross-world relation by understanding it so that a liquid in world W_1 which has the same important physical properties (in W_1) that a liquid in W_2 possesses (in W_2) bears *same$_L$* to the latter liquid.

Then the theory we have been presenting may be summarized by saying that an entity *x*, in an arbitrary possible world, is *water* if and only if it bears the relation *same$_L$* (construed as a cross-world relation) to the stuff *we* call "water" in the actual world (Putnam, 1973b, p. 708).

Putnam's discussion of possible worlds and cross-world relations strongly suggests the following symbolization of the ostensive definition of water:

(8) (w) (x) $(Exists_w(x)$

$\rightarrow [\Pi_{water_w}(x) \leftrightarrow Same_L(x\text{-}in\text{-}w, this\text{-}in\text{-}W_@)])$.

12.2. Time-Slices and Possible World-Slices of Continuant Individuals

A noteworthy feature of Putnam's discussion of cross-world relations is the use of such hyphenated expressions as '*x-in-w*' and '*this-in-W$_@$*'. These expressions are meant to denote philosophical entities that are different from ordinary individuals in important respects. The hyphenated expressions impose a somewhat bizarre ontology of what we shall call "possible world-slices" of individuals. What sort of thing are possible world-slices of individuals? They are best understood on an analogy to time-slices, or momentary phases, of enduring individuals.

A time-slice of an enduring object, such as a statue, is a temporal "part" of the statue, in much the same way that a cross-sectional slice of the statue is a spatial part of the statue. The enduring statue is "constructed" through time, as it were, from its time-slices. A time-slice of an enduring object may have a very fleeting existence. The statue-during-interval-*t* exists throughout *t*, but the statue-at-moment-*t'* comes into existence in a flash and just as quickly disappears never to be seen again. But for its fleeting existence, the statute-at-time-*t* is similar in many of its physical properties to the statute itself. It has the same spatial location that the statue has at time *t*. It also has the same shape, size, weight, and color that the statue has at time *t*. Still, it is only a temporal component of the statue, a brief phase of its existence, and not identical with the statue itself. Different time-slices of a statue are numerically distinct things, although they bear an important equivalence relation to one another. They are slices of the same enduring object, or *gen-identical*.[10]

By analogy, a possible world-slice of a statue is to be a modal "part" of the statue. The statue itself is a cross-world continuant. It exists in many possible worlds, just as it endures through time. This is just to say that the statue has tremendous potential for being other than it actually is. Few of its features are essential—especially if one is willing to count among its features such contrived properties as the property of *being such that the Democrats control the Congress during Richard Nixon's first term as president,* a property that every cross-world continuant has contingently. Possible world-slices of cross-world continuants are quite strange in this respect; they have no potential for being other than they are. A possible world-slice of a statue is the statue *with such-and-such properties,* the statue *as it might have been.* All of the properties of a possible world-slice of a statue, except existence and its cognates, are essential to that possible world-slice, for unlike the statue itself, the possible world-slice exists in only one possible world. In particular, the statue-in-the-actual-world is not the same thing as the statue itself, for the statue could be other than it is. The statue-in-the-actual-world is supposed to be a new and different entity; it is, so to speak, the statue *as it actually is.* The statue itself might have had a slightly different shape or size, but the statue *as it actually is,* the statue-in-the-actual-world, must have the shape and size that the statue actually has. If the statue had been slightly larger, the statue-in-the-actual-world simply would not exist. In its place there would exist a slightly larger possible world-slice of the statue: the statue *as it would have been,* the statue-in-that-world. Aside from dissimilarities in essential and other modal properties, the statue-in-possible-world-*w* is very similar to the statue itself, if the comparison is made with respect to *w*. They share the same

---

[10]One possible exception to the rule that a time-slice of an individual *x* is not identical with the individual *x* of which it is a time-slice may be *x*-during-interval-*t*, where *t* is the entire duration of *x*. This temporal "part" of *x* might be identified with *x* itself. Kaplan (1967a) contains an interesting discussion concerning the differences and relations between possible world-slices of individuals and cross-world continuant individuals. The use of the term 'gen-identical' is due to Kurt Lewin.

spatial location, shape, size, color, weight, and history in *w*. Still, a possible world-slice of the statue cannot be identical with the statue itself. Different possible world-slices of the same cross-world continuant are numerically distinct entities that bear the gen-identity relation to each other. The statue itself is "constructed," as it were, through the realm of possibilities—or "logical space"—from its possible world-slices.

It is evident from the foregoing that a possible world-slice of a sample of water cannot itself be a sample of water. A sample of water is an ordinary sort of thing, with relatively few essential properties. If we are to countenance such a thing as a possible world-slice of a sample of water, a sample of water *as it might have been,* then we must say that although the world-slice looks and tastes like a sample of water, and shares other nonmodal properties with ordinary samples of water, the world-slice itself is a very unusual sort of entity all of whose properties, except existence and its cognates, are essential. With this in mind, a quick glance at (8), our symbolization of Putnam's suggested ostensive definition of water, reveals that, strictly speaking, Putnam's *same$_L$* relation is not a relation between ordinary samples of liquid substances, any more than gen-identity is a relation between ordinary sorts of individuals. Putnam's *same$_L$* relation is the relation that holds between two possible world-slices of liquid samples when they are possible world-slices of samples of the same liquid. It is what might be called the *gen-consubstantial* relation between possible world-slices of liquid samples.

The notion of a time-slice of a continuant individual is employed by philosophers when dealing with questions of cross-time identity and other cross-time relations. For example, if a statue composed entirely of plaster at time t_1 undergoes a very gradual process of disassembly and replenishment with plastic until at time t_2 there stands a statue composed entirely of plastic where the plaster statue once stood, a question of identity arises: Are the plaster and plastic statues the same, and if not, at what point in the process did we get a new statue distinct from the original? One way of rephrasing the question in what appears to be a more illuminating and precise way makes use of the notion of a momentary time-slice of an individual: Is the statue-at-t_1 gen-identical with the statue-at-t_2, and if not, which of the sequence of statue time-slices that spans the interval from t_1 to t_2 is the earliest time-slice not gen-identical with all of its predecessors? In this way the question of what sorts of changes a thing may undergo and still remain numerically the same thing may be recast as a demand for a list of the necessary conditions for gen-identity between two distinct time-slices.

Similarly, questions concerning a thing's essence can be recast as a demand for a list of the necessary conditions for gen-identity between possible world-slices of that thing. Putnam's concern is with cross-world consubstantiality rather than with cross-world identity, but the issues are entirely analogous. Indeed, consubstantiality involves identity in a perfectly straightforward way: Two substance samples x and y are consubstantial if and only if the substance of which x is a sample is identical with the substance of which y is a sample. *Cross-world* consubstantiality involves *cross-world* identity in just the same way: Two possible world-slices x-in-w_1 and y-in-w_2 of substance samples in w_1 and w_2, respectively, are gen-consubstantial if and only if the w_1-slice of the substance of which x is a sample in w_1 is gen-identical with the w_2-slice of the substance of which y is a sample in w_2.

12.3. An Initial Attempt to Eliminate Possible World-Slices

Although the notions of time-slices and possible world-slices of continuant individuals might seem helpful in making precise certain issues involving cross-time and cross-world relations, they are not necessary. It is generally possible to state the issues solely in terms of continuant individuals without any loss in precision. Instead of asking whether the statue-at-t_1 is gen-identical with the statue-at-t_2, for instance, we ask whether the (enduring) statue that is composed of plaster at t_1 is identical with the (enduring) statue that is composed of plastic at t_2. The notion of a possible world-slice of an individual is highly suggestive of a certain metaphysical theory, and though this theory is no doubt coherent, its ontology is bizarre, and bound to generate philosophical controversy. (See Plantinga, 1974, pp. 88–92; and Chisholm 1976, appendix A.) If for no other reason than this, it would be generally desirable to couch discussion of cross-world relations in terms of ordinary continuant individuals instead of possible world-slices of continuant individuals. In particular, it would be desirable to recast Putnam's suggested ostensive definition of water in terms of liquid samples rather than in terms of possible world-slices of liquid samples, especially since the definition is supposed to represent the force of a meaning explanation *in everyday language* of the word 'water'.

It would not do for Putnam's purposes simply to drop all reference to possible worlds, and all quantification over them, from the ostensive definition of water, without any further change. When one does this, the following definition of water results:

> Something is a sample of water if and only if it is a sample of the same liquid as *this*.

Symbolically, this nonmodalized version of an ostensive definition of water might be represented thus:[11]

$$(x) \ [\Pi_{water}(x) \leftrightarrow Consubstantial \ (x, this)].$$

We saw in Section 6.2 that a universally quantified biconditional can serve only to fix the semantical extension of the term 'water' with respect to the actual world, and not its full semantical intension (function from possible worlds to extensions). As we have already said, Putnam's thesis (T5) is best construed as the thesis that the term 'water' rigidly designates the substance water as a formal consequence of the ostensive definition of water. In order to fix the *designation* of the term 'water' so that it rigidly designates water, we must guarantee that the semantical extension of 'water' with respect to an arbitrary possible world w is exactly the class of water samples existing in w. That is, we must fix not just the semantical extension of 'water' but its full semantical intension. This is precisely the intention behind Putnam's use of universal quantification over possible worlds in his suggested ostensive definition of water.

Later, in Section 14.4, we shall be concerned to eliminate quantification over possible worlds from Putnam's ostensive definition of water, but first we must eliminate reference to possible *world-slices* of liquid samples. Putnam points out (1973b, p. 707) that the demonstrative 'this' rigidly designates the actual paradigmatic sample of water involved in the ostensive definition. Indeed, if we assume Kaplan's theory of indexicals, the demonstrative is an obsti-

---

[11]The capitalized adjective '*Consubstantial*' is used here as a predicate for the relevant equivalence relation between liquid samples in order to distinguish this intra-world relation from the gen-consubstantiality relation between possible world-slices of liquid samples. We have symbolized the latter by Putnam's predicate '*Same$_L$*'.

Strictly speaking, the consubstantiality relation is the relation that holds between two substance samples when they are samples of the same substance, whether or not that substance is a *liquid*, as opposed to, say, a gas. Similarly, the conspecificity relation is the relation that holds between two organisms when they are organisms of the same species, whether that species is a species of animals or of plants. Since the paradigm referred to by the demonstrative '*this*' is in fact a liquid sample, the larger equivalence relation of consubstantiality is equally suited to Putnam's purpose.

nately rigid designator of the paradigm water sample. If this is correct, it may seem as if reference to possible world-slices in the definition can simply be replaced with reference to liquid samples thus:

(9′)   In any possible world w, something is a sample of water (in w) if and only if (in w) it is a sample of the same liquid as *this*.

Symbolically, this reformulation of the definition of water might be represented thus:

(9) $(w)\,(x)\,(Exists_w(x)$

$$\rightarrow [\Pi_{water_w}(x) \leftrightarrow Consubstantial_w\,(x,this)]).$$

A moment's reflection reveals that this attempt to eliminate reference to possible world-slices is not adequate for Putnam's purposes. A problem arises if the paradigmatic sample of water denoted by the demonstrative 'this' does not *essentially* exist as a sample of water. Suppose, for example, that the sample of water in question is such that it might have been a sample of liquid carbon dioxide, i.e., that there is a possible world w in which that very thing that actually serves as a paradigmatic sample of liquid H_2O is instead a sample of liquid CO_2. Then according to the reformulated definition suggested above, something is a sample of "water" in w if and only if it is a sample of liquid CO_2 in w. The extension of the term 'water' with respect to w is fixed not to be the class of liquid H_2O samples in w, but the class of liquid carbon dioxide samples in w. If the term 'water' rigidly designates anything according to this definition, it does not rigidly designate the substance H_2O (with varying amounts of impurities) in its liquid form. Rather, it designates the category *Sample of the Same Liquid as P,* or something similar, where 'P' is a name of the paradigmatic sample in question. But this contradicts Putnam's contention that the term 'water' rigidly designates liquid H_2O.

One might object that a counterinstance of this sort is impossible, since whatever is in fact a sample of water is such that it is *essentially* a sample of water, and *could not be* a sample of carbon dioxide. Kripke, for instance, says some things that seem to suggest that he would endorse this essentialist claim. It may even be that the truth of this essentialist claim is a consequence of the theory of singular direct reference propounded by Kripke. Indeed, the question of whether it is or not is one of the central issues of the investigation in Part II of the present work.

Two points are in order here. First, whereas Kripke may hold that any actual sample of water is essentially a sample of water, Putnam gives no indication whatsoever that he is in agreement with Kripke on this point, let alone that he wishes to build this version of essentialism concerning individuals into his theory of natural kind terms. Donnellan, himself a leading proponent of the direct reference theory, has expressed doubts (1974b) concerning Kripke's essentialism concerning individuals, and there is no textual evidence indicating that Putnam, a leading proponent of the direct reference theory of the designation of general terms, sides with Kripke on this issue rather than with Donnellan. Yet, if we rewrite the ostensive definition of water in the manner proposed, then we must commit ourselves to the view that the actual paradigm is a sample of liquid H_2O in every possible world in order to maintain the thesis that the term 'water' rigidly designates the substance water, i.e., H_2O.

Second, even if an actual sample of water is such that it *must be* a sample of water, no water sample is such that it *must exist*. Whatever sample of water is selected as a paradigm, its component molecules might never have existed. There are many possible worlds in which the sample of water actually chosen as a paradigm simply does not exist, and among these possible worlds are many in which other samples of water do exist. Let w be any such possible world. According to the reformulation of the ostensive definition of water proposed here, in order for a liquid sample in w to be a sample of water, it must be a sample of the same liquid that the actual paradigm is a sample of *in w*. But our paradigm sample does not exist in w, and so it seems that there is no liquid substance that can be identified as the liquid that the actual paradigm is a sample of *in w*. This is not because the demonstrative 'this' denotes nothing with respect to w. Even if the demonstrative obstinately designates the actual paradigm, it can hardly be said that this paradigm is a sample of water *in w*, since the paradigm does not even exist in w. Hence it seems that, according to the reformulated definition, *nothing* is to count as a sample of water in w, not even the genuine liquid samples of H_2O that exist in w.

As Putnam explicitly remarks (1973b, p. 708), the purpose of his suggested ostensive definition of water is to "point out a standard"— an existing paradigmatic sample of water—by which it is determined whether individual liquid samples in any possible world are samples of water in that possible world. Liquid samples in other possible worlds are to be compared with some special sample of water that serves as a paradigm. The purpose of the ostensive definition would be thwarted if the comparison were made in such a way that the standard might cease to be a sample of water, and indeed might even cease to exist. The comparison must be made in such a way as to ensure that the paradigm *exists as a sample of water* throughout the comparison. It is precisely for this reason that Putnam makes use of possible world-slices of liquid samples. An arbitrary liquid sample *as it is in a particular possible world* is to be judged against an actual sample of water *as it exists in the actual world.*

If we are going to eliminate all reference to possible world-slices of liquid samples from the ostensive definition of water in favor of reference to ordinary liquid samples, we must do so in such a way as to retain the effect of cross-world consubstantiality between liquid samples in different possible worlds. One way of doing this is to rewrite the ostensive definition of water as follows:

(10′)   For every possible world *w*, something existing in *w* is a sample of water in *w* if and only if it is a sample *in w* of the same liquid that *this* is a sample of *in the actual world.*

It is not clear at first glance exactly how (10′) is best symbolized. In our past symbolizations, we have represented the crucial equivalence relations of consubstantiality and gen-consubstantiality by way of ostensibly unstructured predicates. In keeping with the pattern of earlier symbolizations our latest reformulation of the ostensive definition of water might be symbolized thus:

(10) $(w) (x) (Exists_w(x) \rightarrow [\Pi_{water_w}(x)$

$\leftrightarrow Cross\text{-}world\text{-}consubstantial\ (x,w,this,W_@)])$.

Comparison of this symbolization with (8), our symbolization of Putnam's original formulation, indicates that what we have done, in effect, is simply to replace the binary *same_L* relation between possible world-slices x-in-w_1 and y-in-w_2 with the corresponding four-place relation that holds among the two continuant individuals x and y, and the two possible worlds w_1 and w_2. Our symbolizations, however, are deceptive. More discriminating symbolizations that reveal the internal logical structure of these different consubstantiality relations have much greater philosophical significance. In order to explain what we mean by this we must first consider in some detail the concept of a cross-world relation, a concept that requires philosophical elucidation in any case. The discussion of cross-world relations that follows will prove important when we come to consider thesis (T9) in the next chapter.

13. CROSS-WORLD RELATIONS

13.1. Cross-World Construal of Binary Relations

We have already encountered some binary relations that appear to be naturally construable as cross-world relations. Putnam, in the passage quoted above, illustrates what it means to construe a binary relation as a cross-world relation by means of the *same height* relation. Putnam's account of cross-world relations treats them as binary relations between possible world-slices of individuals rather than as four-place relations among individuals and possible worlds, but nothing of importance rests on this. What Putnam's presentation of his theory of natural kind terms does require is that we construe certain equivalence relations, such as the consubstantiality relation between substance samples and the conspecificity relation between organisms, as cross-world relations. The smallest equivalence relation, identity, is also construable as a cross-world relation (x is numerically the same thing in w_1 that y is in w_2). In fact, most ordinary equivalence relations may be sensibly construed as cross-world relations.

Some binary relations that are not equivalence relations also appear to be naturally construable as cross-world relations. The *taller than* and *shorter than* relations, for instance, may be so construed: If x is a person who exists in w_1 and is six feet tall in w_1, and y is a person who exists in w_2 and is five feet tall in w_2, then x is taller in w_1 than y is in w_2. Physical spatial properties, such as *being to the left of*, are also naturally construable as cross-world relations. (If I were on the left side of the room right now, *my right hand would be to the left of where my left hand actually is,* although my right hand would still be to the right of where my left hand *would be.*)

Not all binary relations seem to lend themselves to construal as genuine cross-world relations, relations holding between individuals *across distinct possible worlds*. Some relations involving physical interaction or contact, for instance, do not. It seems either patently false or senseless to say of a man x who exists in possible world w_1 but not in possible world w_2, and of a second man y who exists in w_2 but not in w_1, that x in w_1 shakes hands with y in w_2. Even if the first man's reach in w_1 is great, it cannot be so great as to extend into the realm of possibilities and shake the hand of a merely possible man *as he might have been.* Other binary relations in addition to the *hand shaking* relation that do not seem to be construable as cross-world relations include *being acquainted with, being married to, being indebted to, studying under, providing financial support for,* and many others. On the other hand, equivalence relations such as *studying under the same person as* are easily construed as cross-world relations.[12]

In construing a binary relation as a cross-world relation, there is considerable temptation to use locutions which, but for the absence of hyphens, are highly suggestive of an ontology of possible world-slices of individuals, e.g., "x in w_1 is taller than y in w_2." Indeed, it is precisely when one considers relations, and in particular the relation of identity, between individuals across possible worlds, or at different times, that the notion of a modal or temporal slice of an individual naturally arises. On the other hand, it is distinctly odd to use such locutions with interactional relations, as, for example, 'Smith in w_1 shook the hand of Jones in w_2.' In many cases one can change the wording of a cross-world assertion in such a way as to eliminate the suggestion of an ontology of possible world-slices by attaching the prepositional phrases 'in w_1' and 'in w_2' to verb phrases and other predicates rather than to the singular terms, e.g., 'x is taller in w_1 than y is in w_2'. Locutions of the latter sort are more suggestive of the corresponding four-place relation among individuals and possible worlds.

That some relations are naturally construable as genuine cross-world relations whereas others are not seems to be connected with the fact that certain relations are, in some sense, *grounded in* intra-world properties whereas other relations are not. The three comparative height relations, *being taller than, being shorter than,* and *being the same height as,* for instance, may be said to be grounded in particular height properties, in the sense that whenever a pair of objects x and y stand in one of these relations, they do so *by virtue of* x's having a certain height and y's having a certain height. If x is six feet tall and y is five feet tall, then x's being taller than y is a state of affairs that is grounded in x's having a height of six feet and y's having a height of five feet, states of affairs that obtain, or do not

---

[12]Similar remarks may be made in connection with cross-time relations, except that interaction through time is possible and consequently some relations involving interaction (causal relations, for instance) are easily construed, in some sense, as cross-time relations.

obtain, *within a possible world.* Similarly, conspecificity may be said to be grounded in particular species memberships, such as the property of *being a tiger,* and so on. The identity relation in particular may be said to be grounded in particular haecceities, in the sense that whenever a pair of objects x and y are numerically identical, they are so by virtue of x's being *this* thing and y's also being *this* thing.

Unfortunately, the exact sense in which these different relations may be said to be "grounded in" intra-world properties, whereas certain interactional relations are not thus "grounded," is unclear. *Any* arbitrary binary relation R is, in *some* sense or other, grounded in certain properties. If a pair of individuals x and y stand in the relation R, then x's bearing R to y may always be said to be grounded, in some sense, in x's having the relational property of *bearing R to y* and y's having the relational property of *bearing the converse of R to x.* It is no trivial matter to specify in an interesting and precise way exactly those features of binary relations that allow for construal as cross-world relations. No complete attempt to do so will be made here. But there is much that may be said concerning the nature of the cross-world relations considered thus far that may help clarify the sense in which these cross-world relations are "grounded in" certain intra-world properties whereas other relations are not.[13]

13.2. *Intra-World Attributes, Extra-World Attributes, and Cross-World Relations*

In the preceding paragraphs we invoked the notion of an *intra-world property.* An intra-world property is a property that an individual

---

[13]It is not true that all and only transitive relations may be naturally construed as cross-world relations. The relation of *being to the left of* is not always transitive, as is demonstrated by the example of people holding hands in a circle. (See footnote 21 below for a possible example of a transitive relation not naturally construable as a cross-world relation.) Nor will it do to say that cross-world relations are grounded in nonrelational properties, such as the property of *being five feet tall,* while relations such as the *hand shaking* relation are grounded only in relational properties. The *same father* relation may also be sensibly construed as a cross-world relation: A father might have sired more offspring than he actually did, and in those possible worlds in which he does, his additional offspring have the same father that his actual offspring have in the actual world. But the *same father* relation is apparently grounded in such relational properties as that of *having so-and-so as father.* In fact, the cross-world relation of identity is grounded in haecceities, intrinsically relational properties whose constitutive relation is identity. We shall suggest below that one of the features that differentiate certain binary relations which are naturally construable as cross-world

either possesses or lacks *within a possible world*. Similarly we may speak of *intra-world relations*. An intra-world *n*-place relation is one that holds or does not hold among the elements of an *n*-ary sequence of individuals *within a possible world*. The predicates of ordinary discourse about actual states of affairs (i.e., the predicates of our symbolic language *before* they are subscripted with an argument place for a possible world) designate intra-world attributes.[14] To each intra-world property P there corresponds a unique binary relation R_P that is defined as holding between an individual x and a possible world w if and only if x has P in w. This relation R_P is not an intra-world relation. We do not say that an individual x has the property P in a possible world w *in a possible world* w', nor would it be appropriate to say that x stands in R_P to w *in a possible world* w'. An individual either stands in R_P to a possible world w or it does not, and it makes no clear sense—or in any case, it is entirely unnecessary—to speak of the state of affairs of x's having P in w as itself obtaining (or failing to obtain) within a second possible world w'.[15] Similarly, to each *n*-place intra-world relation S there corresponds an $(n + 1)$-ary relation R_S that is defined as holding among the elements of a sequence $\langle x_1, x_2, \ldots, x_n, w \rangle$ if and only if w, the last element of the sequence, is a possible world in which S holds among the elements of the sequence $\langle x_1, x_2, \ldots, x_n \rangle$. The relation R_S is not an intra-world relation any more than R_P is. S either holds among the elements of a given *n*-ary sequence in a possible world w or it does not, and it makes no clear sense, or is entirely unnecessary, to relativize the given state of affairs in w to a second possible world w'. In our symbolic language with subscripted predicates, i.e., in "possible world discourse," a predicate Π designates the relation R_A, where A is the attribute designated by Π in ordinary discourse. For instance, the ordinary discourse predicate 'is blonde' designates the intra-world property of *being blonde,* and the possible world

---

relations from those which are not is that the former are often grounded in certain *relational* properties *in a certain way*.

[14]We have not discussed a notion of *designation* for relational (two or more place) predicates, but it is obvious that many of the arguments and theses of the direct reference theory of general term designation are equally applicable to many transitive verb phrases and other relational predicates.

[15]It is not that it is impossible to find an interpretation for such embeddings, but there must be some point at which it makes sense to stop. Otherwise even the simplest of assertions would have an infinite (and therefore unassertable) form: α is ϕ in w_1 in w_2 in w_3. . . .

discourse predicate 'is blonde *in*' designates the binary relation that holds between an individual x and a possible world w when x is blonde in w.

Let us say that an attribute (a property or a relation) is *extra-world* if it is inappropriate in this way to relativize the assertion of something having the property, or of some things standing in the relation, to possible worlds. If A is an intra-world attribute, R_A, is an extra-world relation. The attributes designated by the predicates of possible world discourse are thus extra-world attributes. Other extra-world attributes include the property of *being a world,* and the accessibility relation among worlds (w_1 is *possible relative to w_2*).

Cross-world relations are a strange breed. They do not seem to be intra-world relations, nor do they seem to be extra-world relations. It is inappropriate to speak of a binary cross-world relation *qua cross-world relation* as holding or not holding between a pair of individuals within a *single* possible world. But cross-world relational assertions are clearly relativized in some way to possible worlds. One speaks of the relation R as holding (or not holding) between a pair of individuals *across* a pair of possible worlds. In our symbolic language, in order to assert that an individual x is taller in a possible world w_1 than an individual y is in a possible world w_2, the '*Taller-than*' predicate must be subscripted by two possible world argument places instead of one:

Taller-than $_{w_1/w_2}(x,y)$.

Thus the extra-world relation corresponding to a binary cross-world relation is not a three-place relation but a four-place relation with two additional argument places for possible worlds.

One may initially be skeptical toward cross-world relations. It is fairly clear what it means to say that a pair of individuals stand in a relation within a single possible world (as long as the notion of a possible world is assumed to be coherent). When one moves from the symbolic language of intra-world discourse about actual states of affairs to possible world discourse, attributes become relativized to possible worlds, and hence the number of argument places of each intra-world attribute increases by one. Intra-world properties become binary extra-world relations, binary intra-world relations become ternary extra-world relations, and so on. This is illustrated in our practice of subscripting predicates with singular terms for possible worlds in the transition from the symbolic language of ordinary discourse about actual states of affairs to the two-sorted language of possible world discourse. An individual x has or lacks a property *in a possible world w*. A pair of individuals x and y stand, or fail to stand, in a binary relation *within a possible world w,* and so on. But what can it mean to say that a pair of individuals x and y stand in a binary relation *across two different possible worlds* w_1 and w_2?

13.3. A Mechanism for Generating Cross-World Relations

Skepticism regarding cross-world relations can be alleviated when it is realized that the move from ordinary discourse to possible world discourse already contains within it a mechanism for generating four-place extra-world relations among individuals and possible worlds from certain binary intra-world relations.

We mentioned above certain nontransitive binary relations that are naturally construable as cross-world relations. Another such relation is the *grand-student* relation. This is the special relation that holds between a pair of individuals x and y when x studied under someone who studied under y. Aristotle, for instance, was a grand-student of Socrates, since Aristotle studied under Socrates' pupil, Plato. If an individual x studied under a second individual z in a possible world w_1, and that same individual z studied under a third individual y in a different possible world w_2, then we might say that the *grand-student* relation holds between the individuals x and y *across the possible worlds* w_1 *and* w_2. In this way we arrive at a cross-world construal of the *grand-student* relation.

This example provides the key for understanding how the transition from ordinary nonmodal discourse to possible world discourse automatically generates cross-world relations from certain ordinary binary relations. A pair of individuals x and y stand in the *grand-student* relation across distinct possible worlds w_1 and w_2 when and only when there is an intermediate individual z who *carries across* from w_1 to w_2 in such a way that x studied under z in w_1 and z studied under y in w_2. If one examines each of the other cross-world relations mentioned above, with a little imagination one will find a structural similarity in each case to the *grand-student* relation—except that in some cases there are *two* intermediate entities which carry across possible worlds and which are related to one another in a very special way. Consider for instance the three cross-world comparative height relations, *being taller than, being shorter than,* and *being the same height as.* When a quadruple of elements $\langle x,w_1,y,w_2 \rangle$ stand in one of the corresponding four-place extra-world relations, there is an inter-

121

mediate entity h, which is the height that x has in w_1, and an intermediate entity h', which is the height that y has in w_2, and the relationship that holds between the heights h and h' determines which cross-world height relation the quadruple of elements stand in. Individual x is taller in w_1 than y is in w_2 if and only if $h > h'$; x is shorter than y if and only if $h < h'$; and x is the same height as y if and only if $h = h'$.

A key point is that the relevant relationship that holds between the heights h and h', the intermediate entities, is *world-independent* or *world-invariant*.[16] Whether h is greater than, equal to, or smaller than h', h and h' are so related irrespective of which possible world one is considering. One may compare h and h' in w_1 or in w_2, or in the actual world, and their relationship is preserved. Similar remarks may be made in connection with each of the cross-world relations discussed above. Consider for instance the cross-world conspecificity relation. If x is a natural organism in w_1 and y is a natural organism in w_2, then there is an intermediate entity S which is the species that x is a member of in w_1, and there is an intermediate entity S' which is the species that y is a member of in w_2, and the quadruple $\langle x,w_1,y,w_2 \rangle$ stand in the cross-world conspecificity relation if and

[16]Consider any binary intra-world relation R. We say that R is *world-invariant* if

$$(w_1)\,(w_2)\,(x)\,(y)\,[R_{w_1}(x,y) \leftrightarrow R_{w_2}(x,y)],$$

i.e., whenever a pair of individuals stand in R in one world, they stand in R in all worlds; and we say that R is *world-variant* otherwise. We also say that an extra-world relation S is *world-dependent* or *world-relative* if at least one of its argument places is a possible world argument place, and we say that S is *world-independent* otherwise. Given any binary intra-world relation R, there is a corresponding binary world-independent relation S which is defined by

$$S(x,y) =_{def.} (\exists w)R_w(x,y),$$

i.e., x stands in S to y if and only if x stands in R to y *in some possible world or other*. When R is world-invariant, the corresponding extra-world relation S so defined bears a special relation to R, namely, that

$$(w)\,(x)\,(y)\,[S(x,y) \leftrightarrow R_w(x,y)],$$

i.e., x stands in R to y in a possible world w if and only if x stands in S to y. In other words, when R is world-invariant, the binary world-independent relation S defined from R in the natural way is such that it always agrees with R irrespective of which world one is considering. It is easy to prove that for any binary intra-world relation R, there is a binary world-independent relation S that agrees with R in this way, irrespective of which world one is considering, if and only if R is world-invariant. Hence we shall also say that a binary intra-world relation is *world-independent* if it is world-invariant.

only if $S = S'$. Whether the intermediate entities S and S' are identical or distinct is a world-independent matter.

Each of the binary relations mentioned above as relations that are naturally construable as cross-world relations involve, or may be naturally thought of as involving, intermediate entities that carry across possible worlds. In fact, each of these relations can be *defined* in such a way as to make explicit an internal structure involving intermediate entities. The *grand-student* relation stands apart from the other relations in its logical structure, and its structure will be discussed in a moment. In the case of every other binary relation R mentioned above as being naturally construable as a genuine cross-world relation, there is an additional binary functional (many-one) relation R' and an additional world-independent binary relation R'' such that, necessarily, for any individuals x and y, x bears R to y if and only if $R'(x)$, the unique entity to which x bears R', itself bears R'' to $R'(y)$, the unique entity to which y bears R'. In fact, in each case there is a binary functional relation R' and a binary world-independent relation R'' such that R may be *defined* by the following:

$$R(x,y) =_{def.} R''(R'(x),R'(y)),$$

where $\ulcorner R'(\alpha) \urcorner$ is an abbreviation for the definite description $\ulcorner (\imath z) R'(\alpha, z) \urcorner$. In set theoretic terminology, R is defined by *composition* of the relation R'' and the function R' taken twice. If R is the *taller than* relation, then R' is the binary functional relation that holds between any individual with height and its particular height, and R'' is the binary *greater than* relation among heights. If R is the *same height* relation, then R'' is the relation of identity. If R is the conspecificity relation, then R' is the binary functional relation between an organism and its species, and R'' is the identity relation. Thus, for instance, we have the following definition of the conspecificity relation:

$$Conspecific(x,y) =_{def.} (\imath z)[Species(z) \land x \in z]$$
$$= (\imath z')[Species(z') \land y \in z'],$$

where the symbol '$\in$' is taken as a predicate for the relation that holds between a pair of elements x and y when y is a kind and x is an instance or example of the kind y.

Notice that in each of these definitions, there is overt and explicit reference in the definiens to the so-called intermediate entities by way of functional definite descriptions, e.g., 'the height of y', 'the

123

species of y', etc., whereas the definiendum need not involve any explicit reference to the intermediate entities, e.g., 'x is shorter than y', 'x and y are conspecific', etc. To use Quine's phrase, the definiens involves an *explicit* "ontological commitment" to the intermediate entities. As we shall see below, this difference between the definiens and the definiendum is often a point of considerable philosophical significance.

In the general case, a binary relation R might be definable by composition of a binary relation R'' together with a pair of binary functional relations R' and S', the latter two of which need not be the same, thus:

$$R(x,y) =_{def.} R''(R'(x),S'(y)).$$

Such is the relation that holds, say, between a certain scholar and Henry VIII when the scholar has more degrees than Henry VIII had wives. It is obtained by letting R' be the function *the total number of degrees earned by x*, letting S' be the function *the total number of women that x married*, and letting R'' be the *greater than* relation among natural numbers. This relation between the scholar and Henry VIII may also be sensibly construed as a cross-world relation: there are countless possible worlds in which Quine has more degrees than Henry VIII had wives in the actual world. Indeed, the actual world is probably one of them.

The *grand-student* relation, however, is not defined by composition of a binary relation together with a pair of functions. It is defined as the relative product of the *studied under* relation with itself. A binary relation R is the *relative product* of a pair of binary relations R' and S if it may be defined by the following:

$$R(x,y) =_{def.} (\exists z)[R'(x,z) \land S(z,y)].$$

Thus we have the following definition of the *grand-student* relation:

$$Grand\text{-}student(x,y) =_{def.}$$
$$(\exists z)[Studied\text{-}under(x,z) \land Studied\text{-}under(z,y)].$$

Notice that, as in the case of definition by composition, there is overt and explicit reference in the definiens to an intermediate entity z, here by way of existential quantification, whereas there need not be any such overt reference in the definiendum.

Definitions of binary relations by either the method of composition or of relative product can be put into the general form:

$$R(x,y) =_{def.} (\exists z)(\exists z')[R'(x,z) \land S'(y,z') \land R''(z,z')].$$

124

If R'' is the relation of identity, then R is the relative product of R' and the converse of S'. If R' and S' are functional relations, then R is defined by composition of R'' together with R' and S'.

The compositional analysis of these binary intra-world relations is relevant to their construal as cross-world relations. As we noted above, when one moves from intra-world discourse about actual states of affairs to possible world discourse, intra-world properties become binary extra-world relations, binary intra-world relations become ternary extra-world relations, and so on. Somehow in the transition, some binary relations apparently become four-place relations, or relations that hold *between* two individuals *across* two possible worlds, instead of ternary extra-world relations with a single argument-place for possible worlds. An individual is taller than, shorter than, or the same height in one possible world as another individual in another possible world. The expansion of an intra-world composite binary relation into a four-place extra-world relation is easily accounted for in terms of the structured analysis of the relation into its component relations.

Consider first the case of a binary relation R that is defined as the relative product of a pair of binary relations R' and S. The component binary relations R' and S themselves each become ternary relations, with an additional argument-place for possible worlds, in the transition from ordinary discourse to possible world discourse. The definition of R,

$$R(x,y) =_{def.} (\exists z)[R'(x,z) \wedge S(z,y)],$$

upon transition to possible world discourse, may be expanded into the definition of a four-place relation thus:

$$R_{w_1/w_2}(x,y) =_{def.} (\exists z)[R'_{w_1}(x,z) \wedge S_{w_2}(z,y)].$$

The *grand-student* relation is a case in point. Its definition involves two occurrences of the *studied under* relation, which is an interactional relation that is not itself naturally construable as a cross-world relation. In fact, the relation is *world-variant*. Pairs of individuals that may stand in this relation do so in some possible worlds and not in others. Aristotle, for instance, might not have studied under Plato. The two occurrences of the *studied under* relation in the definition of the *grand-student* relation may be construed as intra-world relations that may hold simultaneously between pairs of individuals within two different possible worlds. When this is made explicit, we obtain the definition of the cross-world *grand-student* relation:

$$Cross\text{-}world\text{-}grand\text{-}student(x,w_1,y,w_2) =_{def.}$$

$$(\exists z)[Studied\text{-}under_{w_1}(x,z) \wedge Studied\text{-}under_{w_2}(z,y)].$$

The cross-world *grand-student* relation involves interaction, but this interaction is with an intermediate cross-world entity *within* possible worlds. It is in this way that the binary *grand-student* relation is construable as a four-place relation among individuals and possible worlds.

The situation is similar if R is defined by composition of a binary relation R'' and a pair of functional relations R' and S', except for one additional complication. In compositional definitions of this kind, there are three occurrences of component relations instead of two. Thus, the definition of R,

$$R(x,y) =_{def.} R''(R'(x),S'(y)),$$

upon transition to possible world discourse, may be expanded into

$$Cross\text{-}world\text{-}R_{w_3}(x,w_1,y,w_2) =_{def.} R''_{w_3}(R'_{w_1}(x),S'_{w_2}(y)),$$

Strictly speaking, then, R becomes a five-place relation. Consider for instance the *taller than* relation. Upon transition to possible world discourse, its definition,

$$Taller\text{-}than(x,y) =_{def.} \text{ the height of } x > \text{ the height of } y,$$

may be expanded into the definition of a five-place relation thus:

$$Cross\text{-}world\text{-}taller\text{-}than_{w_3}(x,w_1,y,w_2) =_{def.}$$

$$\text{the height in } w_1 \text{ of } x >_{w_3} \text{ the height in } w_2 \text{ of } y.$$

That is, one takes the height h that an individual x has in a possible world w_1, and also the height h' that an individual y has in a possible world w_2, and one then compares the heights h and h' in terms of their relative greatness *in some possible world* w_3. The quintuple $\langle x,w_1,y,w_2,w_3\rangle$ stand in this five-place relation if and only if $h > h'$ in w_3. But as we noted earlier, the *greater than* relation between heights is a world-invariant relation. The height h that x has in w_1 is either greater than the height h' that y has in w_2 or it is not, and it does not make any difference whether h and h' are compared in w_1, or w_2, or in some third possible world w_3, or in any other possible world. Since the *greater than* relation between heights is world-invariant, the third possible world argument in the definition of the five-place *taller than* relation serves no real purpose. It might as well be, and generally is, ignored.[17] When the third possible world argument place is dropped from consideration the definition of the five-place *taller than* relation becomes the definition of a four-place cross-world relation thus:

$$Cross\text{-}world\text{-}taller\text{-}than(x, w_1, y, w_2) =_{def.}$$

the height in w_1 of $x >$ the height in w_2 of y.

In general, if a binary relation R is defined by composition of a world-invariant binary relation R'' together with a pair of world-variant functional relations R' and S', then the third possible world argument which appears on R'' in the expanded definition of R may be dropped from consideration to obtain:[18]

[17]This may be accomplished by affixing an existential quantifier on the third of the three possible world arguments. Strictly speaking, then, the ternary world-dependent relation R'' (e.g., the *greater than within* relation among a pair of heights and a possible world) is replaced by the binary extra-world relation obtained by existentially generalizing upon the possible world argument of the ternary R″ (*greater than in some possible world or other*). Since the corresponding binary intra-world relation is world-invariant, it holds between a pair of individuals x and y in a possible world w if and only if x and y stand in R'' *in some possible world or other*. See the preceding footnote.

[18]In the special case of identity, the binary functional relations R' and S' and the world-independent binary relation R'' are all identity itself.

The view that identity is world-invariant, in the sense that

$$(w_1)\,(w_2)\,(x)\,(y)\,[(x =_{w_1} y) \leftrightarrow (x =_{w_2} y)],$$

or equivalently

$$\Box(x)\,\Box(y)\,[\Diamond(x = y) \to \Box(x = y)],$$

should be distinguished from a related doctrine (or cluster of doctrines) that has been called *haecceitism*. Kaplan (1975, pp. 722–723) gives the name 'haecceitism' to the view that it makes perfectly good sense to say that a thing x in one possible world is identical with a thing y in another possible world, in the absolute sense of being one and the very same thing, completely irrespective of similarities or ways of conceptualizing them. Although this may be somewhat vague or ambiguous, at least one version of haecceitism may be described as the view that the logic of possible world discourse includes a binary *absolute* concept of genuine identity between individuals in addition to its ternary *world-relative* concept of identity. If we assume this version of haecceitism, using its binary world-independent concept of identity the relation of cross-world identity between an individual x in a possible world w_1 and an individual y in a possible world w_2 may be defined thus:

$$(\imath z)\,[x =_{w_1} z] = (\imath z)\,[y =_{w_2} z].$$

If we assume, as we have, that extra-world atomic subject-predicate assertions may

(footnote continued on next page)

$$Cross\text{-}world\text{-}R(x,w_1,y,w_2) =_{def.} R''(R'_{w_1}(x),S'_{w_2}(y)).$$

Indeed, since a definition involving either of the methods of composition or relative product can be put into the general form

$$R(x,y) =_{def.} (\exists z)(\exists z')[R'(x,z) \wedge S'(y,z') \wedge R''(z,z')],$$

we can easily generalize our account of this mechanism for generating cross-world relations. In general, whenever a binary relation R is defined in this way in terms of two relations R' and S' to intermediate entities z and z', which themselves stand in a binary relation R'', and the relation R'' between the intermediate entities z and z' is a world-invariant relation, then it is perfectly natural upon transition to possible world discourse to construe R as a relation *between* individuals *across* possible worlds in virtue of the very logic of possible world discourse. The cross-world construal of R is forced upon us as soon as the component relations R' and S' are construed as intra-world relations that simultaneously hold between two pairs of individuals *in two different possible worlds* w_1 and w_2 thus:

$$(\exists z)(\exists z')[R'_{w_1}(x,z') \wedge S'_{w_2}(y,z') \wedge R''(z,z')].$$

R is construed as a cross-world relation by construing its compo-

---

be made using arbitrary definite descriptions from possible world discourse (i.e., that such assertions make sense), e.g., '$G_{w_2}[(\imath x)F_{w_1}(x)]$', then the relation of cross-world identity may be defined independently of absolute identity thus:

$$x =_{w_1} (\imath z)[y =_{w_2} z].$$

Assuming the version of haecceitism mentioned above, we may prove that the following three assertions are equivalent: (*a*) intra-world (or world-relative) identity is world-invariant, and the binary world-independent relation $(w)[x =_w y]$ is (co-extensive with) absolute, world-independent identity (see footnote 16); (*b*) intra-world identicals are absolutely identical, and vice-versa, i.e., $(w)(x)(y)[x =_w y \leftrightarrow x = y]$; (*c*) everything is intra-world identical with itself in at least one world, and furthermore *cross-world* identicals are absolutely identical, and vice-versa, i.e., $(x)(\exists w)[x =_w x]$ and $(w_1)(x)(w_2)(y)[(x =_{w_1} (\imath z)[y =_{w_2} z]) \leftrightarrow x = y]$. Thus, if we assume haecceitism, the further assumption that things are intra-world identical in a possible world if and only if they are absolutely identical (or equivalently that intra-world identity is world-invariant and things are absolutely identical if and only if they are intra-world identical in every world) confirms our definition of cross-world identity. Also, there is a sense in which one who holds that intra-world identity is world-invariant can become a haecceitist simply by letting $(w)[x =_w y]$ be the absolute, world-independent concept of identity, provided that he or she allows that $\Box(x)\Diamond[x = x]$, and that the world-independent relation defined by $(w)[x =_w y]$ is a congruence relation, i.e., that it preserves Leibniz's Law in possible world discourse. The haecceitist convert is then committed to (*b*) and (*c*) above.

128

nent intra-world relations as ternary extra-world relations in just the ordinary way, while construing the world-invariant relation R'' between the intermediate entities z and z' as a binary extra-world relation that holds between z and z' independently of any possible world. The binary relations mentioned above which are not naturally construed as cross-world relations are relations that are not, or are not naturally thought of as, defined using two occurrences of world-variant relations to intermediate entities which carry across possible worlds and which are world-independently related.

One might gather from the account of cross-world relations given thusfar that, in general, whenever a binary relation R has an internal logical structure involving two occurrences of world-dependent attributes, whether properties or relations, it will be natural upon transition to possible world discourse to construe the binary relation R as a cross-world relation. For one can always construe the two component world-dependent attributes as attributes which hold among two sequences of individuals in two different possible worlds. Thus, for instance, consider the contrived relation R that holds between a pair of individuals x and y whenever x is hungry and y is angry. We might say that a pair of individuals x and y stand in R *across* possible worlds w_1 and w_2 when x is hungry in w_1 and y is angry in w_2. (In this case, the world-dependent attributes are monadic properties rather than binary relations to intermediate entities.) Hence, it seems that the middlemen may be bypassed. The interesting fact is that the situation here does not seem to generalize as smoothly as the situation with the *taller than* relation, particularly to cases in which one of the defining attributes already involves a relation between x and y. Consider for instance the special relation that holds between a pair of individuals x and y when x loves y and at the same time y does not love x. One might call this the *unrequited love* relation. The transition to possible world discourse does, of course, generate a four-place relation from this binary relation. This four-place relation is the special relation that holds among the elements of a quadruple $\langle x, w_1, y, w_2 \rangle$ when x loves y in w_1, and at the same time y does not love x in w_2. Here is a relation that, in some sense, holds between individuals in different possible worlds. Would it be appropriate or natural to say that this relation corresponds to the "cross-world *unrequited love* relation"? Notice that this four-place relation holds among the elements of a quadruple $\langle x, w_1, y, w_2 \rangle$ even if x's love for y is requited in w_1 and neither one of x and y is acquainted with the other in w_2. Would it be natural to say in this case that "x in w_1

unrequitedly loves y in w_2," or that x and y "stand in the *unrequited love* relation *across* the worlds w_1 and w_2"? The issue is debatable, but there is a strong temptation to say that there is no such thing as a cross-world *unrequited love* relation, unrequited love between individuals *across* possible worlds. This is not to deny that the four-place relation defined above exists. It is only to deny that it is the natural cross-world construal of the binary *unrequited love* relation. It is unnatural to construe the *unrequited love* relation in just the same way as the *taller than* relation, as a relation that may hold between individuals across distinct possible worlds. On the other hand, the relation of *loving the same man as*, as well as certain other binary love-triangle relations, can clearly be construed as cross-world relations. The concept of a cross-world relation seems to preclude the two relata from being intra-world related as part of the cross-world relation. And intermediate entities that carry across possible worlds and are related in a world-independent way, though perhaps not absolutely required, seem to provide an important element in the original, intuitive idea.

We have considered the question of whether every structured binary relation defined by way of two occurrences of world-dependent attributes has a natural cross-world construal. What about the converse? Is it the case that every binary relation that is naturally construable as a cross-world relation has, or may be thought of as having, an internal logical structure involving two occurrences of world-dependent attributes? Here again the issue is not clear-cut. Perhaps some primitive, unstructured binary relations are also naturally construable as cross-world relations.[19] It certainly seems to be true that binary relations involving a much more complex structure than any of those so far considered may also have natural cross-world construals. We are not asserting the philosophical thesis that the binary relations which are construable as genuine cross-world relations are precisely those which are logically composed out of two occurrences of world-dependent relations to intermediate entities. What is clear is that certain binary relations defined using world-dependent relations to intermediate entities are naturally construed as genuine four-place, or cross-world, relations when their component world-dependent relations are construed as intra-world relations in two different possible worlds. The analyzed logical structure of these composite binary relations is crucial to the

---

[19]Relations such as *loves* and *thinks of* may be examples of this sort (he is in love with her the way she might have been).

construal of the relation as a cross-world relation. Interactional relations, such as the *hand shaking* and *marries* relations, are not defined in this way, nor are they naturally construed as cross-world relations.[20]

We noted above that in the case of the conspecificity and *same height* relations, the component world-independent relation R'' is the relation of identity. In fact, whenever a binary relation R is defined by composition of a binary relation R'' together with a functional relation R' taken twice, R will be an equivalence relation whenever R'' is, and in particular whenever R'' is the relation of identity. Most ordinary binary equivalence relations that come readily to mind, and all of the binary equivalence relations discussed above, may be seen as defined by composition of identity together with some function taken twice.[21] This helps to explain why so many equivalence relations are naturally construable as cross-world relations.

[20]The compositional analysis of relations such as the comparative height relations and the other equivalence relations mentioned above provides a special technical sense in which some cross-world relations can be said to be "modally grounded in" certain more fundamental properties while other relations cannot. Whether a binary relation R is defined by composition of a world-dependent binary relation R'' together with a pair of world-dependent functional relations R' and S', or instead as the relative product of a pair of world-dependent relations R' and the converse S of a binary relation S', the relation R is defined in either case by means of an important world-independent relation R'' so that an arbitray pair of individuals x and y stand in the relation R when and only when there are intermediate entities z and z' such that x has the intra-world relational property of bearing R' to z, y has the intra-world relational property of bearing S' to z', and z bears the world-independent relation R'' to z'. This is one very special sense in which one might define the phrase 'R is *modally grounded in* the intra-world properties of bearing R' to something and of bearing S' to something'. In this special sense of the phrase, a relation such as the *hand shaking* relation cannot be said to be modally grounded in certain properties, not even in the property of *bearing the hand shaking relation to something*. For there is no world-independent relation R'' by means of which the *hand shaking* relation may be defined as the relation that holds between an arbitrary pair of individuals x and y when and only when there are intermediate entities z and z' such that x shakes the hand of z, z' shakes the hand of y, and z bears R'' to z'.

[21]When the intermediate entity that is the value of the relevant function for a given relatum is a class of individuals, the relation may be put in the form

$$(z)[R'''(x,z) \leftrightarrow R'''(y,z)]$$

rather than the form $R'(x) = R'(y)$, where $R'(x) = \hat{z}[R'''(x,z)]$.

Not all binary equivalence relations are naturally thought of as defined by composition of identity together with a couple of functions. Set theoretically, any binary relation R can be "blown up" into an equivalence relation by simply adding all the ordered pairs needed to make the relation into an equivalence relation thus:

(footnote continued on next page)

The compositional definition of an equivalence relation can often be read off directly from the standard specification of the relation in natural language. In English, these specifications often take the form $\ulcorner\tau$ the same ν as$\urcorner$, where τ is a transitive verb phrase and ν is a common noun, for example, 'is the same height as', 'is a member of the same species as', etc. The occurrence of the word 'same' indicates a predication of identity. The functional relation R' is precisely that designated by the occurrence of the transitive verb phrase τ, e.g., 'is a member of'. (See footnote 14.) The corresponding function R' is that "expressed" by the gappy phrase $\ulcorner$the ν that —— $\tau\urcorner$, e.g., 'the species that —— is a member of', often abbreviated $\ulcorner$the ν of$\urcorner$. In fact, the transitive verb phrase $\ulcorner\tau$ the same ν as$\urcorner$ might be taken as shorthand for $\ulcorner$the ν that —— τ, is identical with the ν that —— $\tau\urcorner$, e.g., 'the species that —— is a member of is identical with the species that —— is a member of', thus laying bare the relational composition.

From the point of view of English syntax, it may be more plausible to treat a verb phrase of the form $\ulcorner\tau$ the same ν as$\urcorner$ as shorthand for $\ulcorner$—— τ the ν that —— $\tau\urcorner$, e.g., '—— is a member of the species that —— is a member of'. In the special case where an equivalence relation R is defined by composition of the relation of identity together with a functional relation R' taken twice, the definition of R may be rewritten in the form

$$R(x,y) =_{def.} R'(x,R'(y)).$$

Indeed, given that R' is a function, i.e., a many-one relation, the two formulations of the definition of R are equivalent, in the sense that each is logically derivable from the other.[22] Thus for instance, if

---

$$(F)[(F \text{ includes } R \wedge F \text{ is reflexive} \wedge F \text{ is symmetric}$$
$$\wedge F \text{ is transitive}) \rightarrow F(x,y)],$$

i.e., the pair of elements $\langle x,y \rangle$ stand in every equivalence relation that includes R. (I owe this point to Kaplan.) Plugging the *kissing* relation, for example, in place of R in this formula, one obtains a new relation, *kissing**, that holds between any individuals x and y when either kisses the other, and also when one kisses someone who kisses the other, and also when one kisses someone who kisses someone who kisses the other, and so on. Moreover, anyone who kisses someone or is kissed by someone, kisses* himself or herself. Whether the *kissing** relation is naturally construable as a cross-world relation depends on what counts as natural or unnatural.

[22] It is assumed here that any inference of the form

$$\psi[(\imath x)\phi(x)] \therefore (\exists y)[(x)(\phi(x) \leftrightarrow x = y) \wedge \psi(y)]$$

is valid where $\ulcorner\psi(\alpha)\urcorner$ is an atomic formula formed from an n-place predicate and n occurrences of singular terms, one of which is α. It is *valid* in the sense of we may assume as an axiom that any natural organism is a member of at most one species and not several,[23]

($Sp1$) $(x)(y)(z)[Species(y) \land Species(z)$

$$\land\, x \in y \land x \in z \rightarrow y = z],$$

we have the following redefinition of the conspecificity relation:

$$Conspecific(x,y) =_{def.} x \in (\imath z)[Species(z) \land y \in z].$$

This definition informs us quite literally that a pair of individuals x and y are said to be *conspecific*, by definition, if and only if x is a member of the species that y is a member of. Notice that here again there is explicit reference in the definiens to the intermediate entity by way of the definite description 'the species that y is a member of', though not in the definiendum.

13.4. *Nondenoting Singular Terms*

One more point which will prove important in later sections should be noted here before returning to the logical form of Putnam's suggested ostensive definition of water. When one individual has a height that is less than that of another individual, we say that the first individual is shorter than the second individual, and when one individual has a height that is greater than or equal to that of a second individual, we say that the first individual is *not* shorter than the second individual. This much accords perfectly with a compositional definition of the *shorter than* relation in terms of the height

---

'truth-preserving', since its premise cannot be true unless its component definite description is proper. Thus, the two definiens '$R'(x) = R'(y)$' and '$R'(x,R'(y))$' are equivalent in the sense that one is true of a pair of individuals if and only if the other is. In a moment we shall make a further simplifying assumption that atomic subject-predicate sentences with nondenoting terms are false. It will follow from this further assumption that when R' is *atomic* or *primitive* (not analyzable into component attributes), it is also the case that each of the two definiens is *false* of a pair of individuals if and only if the other is.

[23]Axiom ($Sp1$) is intended as an axiom of the theory of natural kinds. It may be taken to play the same role in that theory that the axioms of set theory play in set theory. Axiom ($Sp1$) is itself very plausible, but it has not been substantiated here. It may be thought of as an assumption that we are prepared to grant in constructing the strongest possible case for the derivability of nontrivial essentialism from the theory of direct reference. In particular, the criticisms that will be raised in Part II do not challenge this assumption in any way.

For valuable related discussion concerning the theory of natural kinds and its axiomatization see Thomason, 1969.

function taken twice and the *less than* relation among heights. But suppose we are comparing an object that has height with another object that does not have height. Say, for instance, we are comparing a lectern with an abstract object such as a number or a class. There is a problem in evaluating the statement 'This lectern is shorter than the null class'. Certainly the statement is not true, but is it false? Can we say, for instance, that the lectern is *not* shorter than the null class? Some philosophers would say that both the quoted statement and its negation lack truth-value—that they are neither true nor false—since they are "sortally incorrect" and involve a "category mistake." Others would say that the quoted statement is false and that its negation is true. By our proposed compositional definition of the *shorter than* relation, the question of how to evaluate the quoted statement reduces to a problem of how to evaluate an atomic subject-predicate sentence when one of its component singular terms is nondenoting. For by our definition of the *shorter than* relation, the statement 'This lectern is shorter than the null class' has the following analysis:

the height of this lectern < the height of the null class.

It therefore implicitly contains a nondenoting definite description, 'the height of the null class'. Some semantical theories of nondenoting terms count such a statement false. Other theories count such a statement as lacking truth-value. In general, the functions R' and S' that appear in the definition of a binary relation R by composition may be partial functions. That is, they may not yield a value for every argument. The height function yields no value when an abstract object is taken as an argument, since abstract objects do not have height.[24] Similarly, the species function yields no value when an inanimate object such as a table or chair is taken as an argument, since tables and chairs are not members of biological species. This presents a problem in evaluating statements such as 'This lectern and the world's largest living mammal are conspecific' and 'This lectern is shorter than the null class'. If statements such as these were counted neither true nor false, several technical questions and complications would arise in what follows, questions and complications which are easily resolved but which are of little interest from the point of view of the main concerns of the present work. In order to

---

[24]In saying that abstract objects do not have height, I do not mean that they have a height of 0 (units), but that the height function yields no value at all, not even 0, when an abstract object is taken as argument.

134

avoid these complexities, we shall simply assume that these statements are to be counted false.

There are several things that we can do in order to ensure that these statements are counted false, while maintaining a structured analysis of relations such as the *shorter than* and conspecificity relations for the purpose of cross-world construals. We might adopt a semantical theory according to which atomic subject-predicate sentences involving nondenoting singular terms are counted false. Alternatively, we might modify the general form of the definition of a binary relation by composition. The general form of the definition might be rewritten as[25]

$$R(x,y) =_{def.} (\exists z)R'(x,z) \wedge (\exists z')S'(y,z') \wedge R''(R'(x),S'(y)),$$

or in the more familiar form

$$R(x,y) =_{def.} (\exists z)(\exists z')[R'(x,z) \wedge S'(y,z') \wedge R''(z,z')].$$

It will be most convenient for what follows simply to adopt a semantical theory that counts atomic formulae with nondenoting terms false. This also means that atomic formulae containing singular terms that denote nothing *with respect to a possible world w* will be counted false *with respect to w.*[26]

---

[25]It is not necessary to expand the definiens further by adding uniqueness clauses, since we are *given* that R' and S' are functions, i.e., many-one relations. Notice that however we choose to formulate the definition of a binary relation R, by the methods of either composition or relative product, in each case the definition involves overt and explicit reference in the definiens to the intermediate entity or entities, by way of existential quantification or definite descriptions, whereas the definiendum need not involve any explicit reference to the intermediate entities.

[26]In particular, an identity statement $\ulcorner \alpha = \beta \urcorner$ will be counted false with respect to any possible world w if either α or β denote nothing with respect to w. This does not mean that $\ulcorner \alpha = \beta \urcorner$ will automatically be counted false with respect to a possible world w if either α or β denote something with respect to w that does not exist in w (i.e., something that is not in the domain over which bound variables range with respect to w). The formula $\ulcorner \alpha = \beta \urcorner$ is true with respect to a possible world w if and only if α and β denote the same thing with respect to w, whether or not that thing exists in w. (See Sections 3.1 and 3.2 on the distinction between a term denoting nothing with respect to a possible world and a term denoting, with respect to a possible world, something that does not exist in that possible world.)

Given our treatment of variables bound from within a modal operator, the existence predicate '*Exists*' occurring in (10) is definable by the following:

$$Exists(\alpha) =_{def.} (\exists \beta)[\alpha = \beta],$$

where β is any individual variable that does not occur free in α. If α denotes something
(footnote continued on next page)

135

14. REFORMULATIONS

14.1. A New Attempt at Formalization

We return to Putnam's suggested ostensive definition of water. In eliminating all reference to possible world-slices of liquid samples from the definition, we found ourselves construing the consubstantiality relation between liquid samples as a four-place, or cross-world, relation—a relation between liquid samples across possible worlds. We have seen that equivalence relations like the consubstantiality and conspecificity relations are naturally construable as cross-world relations in virtue of their compositional structure. The consubstantiality relation may be defined in a manner entirely analogous to the definition given above of the conspecificity relation thus:

$$Consubstantial(x,y) =_{def.}$$

$$(\imath z)[Substance(z) \wedge x \in z] = (\imath z)[Substance(z) \wedge y \in z],$$

or more simply by

$$Consubstantial\ (x,y) =_{def.} x \in (\imath z)[Substance(z) \wedge y \in z],$$

where '$\in$' is taken as the predicate for the relation that holds between a substance sample and the substance of which it is a sample. In English, these definitions inform us that a pair of individuals x and y are *consubstantial*, by definition, if and only if x is a sample of the same substance that y is a sample of. Upon transition to possible world discourse, the first definition becomes

$$Cross\text{-}world\text{-}consubstantial(x,w_1,y,w_2) =_{def.}$$

$$(\imath z)[Substance_{w_1}(z) \wedge x \in_{w_1} z] =$$

$$(\imath z)[Substance_{w_2}(z) \wedge y \in_{w_2} z].$$

Likewise, the second definition becomes

---

with respect to a possible world w which is not a member of the domain over which the bound variable β ranges with respect to w, i.e., which does not exist in w, the definiens, and hence also the definiendum, $\ulcorner Exists(\alpha)\urcorner$, is false with respect to w, as it should be. Also, given our decision to count an identity statement false when one of its components is nondenoting, the definiens, and hence also the definiendum, is false if α denotes nothing. Thus the statement 'The present king of France exists' is also counted false.

136

Cross-world-consubstantial$(x,w_1,y,w_2) =_{def.}$

$$x \in_{w_1} (\imath z)[Substance_{w_2}(z) \wedge y \in_{w_2} z].$$

Either of these might be taken as appropriate symbolizations for the cross-world relational phrase 'x is a sample in w_1 of the same substance that y is a sample of in w_2'. The second definition of cross-world consubstantiality is a trivial consequence of the first. Indeed, on certain plausible assumptions, the two definitions are equivalent. The assumptions needed may be stated as the necessitations of two axioms on the relevant concept of a (chemical) substance. The first axiom is entirely analogous to axiom $(Sp1)$ for species, which asserts that any natural organism is a member of at most one species. Here we must assert the same thing for substance samples *in every possible world*. That is, we need to assume the necessitation of the following axiom of the theory of natural kinds:

$(Sub1)$ $(x)(y)(z)[Substance(y) \wedge Substance(z) \wedge$

$$x \in y \wedge x \in z \rightarrow y = z].$$

Further we need to assume a certain general principle of essentialism regarding substances, namely, that anything that is a substance in some possible world is a substance in every possible world in which it exists.[27] This assumption may be expressed as the necessitation of the following principle of essentialism:[28]

$(Sub2)$ $(x)(Substance(x) \rightarrow \Box[Exists(x) \rightarrow Substance(x)]).$

[27]This general principle of essentialism regarding *substances* is not to be confused with the corresponding general principle of essentialism regarding *substance samples*, which states that anything that is a substance sample in some possible world is a substance sample in every possible world in which it exists. See also Chapter Three, footnote 5.

[28]For technical reasons, $(Sub1)$ and $(Sub2)$ unnecessitated may not be sufficient, depending on the treatment of bound variables in a language with modal operators, i.e., in "subjunctive" or modal operator discourse. The general principles expressed by $(Sub1)$ and $(Sub2)$ must be asserted for possible substances that may not exist in the actual world, assuming that there might have existed different substances than those that actually exist. (The prospect of possible but nonactual substances was discussed briefly in Section 6.1. See also footnote 36 below.) As we have already noted, the domain over which a bound variable ranges with respect to a possible world w is presumed throughout the present work to be precisely the class of possible individuals that exist in w. In order to ensure that the initial universal quantifiers of $(Sub1)$ and of $(Sub2)$ range over all possible substances, actual or not, it is necessary to assert the necessitations of $(Sub1)$ and $(Sub2)$.

137

As with axiom (*Sp*1), axioms (*Sub*1) and (*Sub*2) are plausible, but neither has been substantiated here. Indeed, from the point of view of the main inquiry of Part II of the present work, there is still a question whether the essentialist (*Sub*2) follows somehow as a consequence of the theory of direct reference. All three of these assumptions can be eliminated by taking the first formulations of the definitions of the conspecificity and consubstantiality relations instead of the second. In an effort to keep our symbolizations as close to English as possible, however, we shall retain the second formulations. Axioms (*Sp*1), (*Sub*1), and (*Sub*2) may be taken as further assumptions that we are prepared to grant in constructing the strongest possible case for the derivability of nontrivial essentialism from the theory of direct reference.

We are now in a position to give a more perspicuous symbolization for (10′). We obtain it directly from (10) and the second definition of the consubstantiality relation given above:

(11) $(w)(x)[Exists_w(x) \rightarrow (\Pi_{water_w}(x)$

$$\leftrightarrow x \in_w (\imath z) \, [\text{Substance}_{w@} \, (z) \land (this \in_{w@} z)])].$$

Notice that (11) makes overt and explicit reference, by way of a definite description, to a certain intermediate entity, namely, the substance that the paradigm referred to by the demonstrative '*this*' is a sample of in the actual world. Overt reference to this substance is absent from (10), and this is one reason why (11) is superior to (10) as a symbolization of (10′).

The substance referred to, of course, is water. As we have seen, reference to this substance is crucial for the cross-world construal of the consubstantiality relation. It is precisely by carrying this substance across possible worlds, as an intermediate entity to which water samples are intra-world related, that these samples are construed as *consubstantial* across possible worlds.

It should be noted here that Putnam, in a brief prolegomenon to his presentation of his direct reference theory of natural kind terms, remarks that "we shall assume ... that in at least some cases it is possible to speak of the same individual as existing in more than one possible world" (1975a, p. 230). In a footnote to this sentence, however, he qualifies the remark: "This assumption is not actually needed in what follows. What *is* needed is that the same *natural kind* can exist in more than one possible world" (p. 230n).

Kaplan (1975, pp. 722–723) gives a name to the doctrine that it makes perfectly good sense to identify, in an *absolute* sense irrespective of similarities or qualitative concepts, a thing x of kind k in one possible world with something y of kind k in another possible world. He calls it 'haecceitism with respect to entities of kind k'. (See footnote 18 above.) In Kaplan's terminology, Putnam points out in his footnote that his theory presupposes *haecceitism with respect to natural kinds*. This footnote of Putnam's strongly suggests that a symbolization for (10′) that makes use of our compositional analysis of cross-world consubstantiality is closer to Putnam's intentions than one that conceals any mention of the substance water as a cross-world entity. Expression (11) does indeed make explicit reference to a certain natural kind as a cross-world entity, whereas (10) gives no hint of any commitment to haecceitism in any form. This is a second reason why (11) is a superior symbolization of (10′).

14.2 Thesis (T3)

To arrive at the logical form of an ostensive definition for a species term such as 'tiger' one simply substitutes in (11) the term 'tiger' for 'water' and the term 'species' for 'substance', to obtain

$$(w)(x)[Exists_w(x)$$
$$\rightarrow (\Pi_{tiger_w}(x) \leftrightarrow x \in_w (\imath z)[Species_{W_@}(z) \wedge this \in_{w_@} z])].$$

In English we have:

> For every possible world w, something existing in w is a tiger in w if and only if it is a member in w of the same species that *this* is a member of in the actual world,

to be said with reference to a particular tiger serving as a paradigm.

Generalizing upon the logical form of the ostensive definitions, Putnam's thesis (T3) may be interpreted as the thesis that one may "explain the meaning," and thereby fix the designation, of a natural kind common noun v in an "ostensive definition" whose intended logical form is given by the following:

$$(w)(x)[Exists_w(x)$$
$$\rightarrow (\Pi_{v_w}(x) \leftrightarrow x \in_w (\imath z)[K_{w_@}(z) \wedge this \in_{w_@} z])].$$

where '$\in$' is a binary predicate for the relation that holds between an individual x and a kind k when x is an instance of kind k, K is a generic natural kind predicate like 'is a substance' or 'is a species',

and the demonstrative '*this*' is used with reference to an actual
paradigm of the natural kind designated by *v*.

14.3. Reductionism and Analysis

There is an interesting sidenote to our analysis of Putnam's suggested
ostensive definition of water. We noted repeatedly in our discussion
of composite relations that when a binary relation is defined either by
composition of a binary relation R'' together with a pair of functions
R' and S', or as the relative product of a pair of relations R' and S,
there is overt reference in the definiens, either by way of definite
descriptions or by way of existential quantification, to the intermediate entity or entities, whereas there need not be any overt reference
to these intermediate entities in the definiendum. This difference
between definiens and definiendum is often significant in connection
with certain reductionist programs in philosophy. If the definition of
a relation R is intended as a strict synonymy definition, then the
definiens is supposed to fix not only the semantical extension of the
definiendum but its sense as well. The definiens is intended to
capture not only the metaphysical extension of the relation R, or
what is sometimes called the *relation-in-extension* or *course of
values* (a class of ordered pairs), but also what is sometimes called
the *relation-in-intension,* that is, the binary relation itself, an *attribute* analogous to a property—except that, whereas an object *has* a
property, a *pair* of objects *stand in* a binary relation. Thus when the
definition of a binary relation R by either of the methods of
composition or of relative product is taken as a strict synonymy
definition, the predicate for R is understood as involving reference,
albeit covert reference, to the intermediate entities, and the notion of
intermediate entities of the sort that serve as second relata for R' and
S' (the converse of S) is conceptually prior to, or constitutive of, the
notion expressed by the predicate for R. This is true despite the fact
that the predicate's semantical extension involves only the relata of R
and not the intermediate entities. Many philosophers have found it
theoretically preferable to take advantage of the fact that the
metaphysical extension of a relation R involves only its relata, and to
redefine a compositional relation R independently of its component
relations R' and S', or to take R as primitive. This often makes it
possible to eliminate the category of the intermediate entities in favor
of the relation R itself, or to regard the intermediate entities as
"logical constructs," now definable without circularity in terms of
the relation R.

Consider for instance the equinumerous relation between classes. This equivalence relation is definable by composition as an identity between the cardinalities of a pair of classes, thereby treating the cardinalities as intermediate entities. One of Frege's many remarkable achievements was to show that the equinumerous relation can also be defined independently of the notion of the cardinality of a class using only notions from "logic" (i.e., higher order logic, or logic plus class theory proper). This elimination of reference to numbers in the equinumerous relation enabled the logicists to define the notion of *cardinality,* and the more general notion of *number,* without circularity in terms of the equinumerous relation between classes.

Structurally similar attempts have been made or suggested more recently in connection with the notion of the "meaning," or *sense,* of an expression. The synonymy relation between expressions is definable by composition as an identity between the senses of a pair of expressions, thereby involving senses as intermediate entities. Some philosophers of language have suggested that we redefine the notion of synonymy independently of the notion of the sense of an expression, or that we take some synonymy notion as primitive and then explicate the notion of sense in terms of, or eliminate the notion of sense in favor of, the independently defined or primitive synonymy relation.[29]

Of course, each of these reductionist programs involves an implicit rejection of the strict synonymy alleged in the compositional definition of the relation R in question. One cannot analyze the notion of a number in terms of the equinumerous relation among classes if the equinumerous relation among classes is in turn to be analyzed in terms of the notion of a number. Similarly, one cannot "reduce" linguistic meanings to synonymy relations among expressions if synonymy is in turn to be analyzed in terms of the notion of meaning. If the category of the intermediate entities is conceptually constitutive of the relation R, then a genuine "reduction" of the former in terms of the latter is impossible, at least without a "revision in our conceptual scheme." Following this line of thought, one might wish to reject the analysis that we have proposed for the conspecificity and consubstantiality relations in terms of species and substances in order to "reduce" species to conspecific organisms, and substances to consubstantial samples. In this way one might hope to lay a

---

[29]The move is suggested in several places in the work of Quine. See 1969, p. 295, for an explicit instance. A similar idea is suggested by Davidson's use of his *samesaying* relation (1969).

philosophical foundation for the intuition that natural kinds such as species and substances are "nothing over and above" the instances that make them up. (But see Chapter Three, footnote 6.)

14.4. Translation Into Modal Operator Discourse

We have already seen one important advantage in upholding the strict synonymy alleged in a compositional definition of a binary relation; doing so yields a plausible account of why it is that certain binary relations are naturally construable as cross-world relations. There is another advantage in maintaining the compositional analysis of relations like conspecificity and consubstantiality, for there is another reductionist program in philosophy that is served well by compositional analysis of these equivalence relations. This is the program that hopes for the ultimate elimination of possible world discourse in favor of modal operator discourse.[30]

Our analysis of the cross-world consubstantiality relation occurring in Putnam's suggested ostensive definition of water was originally motivated by a desire to eliminate reference to these bizarre possible world-slices of liquid samples from (8) and (8'). As a byproduct, this analysis also provides for the easy elimination of still another potentially undesirable feature of Putnam's original formulation, namely, quantification over possible worlds. Putnam, of course, recognizes that the notion of a possible world is found objectionable by some philosophers.[31] He provides a brief apology for his use of the notion with the following words: "We feel that in several senses the notion makes sense and is scientifically important even if it needs to be made more precise."[32] This may be correct (I believe that something along these lines is correct), but until there is more widespread agreement on this point it may be desirable to formulate theories in ordinary, more familiar terms, without reference to possible worlds, whenever it is possible to do so, and especially when the subjunctive locutions of everyday language seem better suited to the topic under investigation (e.g., how we explain the meanings of the natural kind terms of everyday language). Thus, for instance, instead of saying "In every possible world, it is the case that p" we might use the form "It is necessarily the case that p" or

---

[30]See Fine, 1977a, for an illuminating discussion of the details of such a reductionist program.

[31]See Loux, 1979, and, for instance, Quine, 1972, pp. 492–493.

[32]In 1975a, p. 230. Compare also Kripke's defense of possible worlds (1972a, pp. 48n, 15–20) with Lewis's (1973, pp. 84–91).

"It must be the case that *p*" or "It could not fail to be the case that
p." In formal terms, we should replace universal quantification over
possible worlds with the sentential necessity operator, existential
quantification over possible worlds with the sentential possibility
operator, and the actual world constant with the sentential actuality
operator. This proposed translation of possible world discourse into
the subjunctive discourse of modal operators might be seen in the
material mode as an attempt to "reduce" nonactual possible worlds
to unreified *modes* or ways in which some particular thing may be
the case (by necessity, impossibility, contingency, etc.).

There are a number of well-known complications involved in this
proposal to translate possible world discourse formulations into
subjunctive discourse formulations. These complications result from
the fact that discourse involving possible worlds is essentially richer
than the usual first-order discourse involving modal operators.[33] In
particular, a reduction of possible world discourse to subjunctive
discourse often cannot be made in the simple manner suggested
above with formulations that involve ineliminable overlay of quantification over possible worlds. It would be a mistake, for instance, to
rephrase the formula

$$(\exists w_1)(w_2)(x \text{ is taller in } w_1 \text{ than } y \text{ is in } w_2)$$

as

$$\Diamond \Box (x \text{ is taller than } y).$$

The second formula expresses the assertion that *x* might necessarily
have been taller than *y*, whereas the first formula expresses the
somewhat stronger assertion that *x* might have been so tall that *x*'s
height would be greater than any *possible* height of *y*.[34] This means

---

[33]Every statement in customary first-order modal operator discourse is equivalent to
a statement in possible world discourse in which all overlaid quantifiers over possible
worlds, if any, have matrices (equivalent to one) of a specific form involving an
"accessibility" clause, whereas not every statement in possible world discourse is
equivalent to one of this form. See Fine (1977a) and Hazen (1976) on the translation
of possible world discourse into modal operator discourse. A second reason why
possible world discourse is essentially richer than customary first-order modal operator discourse is discussed below in footnote 35.

[34]The first formula would be false even while the second is true, if, for instance, *x* is
essentially taller than *y*, but there is necessarily no upper limit on *y*'s possible height,
so that necessarily, for any height *h*, *y* might have had a height greater than *h*. In
possible world discourse, the second formula translates into

(footnote continued on next page)

that an ultimate reduction of possible world discourse to discourse involving modal operators must be considerably subtler than a simple and straightforward substitution of modal operators for quantifiers on possible worlds.

Fortunately, our last formulation of Putnam's suggested ostensive definition of water, (11), does not involve any overlay of quantification over possible worlds. If the occurrences of '$W_@$' in (11) are replaced by an occurrence of the sentential actuality operator 'A', and the initial quantifier on possible worlds is replaced by a necessity operator, we obtain

$$\Box(x)(Exists(x) \rightarrow$$

$$[\Pi_{water}(x) \leftrightarrow x \in (\imath z)(A[Substance(z)] \wedge A[this \in z])]),$$

which can be reduced[35] to

$$(\exists w_1)(w_2)[w_2 \text{ is accessible to } w_1 \rightarrow \text{ in } w_2, x \text{ is taller than } y],$$

an assertion that fails to make any height comparisons between x and y *as they are in different possible worlds*. This last expression illustrates a further point: Some sentences that involve ineliminable overlay of quantification over possible worlds do have equivalent formulations in customary first-order modal operator discourse. Such is the case with certain expressions involving nested modalities.

[35] Given our treatment of bound variables in modal operator discourse, the antecedent '$Exists(x)$' occurring in the first translation is eliminable since, with respect to any possible world w, the bound variable 'x' ranges only over things that exist in w. See footnote 26 above on the definition of the existence predicate.

There is a second complication in reducing possible world discourse to modal operator discourse, a complication that our translation of (11) into (12) completely ignores. Possible world discourse presupposes an ontology of not only the actual individuals, but also possible but nonactual individuals. The quantifiers of possible world discourse are the so-called "outer domain" or "possibilist" quantifiers. Thus a sentence such as '$(\exists w)(x)Male_w(x)$' asserts that in some possible world w, every *possible* individual x is male in w, whether x exists in w or not. It is necessary to introduce into possible world discourse a primitive predicate for existence in a possible world in order to distinguish those possible individuals that exist in a possible world from those that do not. This predicate has already made its appearance in (8)–(11). The situation is slightly different with bound variables in modal operator discourse. As we noted above, it is presumed throughout the present work that the domain over which a bound variable ranges with respect to a possible world w is precisely the class of possible individuals that exist in w. Unfortunately, this difference between the variables of possible world discourse and modal operator discourse creates a difficulty in translating the definite description '$(\imath z)[Substance_{w_@}(z) \wedge this \in_{w_@} z]$' occurring in (11). The definite description '$(\imath z)A[Substance(z) \wedge this \in z]$' occurring in (12), our proposed translation of (11), is in the terminology of Section 3.1 a persistent designator of water. Its exact translation into possible world discourse is '$(\imath z)[Exists_w(z) \wedge Substance_{w_@}(z) \wedge this \in_{w_@} z]$', which denotes the substance water when

(12) $\Box(x)\ (\Pi_{water}(x)\ \leftrightarrow\ x\ \in\ (\imath z)A[Substance(z)\ \wedge$
$$(this\ \in\ z)]).$$

In English we have:

(12′)   It is necessarily the case that: something is a sample of water if and only if it is a sample of the same *actual* substance that *this* is *actually* a sample of.

Formula (12) employs a definite description of the form $\ulcorner(\imath\alpha)A\phi\urcorner$ for the substance water. We saw in Section 3.1 that an indexical definite description of the form $\ulcorner(\imath\alpha)A\phi\urcorner$ is a rigid counterpart of the description $\ulcorner(\imath\alpha)\phi\urcorner$ omitting the actuality operator. In English, the description 'the (same) actual substance that *this* is actually a sample of' occurring in (12′) is a rigid counterpart of the description 'the (same) substance that *this* is a sample of'. We also saw that another way to "rigidify" a definite description is to enclose it within Kaplan's indexical '*dthat*'-operator. Indeed, (11) might also be translated into modal operator discourse by way of

(13) $\Box(x)[\Pi_{water}(x)$

$$\leftrightarrow x\ \in\ dthat((\imath z)[Substance(z)\ \wedge\ (this\ \in\ z)])],$$

as well as by way of (12).[36] In English (augmented with the '*dthat*'-operator) we have:

_____

the value of the possible world variable 'w' is a possible world in which the substance water exists, and denotes nothing when the value of 'w' is a possible world in which the substance water does not exist. By contrast the definite description occurring in (11) denotes the substance water regardless of the choice of value for the variable 'w', since 'w' does not occur in it. This point of disanalogy between (11) and (12) does not prevent at least a loose translation of (11) into modal operator discourse by way of (12), given our earlier decision to count atomic formulae with nondenoting terms false. (See Section 13.4.) A better translation of (11) into modal operator discourse would employ a singular term that "describes" the substance water as the substance that the paradigm is a sample of, and yet denotes the substance water with respect to every possible world, whether the substance exists there or not. That is, an obstinate designator of water is needed, but one that is, in some sense *descriptive*. (See Chapter One, footnote 11.) Such a translation for (11) will be given by (13). There is, therefore, a technical reason for preferring (13) over (12).

[36]The only difference between (12) and (13) is that (13) contains an occurrence of a singular term of the form $\ulcorner dthat[(\imath z)\phi(z)]\urcorner$ where (12) contains an occurrence of a singular term of the form $\ulcorner(\imath z)A\phi(z)\urcorner$, both of which are rigid counterparts of a definite description $\ulcorner(\imath z)\phi(z)\urcorner$ denoting the substance water, but as noted in the previous footnote, the term formed by means of the '*dthat*'-operator is obstinate, whereas the term formed by means of the actuality operator is persistent. If the substance water is the sort of entity that exists in every possible world, then both terms

(footnote continued on next page)

(13′)   It is necessarily the case that: something is a sample of
          water if and only if it is a sample of *dthat*(the same
          substance that *this* is a sample of).

The elimination of quantification over possible worlds from the
ostensive definition of water was accomplished in three steps. First,
reference to possible world-slices of liquid samples was eliminated
from (8), our symbolization of Putnam's original formulation, in
(10) by replacing the binary gen-consubstantiality relation with the
corresponding four-place relation. Second, the cross-world consubstantiality relation expressed in (10) was analyzed into its component
relations in (11), thus making explicit reference by way of a definite
description to a certain intermediate cross-world entity, the
substance water. Third, the remaining reference to possible worlds in
(11) was replaced by modal operators in two different but similar
ways to obtain (12) and (13). Both (12) and (13) retain the feature
of explicit reference to the substance water and both gain an
occurrence of an indexical operator—features that are conspicuously
absent from (8), Putnam's original formulation.

Reference to possible worlds cannot be directly and immediately
eliminated from (10) in favor of modal operators while retaining an
unstructured predicate for the consubstantiality relation. Upon elim-

---

are strongly rigid, and there is no important difference between (12) and (13), at least
as far as their truth-conditions are concerned.

Presumably, any possible world in which there is some water is a possible world in
which water (the substance) exists. But perhaps it may be said that the substance
water fails to exist in any possible world in which there are no water samples. Even
then, it is easily verified that (12) and (13), which are "definitions" and hence must be
"true by definition," have exactly the same truth-conditions, and fix exactly the right
semantical intension for the term 'water'. The troublesome case that needs checking is
that of a possible world w in which there are no water samples and hence there is no
substance water. The adequacy of (13) as a definition of water depends only on our
assumption that where there is no substance water, there is no water. The adequacy of
(12) follows directly from our decision to count false with respect to w all atomic
subject-predicate formulae containing nondenoting singular terms with respect to w.
This decision is especially significant here. If instead we had decided to count such
formulae neither true nor false, the adequacy of (12) as a definition of water would
depend crucially on the details of three-value modal semantics. On one popular
three-valued truth-table for the biconditional, for instance, (12) would prove inadequate as a definition of water. Formula (13), on the other hand, avoids these
difficulties. Thus there may be a second technical reason why (13) may be superior to
(12) as a modal operator formulation of the ostensive definition of water presented in
Putnam's theory of natural kind terms.

146

ination of reference to possible worlds the unstructured consubstantiality predicate becomes an unstructured binary predicate. Whenever a sentential modal operator modifies a sentence involving an atomic subject-predicate relational assertion, the relation is asserted to hold only in an intra-world sense. Yet we have already seen that Putnam's theory of substance terms requires that the relation of consubstantiality be asserted to hold not in an intra-world sense but in a cross-world sense. In order to eliminate reference to possible worlds from (10), one must first perform the second step of analyzing the cross-world consubstantiality relation into its components, thereby making reference to an intermediate cross-world entity, the substance water. The reference to possible worlds by way of variables and a constant in (8) is avoided, but only by making reference to the substance water by way of a definite description. In a manner of speaking, then, reference to possible worlds is traded for reference to a cross-world substance.[37]

[37]It is interesting to note in this connection that philosophers dealing with cross-world relations or cross-time relations, or anything similar, generally find reference to the intermediate entities unavoidable, unless they resort to slices. Adams (1971) is a case in point. In attempting to formalize Anselm's Ontological Argument, which employs a cross-world *greater than* relation between "beings," he remarks: "I have found it necessary also to introduce the notion of a *magnitude* of greatness" (p. 29). Consider also Russell's formulation (1905) of the following anecdote concerning propositional attitudes: "I have heard of a touchy owner of a yacht to whom a guest, on first seeing it, remarked, 'I thought your yacht was larger than it is;' and the owner replied, 'No, my yacht is not larger than it is.' What the guest meant was, 'The size that I thought your yacht was is greater than the size your yacht is;' the meaning attributed to him is, 'I thought the size of your yacht was greater than the size of your yacht' " (p. 52 of Russell, 1956).

Cross-world relations thus present a certain dilemma for the reductionist philosopher. We noted above that it might be hoped that such notions as that of a *substance* and that of a *species* are ultimately explicable in terms of, "logically constructed" out of, or eliminable in favor of certain equivalence relations, such as consubstantiality and conspecificity—the latter being defined independently of the former, or taken as primitive. Such "reductions" necessarily involve a rejection of any analysis of the latter in terms of the former. But it is just such an analysis that allows for the reduction of possible world discourse to customary first-order modal operator discourse with respect to general assertions of cross-world consubstantiality or conspecificity. Thus, in attempting to "reduce" natural kinds to relations among their members ("natural kinds are *nothing over and above* their members"), the reductionist philosopher is deprived of a key method for reducing discourse ostensibly about possible worlds to customary first-order subjunctive discourse. Conversely, in using this method to reduce possible world discourse to subjunctive discourse, the reductionist is deprived of a key method for reducing natural kinds to relations among their members. See also Chapter Three, footnote 6.

In the general case, we have the following alternative forms of an ostensive definition for a natural kind common noun v;

(14) $\quad \Box(x)\,(\Pi_v(x) \leftrightarrow x \in (\imath z)A[K(z) \wedge (this \in z)])$

and

(15) $\quad \Box(x)\,[\Pi_v(x) \leftrightarrow x \in \text{dthat}((\imath z)[K(z) \wedge (this \in z)])]$,

where '$\in$' is the predicate for the relation between an individual and a kind that the individual is an instance of, K is a generic natural kind predicate like 'is a substance', 'is a species', etc., and the demonstrative '*this*' is used with reference to an actual paradigm of the natural kind designated by v. Thus for instance we have the following definition for the term 'tiger':

$$\Box(x)[\Pi_{tiger}(x) \leftrightarrow x \in dthat((\imath z)\,[Species(z) \wedge$$

$$(this \in z)])].$$

or in English:

> It is necessarily the case that: something is a tiger if and only if it is a member of *dthat*(the same species that *this* is a member of).

(Compare the sentence displayed on page 74.)

Thesis (T3) may thus be reinterpreted as the thesis that the "meaning" of a natural kind common noun v may be "explained," and its designation thereby fixed, in an ostensive definition having the logical form of either (14) or (15). This will be our preferred interpretation.

15. FURTHER EXEGETICAL REMARKS

15.1. Theses (T5) and (T6)

We are now in a position to clarify exactly that role indexicality plays in fixing the designation of a natural kind term. The function performed by indexicality in fixing the designation of the term 'water' arises in connection with Putnam's thesis (T5), the thesis that the term 'water' rigidly designates the substance water as a formal consequence of its ostensive definition. There are two indexical expressions occurring in (12): the sentential actuality operator and the demonstrative '*this*'. Similarly, there are two indexical expressions occurring in (13): the '*dthat*'-operator and the demonstrative '*this*'. Putnam emphasizes the latter of the two occurrences of indexicality, pointing out (1973b, p. 707) that the demonstrative rigidly designates the paradigmatic sample of water that is the object of the ostension. But emphasis on this occurrence of indexicality is misleading. In both (12) and (13), the demonstrative occurs within the scope of an indexical operator, and therefore its denotation with respect to the actual world is all that is relevant to the truth-conditions of the containing sentence.[38] The fact that the demonstrative '*this*' is rigid is quite irrelevant to the truth-conditions of (12) and (13). Indeed, as Donnellan points out (1973b), any singular term denoting the paradigm sample of water, even a nonrigid definite description, would serve the same purpose, at least as far as the truth-conditions of (12) and (13) are concerned.[39]

It is not crucial for (T5), therefore, that the actual paradigm be rigidly designated in the definition of water. What is crucial for (T5) is that the *substance* the paradigm is a sample of be rigidly designated in the definition of water. To see this, suppose that, instead of the rigid description 'the actual substance that *this* is actually a sample of', we had used a nonrigid definite description to denote the substance water, e.g., 'the liquid substance that covers two-thirds of the surface of the earth'. The latter description is nonrigid since there are possible worlds in which two-thirds of the surface of the earth is covered with tomato juice instead of water, and with respect to such a world the description denotes tomato juice. Our "definition" of water then becomes:

> It is necessarily the case that: something is a sample of water if and only if it is a sample of the liquid substance that covers two-thirds of the surface of the earth.

[38]This is a consequence of the modal semantical behavior of these indexical operators. See Kaplan, 1973b. Indeed, the point of the actuality operator in (12) is precisely to ensure that its operand is evaluated only with respect to the actual world. The truth-value of its operand with respect to the actual world in turn depends on the denotations with respect to the actual world of the singular terms occurring referentially within it. The situation is entirely similar in the case of (13).

[39]As we shall see shortly, this is not to say that demonstrative reference to a paradigm plays no important role with regard to the status of (12) *as an ostensive definition*. The immediate presence of an actual sample of water may give the audience an idea of some of the typical, or "stereotypical," properties of water—properties such as that of *being a colorless liquid, being odorless*, etc. A definite description, if used attributively in Donnellan's sense, may not, e.g., 'the liquid sample, whatever kind it is, that Smith will consume with her dinner tomorrow evening'.

Or in possible world discourse,

> In every possible world w, something is a sample of water in w if and only if it is a sample in w of the liquid substance that covers two-thirds of the surface of the earth in w.

According to this "definition" of water, something is a sample of *water* in a "tomatoey" possible world if and only if it is a sample of tomato juice in that world, and hence not a sample of H_2O. This definition thus fails to yield the consequence that the term 'water' is a rigid designator of water. The situation would not be very different were we to use the definite description 'the same liquid that *this* is a sample of', said with reference to the paradigm sample of water, as one can readily judge from the considerations that led to the rejection of (9) and (9′) as a definition of water. In order to satisfy thesis (T5), the latter descriptions must be rigidified in some way.

There are many ways in which one might modify the nonrigid definite description so as to accommodate (T5). One way to do this is to add explicit reference to the actual world in the manner of (11). Another way is to "analyze away" the definite description in accordance with Russell's Theory of Descriptions, treating the description as having what Russell called "primary occurrence" or "large scope." For present purposes this is tantamount simply to replacing the definite description with an individual variable, setting the variable and the description equal, and "quantifying in" in the manner of (5). A third way is to invoke the actuality operator in the manner of (12). A fourth way is to enclose the entire definite description within Kaplan's indexical '*dthat*'-operator in the manner of (13). What each of these methods has in common is that the nonrigid definite description is replaced with a rigid counterpart. Formulae (12) and (13) in particular employ indexical operators just for this purpose.

In Section 6.2 we found that the designation of a common noun v could be fixed in the object language, using but not mentioning v, in a "definition" having the logical form of either (5) or (6). We adopted as a criterion for a common noun v being a rigid designator of an appropriate universal k that some sentence of the form of either (5) or (6) be true, where β is a singular term which denotes the individual k. A quick inspection of (13) reveals that, lo, it has precisely the logical form of (6), with β taken to be the definite description '$(\imath z)$ [*Substance* $(z) \wedge (this \in z)$].' Thus, if (13) gives the logical form of Putnam's ostensive definition of water, then by our criterion for common noun designation (= rigid designation), it is indeed a formal consequence of the ostensive definition of water that the term 'water' is a rigid designator of the substance water. Since (12) has exactly the same truth-conditions as (13), the truth of (12) may also be taken as a criterion for the term 'water' being a rigid designator of the substance water. Hence if (12) is taken as giving the logical form of Putnam's ostensive definition of water, then it is again a formal consequence of the ostensive definition that 'water' rigidly designates water.

In the general case, by our criterion for common noun (rigid) designation, it is a formal consequence of any ostensive definition having either the logical form of (14) or (15) that the common noun v is a rigid designator of the universal denoted by the definite description $\ulcorner (\imath z)[K(z) \wedge (this \in z)]\urcorner$. Thus, given our interpretation of Putnam's thesis (T3), our criterion for common noun rigidity is precisely what is needed to vindicate Putnam's thesis (T5).[40]

We mentioned above that (12) and (13) employ indexical operators for the purpose of rigidifying the definite description '$(\imath z)[Substance(z) \wedge (this \in z)]$' occurring within it. This is one crucial role played by indexicality, as alluded to in Putnam's thesis (T6). It is the indexical operator occurring in the ostensive definition—the actuality operator in the case of (14), the '*dthat*'-operator in the case of (15)—that is crucial to thesis (T5), and not the occurrence of the demonstrative '*this*'. Even if one had attempted to define water by the following,

> It is necessarily the case that: something is a sample of *water* if and only if it is a sample of *dthat*(the liquid substance that covers two-thirds of the surface of the earth).

it would still be a consequence of our definition that the term 'water' applies with respect to every possible world to the same liquid substance, even possible worlds in which tomato juice displaces water

---

[40]For a full and proper understanding of Putnam's thesis (T5) one must appreciate a point to be made in the next footnote. The semantical intension of a term is, on a full development of Putnam's theory, a *component* of the meaning of the term. Hence any definition that represents an attempt to "explain the meaning" of a term must fix its intension. Given our notion of *designation* for general terms, this is tantamount to fixing the designation of the term. Hence, if the term 'water' (rigidly) designates the substance water, then this should be a derivable consequence of any "definition" intended to explain the meaning of 'water'.

as the earth's most abundant liquid. As we have already noted, an occurrence of an indexical operator is not indispensible. The Russellian device of scope and quantification-in would do just as well. But *some* rigidifying device is required, and indexical operators like the '*dthat*'-operator serve this purpose handily. Putnam's thesis (T6) may be interpreted, at least in part, as the thesis that "meaning explanations" of natural kind terms, when fully analyzed, are found to make crucial use of indexicality, and in particular of some usually unnoticed occurrence of indexicality, an occurrence that is quite distinct from the obvious indexicality manifested by the demonstrative of an ostensive definition. An ostensive definition for a natural kind term makes crucial but subtle use of an unnoticed indexical operator *in addition to* its blatant demonstrative reference to a paradigm of the kind in question. Although Putnam takes notice of this further indexicality, he does not make it completely transparent. The crucial indexical operator in the ostensive definition of water is not uncovered and laid bare until (8), Putnam's original formulation of the definition, is finally recast in modal operator discourse in the form of either (14) or (15).

It would be a mistake, however, to suppose that the indexical operator occurring in either (14) or (15) is the *only* "unnoticed indexical component" to which Putnam is referring in his thesis (T6). In order to explain what more is meant by (T6), we must first clarify theses (T4) and (T7).

15.2. Thesis (T4)

We have twice noticed that the demonstrative 'this' occurring in (12') and (13') may be replaced with any singular term denoting any paradigmatic sample of water, even with a descriptional term, without doing violence to thesis (T5). An important part of Putnam's reconstruction of the notion of "meaning" for natural kind terms that we have mentioned only briefly is his notion of a *stereotype*. According to Putnam, there is associated with each natural kind term a certain set of descriptive properties, properties which are commonly believed to be had by (instances of) the natural kind in question, and which must be associated with the natural kind term in a certain way by a given speaker before it is appropriate to say that the speaker in question has "acquired" the term. This set of properties Putnam calls the *stereotype* associated with the term. He argues that the stereotype associated with a natural kind term should be regarded as a component of the "meaning" of the term, although, to couch his view

152

in our terminology, the term is quite definitely not descriptional in terms of its stereotype.[41] It is partly for this reason that the occurrence of the demonstrative '*this*' in the ostensive definition of water, though not crucial for thesis (T5), may be crucial to Putnam's conception of the *definitional*, or *meaning explanatory*, status of (12) and (13). For if the definition is going to convey the "meaning" of the term defined, then according to Putnam it must convey the stereotype associated with the term—*a colorless liquid, odorless, thirst-quenching, tasteless*, etc. One way in which this might be accomplished is by pointing to a paradigm which is present to the audience and which manifests the properties included in the stereotype.[42] Putnam contends in his thesis (T4) that there is a second way in which the meaning of a natural kind term may be conveyed, namely by way of an operational definition describing the natural kind in terms of its stereotype. Thus the definite description 'the same substance that *this* is a sample of' occurring in (12') and (13') might be replaced with some stereotypical description like 'the colorless, odorless, tasteless, liquid substance that quenches thirst

[41]The other components of the meaning of a term on Putnam's theory are a syntactic marker (e.g., 'NOUN'), a semantic marker (e.g., 'LIQUID SUBSTANCE'), and the semantical extension. What Putnam fails to notice (1975a) is that it is not merely the semantical *extension*, but the entire semantical *intension* (function from possible worlds to extensions) that plays the role of the fourth component of meaning in his theory of natural kind terms. It is for this reason that Putnam's suggested "meaning explanations" for natural kind terms are not mere nonmodal universally quantified biconditionals, but involve quantification over possible worlds, thus fixing intension as well as extension. This point is important for a full understanding of theses (T3), (T5), (T6), and (T8).

More accurately, Putnam's fourth component of meaning should be replaced by Kaplan's notion of *character*. See Kaplan, 1973b. The character of an expression is represented (roughly) by that function which assigns to each context the intension that the expression takes on with respect to that context. In the case of natural kind terms, as with all nonindexical expressions, the character is a constant function, and so for practical purposes may simply be replaced with the intension of the term. It is only when considering genuinely indexical expressions that the distinction between character and intension is important.

[42]It is Putnam's contention (1970) that conveying the stereotype associated with a particular natural kind term is generally necessary and sufficient to enable the listener to use the term correctly. The central problem of semantic theory, according to Putnam, is to explain how it is that in acquiring the stereotype one thereby also acquires the correct use of a term, and vice-versa. Putnam also puts forth (1970) his view that one may entirely convey the meaning of a natural kind term in an ostensive definition by simply pointing out an instance. It seems to follow from Putnam's views, then, that the stereotype associated with a natural kind term is somehow automatically conveyed in an appropriate ostensive definition. See footnote 39 above.

and fills our lakes and rivers and oceans'. More accurately one might employ the description 'the liquid substance whose *stereotypical* properties include *being colorless, odorless, tasteless, thirst-quenching,* and *filling those lakes and rivers and oceans*'. Thus, taking (T3) and (T4) together, the general form of a definition for a natural kind common noun v may be given by

(16) $\Box(x)\,(\Pi_v(x) \leftrightarrow x \in (\imath z)A[K(z) \land \phi(z)])$

or

(17) $\Box(x)[\Pi_v(x) \leftrightarrow x \in dthat((\imath z)[K(z) \land \phi\,(z)])]$,

where K is a generic natural kind predicate like 'is a liquid substance' or 'is a species of animal', etc., and the definite description $\ulcorner(\imath z)[K(z) \land \phi(z)]\urcorner$ describes the natural kind designated by v either in terms of its stereotype or as "the natural kind of type K that *this* (a paradigm) is an instance of."

The important point is that, whether the definition is ostensive or operational, the description $\ulcorner(\imath z)[K(z) \land \phi(z)]\urcorner$ must be rigidified in order that the intension of the definiendum v be fixed in such a way that v designates the relevant natural kind. For suppose the indexical operator occurring in either (16) or (17) were omitted from the operational definition of water thus:

> It is necessarily the case that: something is a sample of *water* if and only if it is a sample of the colorless, odorless, tasteless, thirst-quenching liquid that fills such-and-such lakes and rivers and oceans.

We would then be forced to conclude from this definition that the term 'water' designates not the substance water, but the general category *Colorless Odorless Tasteless Thirst-Quenching Liquid . . .* , a category that includes the substance water in the actual world, but includes Putnam's imaginary "fool's water" XYZ instead of water in other possible worlds. The indexical operators occurring in (16) and (17) thus play a crucial role. Thesis (T6) applies equally to operational definitions as well as to ostensive definitions.

It is important for later developments to notice that, unlike natural kind term ostensive definitions of either the form of (14) or (15), operational definitions of either the form of (16) or (17) need not make any use whatsoever of a cross-world *same-K* relation, such as cross-world consubstantiality or cross-world conspecificity. Thus for instance the following so-called operational definition of water makes no mention of consubstantiality:

154

It is necessarily the case that: something is a sample of *water* if and only if it is a sample of *dthat*(the Colorless, odorless, tasteless, thirst-quenching liquid that fills those lakes and rivers and oceans).

In general, the definite description $\ulcorner(\imath z)[K(z) \wedge \phi(z)]\urcorner$ occurring in (16) and (17) need not make any reference to any particular instance of the natural kind in question. In particular, the open formula $\ulcorner\phi(z)\urcorner$ need not be of the form $\ulcorner\alpha \in z\urcorner$, where α is a singular term denoting a particular instance of the kind in question. It is only when considering a so-called ostensive definition that the open formula $\ulcorner\phi(z)\urcorner$ must be of this form, where α is a demonstrative, or something similar.

15.3. Thesis (T7)

It should not have escaped the reader's notice that even the description of water in terms of its stereotype employs some indexicality. Water is the liquid that fills *these* lakes and rivers and oceans; it is the stuff that one finds *over here* and *over there*. The stereotype might be modified by describing water as the liquid that fills Lake Tahoe, or the stuff that fills the lakes and rivers and oceans on Earth, etc., but even this description involves certain nondescriptional elements ('Tahoe', 'Earth', etc.). Of course, all reference to the location of water may be omitted from the stereotype of water. Water may be simply characterized as a colorless, odorless, tasteless, thirst-quenching liquid. This description may underdetermine the extension of the term 'water', since there may be liquids other than H_2O that also fit the description, but this is permissible since Putnam insists that the stereotype associated with a natural kind term may underdetermine its extension, and may even determine the *wrong* extension. It seems very likely, however, that any stereotypical description of water rich enough to determine uniquely the extension of 'water' will be *relationally* descriptional, in the sense of Section 1.3. It will be descriptional relative to a paradigmatic sample perhaps, or to this or that body of water, or to this planet, or to a certain location on this planet, or so on. The part of the stereotype that is thoroughly descriptional and purely qualitative—the sense$_1$ of 'water', the fragment of the stereotype that may be included in a wholly internal "psychological state"—will invariably underdetermine the extension. This much is established by Putnam's Twin Earth argument. Thesis (T1), the thesis that the psychological

155

concept of water underdetermines its metaphysical extension, holds true precisely because even the stereotypical definite description occurring in the operational definition of water must contain certain nondescriptional elements if it is to be rich enough to determine a unique denotation. The designation of these nondescriptional elements is determined by "the context"—in a broad sense of 'context' that may include historical or social ("causal") linguistic acquisition chains and structured cooperation between experts and nonexperts—and not solely by expressed *general* properties. The qualitative or psychological concept of water—the fragment of the stereotype that is left over when the intrinsically relational features are removed—is too broad to determine the proper extension of 'water'. Thesis (T1) is thus indeed true of natural kind terms for the same reason that it is true of indexical terms such as the demonstratives 'this' and 'here', and even the first-person pronoun 'I'. The stereotypical concepts (or more generally the sense$_{1'}$) associated with particular uses of these expressions either include intrinsically relational properties or else are too broad to determine the proper extension. In either case, the qualitative part of the stereotype, the psychological concept, underdetermines the extension. There is a certain inevitable reliance on context, in a broad sense, for the determination of extension from the ordinary concept of a given natural kind or substance, or even from one's psychological self-concept. This is what is meant in Putnam's thesis (T7).

15.4. Thesis (T6) Again

There are, then, not one but two "unnoticed indexical components" in the meaning of a natural kind term, according to Putnam's theory. There is first the occurrence of the actuality operator in (16), or alternatively the occurrence of the '*dthat*'-operator in (17), and both of these indexical operators play a crucial role in "explaining the meaning" of a natural kind term using a definition having either the form of (16) or (17). Without the rigidifying powers of these indexical operators, such definitions would give the wrong intension (function from possible worlds to extensions) to the term defined. But there is another unnoticed element of context-sensitivity, in a broad sense, in the meaning of a natural kind term, and that is the context-sensitivity inherent in the nondescriptional elements contained *within* the definite description $\ulcorner(\imath z)[K(z) \wedge \phi(z)]\urcorner$ occurring in (16) and (17). Water may be defined "ostensively" as the liquid substance that *this* paradigm is a sample of, or "operationally" as the colorless, odorless, tasteless, thirst-quenching liquid that fills *this* lake or *that* ocean, the clear liquid that one finds *over here* and *over there*. The stereotypical description associated with a natural kind term like 'water' will generally include such relationally descriptional features as these if the description is going to be rich enough to determine the extension of the term. This sort of context-sensitivity in the ordinary concept of water is the second "unnoticed indexical component" referred to in thesis (T6).

II

THE PROGRAM TO DERIVE ESSENTIALISM FROM THE THEORY OF REFERENCE

FIVE · *The* K *and* I *Mechanisms*

We turn now to Putnam's thesis (T9), the thesis that the theory elaborated and developed in the previous chapter has the consequence that there are truths, like 'Water is H_2O', that are metaphysically necessary but conceptually contingent.

16. PUTMAN ON (T9)

Putnam is comparatively brief when it comes to substantiating his thesis (T9). The most prominent passage is the following:

> Suppose, now, that I have not yet discovered what the important physical properties of water are (in the actual world)—i.e., I don't yet know that water is H_2O. I may have ways of *recognizing* water that are successful (of course, I may make a small number of mistakes that I won't be able to detect until a later stage in our scientific development) but not know the microstructure of water. If I agree that a liquid with the superficial properties of 'water' but a different microstructure *isn't really water,* then my ways of recognizing water (my 'operational definition', so to speak) cannot be regarded as an analytical specification of *what it is to be* water. Rather, the operational definition, like the ostensive one, is simply a way of pointing out a standard—pointing out the stuff *in the actual world* such that for x to be water, in *any* world, is for x to bear the relation same$_L$ to the *normal* members of the class of *local* entities that satisfy the operational definition. 'Water' on Twin Earth is not water, even if it satisfies the operational definition, because it doesn't bear *same$_L$* to the *local* stuff that satisfies the operational definition, and local stuff that satisfies the operational definition but has a microstructure different from rest of the local stuff that satisfies the operational definition isn't water either, because it doesn't bear *same$_L$* to the *normal* examples of the local 'water'.
>
>   Suppose, now, that I discover the microstructure of water—that water is H_2O. At this point I will be able to say that the stuff on Twin Earth that I earlier *mistook* for water isn't really water. In

the same way, if you describe not another planet in the actual universe, but another possible universe in which there is stuff with the chemical formula XYZ which passes the 'operational test' for *water*, we shall have to say that that stuff isn't water but merely XYZ. You will not have described a possible world in which 'water is XYZ', but merely a possible world in which there are lakes of XYZ, people drink XYZ (and not water), or whatever. In fact, once we have discovered the nature of water, nothing counts as a possible world in which water doesn't have that nature. Once we have discovered that water (in the actual world) is H_2O, *nothing counts as a possible world in which water isn't H_2O*. In particular, if a 'logically possible' statement is one that holds in some 'logically possible world', *it isn't logically possible that water isn't H_2O*.

On the other hand, we can perfectly well imagine having experiences that would convince us (and that would make it rational to believe that) water *isn't* H_2O. In that sense, it is conceivable that water isn't H_2O. It is conceivable but it isn't logically possible! Conceivability is no proof of logical possibility (1973b, pp. 708–709; also in 1975a, pp. 232–233).

His discussion of thesis (T9) is continued in a later passage:

x bears the relation same$_L$ to y just in case (1) x and y are both liquids, and (2) x and y agree in important physical properties. The term 'liquid' is itself a natural-kind term that I shall not try to analyze here. The term 'property' is a broad-spectrum term that we have analyzed in previous papers. What I want to focus on now is the notion of *importance*. Importance is an interest-relative notion. Normally the 'important' properties of a liquid or solid, etc., are the ones that are *structurally* important: the ones that specify what the liquid or solid, etc., is ultimately made out of —elementary particles, or hydrogen and oxygen, or earth, air, fire, water, or whatever—and how they are arranged or combined to produce the superficial characteristics. From this point of view the characteristic of a typical bit of water is consisting of H_2O. But it may or may not be important that there are impurities; thus, in one context 'water' may mean *chemically pure water,* while in another it may mean the stuff in Lake Michigan. And a speaker may sometimes refer to XYZ as water if one is *using* it as water. Again, normally it is important that water is in the liquid state; but sometimes it is unimportant, and one may refer to a single H_2O

molecule as water, or to water vapor as water ('water in the air'). . . .

To sum up: if there is a hidden structure, then generally it determines what it is to be a member of the natural kind, not only in the actual world, but in all possible worlds. Put another way, it determines what we can and cannot counterfactually suppose about the natural kind ('water could have all been vapor?' yes / 'water could have been XYZ' no) (1975a, pp. 238–239, 241).

17. DONNELLAN'S ELUCIDATIONS OF (T9)

Donnellan (1973b and 1974b) has elucidated Putnam's attempt to derive from his theory of natural kind terms the consequence that certain *a posteriori* statements, like 'Water is H_2O', are metaphysically necessary. Donnellan spells out in some detail Putnam's "mechanism," as he calls it, for "generating" necessary *a posteriori* truths concerning natural kinds from ostensive definitions of the form of either (14) or (15). As the mechanism is described by Donnellan, in order to generate a necessary *a posteriori* truth involving a natural kind term we need in addition to the ostensive definition only two further pieces of information. First, we need to know the actual hidden nature of the paradigm mentioned in the definition. Second, at least in some cases, we also need to know—to use Donnellan's phrase—what being an instance of the same K as something (same liquid substance, same species of animal, etc.) "consists in." For example, given Putnam's suggested ostensive definition of water, in order to generate the necessary truth that water is H_2O, we need to know that the paradigmatic sample has the chemical composition H_2O, and we also need to know that being consubstantial with a sample of a given substance "consists in" having the same chemical composition. From these three ingredients—the ostensive definition of water, the fact that the paradigm has the chemical structure H_2O, and the fact that consubstantiality consists in having the same chemical structure—we easily generate the necessary *a posteriori* truth that water is H_2O, or more accurately that every sample of water has the chemical composition of *two parts hydrogen and one part oxygen.* In order for something in another possible world to be a sample of water, it must be cross-world consubstantial with the paradigm water sample in the actual world. In order for it to be cross-world consubstantial with the actual paradigm, it must have the same chemical composition that the paradigm has in the actual

163

world. Hence, since the paradigm has the chemical composition H_2O, in order for something in another possible world to be a sample of water, it must have the chemical composition H_2O.

Notice that each of the three ingredients, particularly the full modal force of the ostensive definition of water, is actually used in this piece of reasoning. The definition fixes the semantical intension of the term 'water' to coincide with the metaphysical intension of a certain substance, and thereby precludes the term from designating a more general kind or category, such as *Sample of the Most Abundant Liquid Substance on Earth*. Without this stipulation, the reasoning to the necessity of 'Water is H_2O' would be fallacious. The two facts that supplement the ostensive definition of water, taken by themselves without the definition, no more yield the conclusion that it is necessary that water is H_2O than they yield the falsehood that it is necessary that the most abundant liquid substance on earth is H_2O—even given the further premise that the paradigm is in fact a sample of the most abundant liquid substance on earth. By the same token, the ostensive definition of water taken together with the fact that the paradigm sample has the chemical structure H_2O do not by themselves yield the conclusion that it is necessary that water is H_2O, without relying on the additional information that being consubstantial with something consists in having the same chemical composition. It is this appeal to the further information that consubstantiality consists in having the same chemical composition that Putnam is alluding to in his remarks, quoted in the previous section, concerning what normally counts as "important physical properties."

One of the questions that Donnellan addresses (1973b and 1974b) is this: What is it about natural kind terms in virtue of which there can be necessary *a posteriori* truths concerning a natural kind, whereas formally analogous necessary truths concerning a nonnatural kind like bachelorhood, e.g., "All bachelors are unmarried', seem generally to be *a priori*? According to Donnellan, there are two features of (single word) natural kind terms, like 'water' and 'tiger', which separate them from other (single word) general terms (nonnatural kind terms) like 'bachelor', and which account for the special *a posteriori* character of generated necessary truths, like the necessary truth that water is H_2O. The peculiar character of natural kind terms, according to Donnellan, is that (*i*) they are *paradigmatic,* in the special sense that they are "definable" ostensively by way of reference to actual paradigmatic samples of the natural kind in question, and (*ii*) their ostensive definitions involve a cross-world

164

relation, *being an instance of the same K,* which is a theoretical relation. On Donnellan's view, it is an empirical matter to determine the "nature" of a given object in order to settle whether it has the necessary features to be an instance of a given natural kind. Thus for instance it is an empirical matter to determine the chemical structure of a given portion of stuff to settle whether it is H_2O or not. Moreover, on Donnellan's view, the question of what constitutes a criterion for two objects being of the same natural kind is also an empirical scientific matter. Concerning the latter, Donnellan says,

> I am inclined to think that we believe [the required principle that two liquid samples are consubstantial only if they have the same chemical structure] on *a posteriori* grounds or, at least, not merely by consulting our linguistic skills. It strikes me as either being the product of scientific discovery, of scientific theories, or, perhaps, change in scientific outlook. For I suppose that just as there was a time when it was not known or believed that water (or the stuff called "water") is H_2O, so there was a time when it was not known or believed, or perhaps I should say, not a part of man's views about liquids, that the same chemical structure is a necessity for [consubstantiality]. For, I suppose, there was a time when the whole notion of chemical structure, at least as we know it when we represent a chemical structure as, e.g., H_2O, was foreign to the natural philosophy of the time (1973b and 1974b).

Donnellan points out that other general terms could be introduced into the language *paradigmatically* by way of an ostensive definition, although he adds that it happens that they are not. Thus, to use his example, we could introduce a new marital status term 'whatchamaycallit' into English by way of the following ostensive definition:

> It is necessarily the case that: someone is a *whatchamaycallit* if and only if he has the same marital status that *he* (pointing) actually has,

said with reference to a particular bachelor. It would then turn out to be a necessary *a posteriori* truth that whatchamaycallits are unmarried. In order to generate this necessary truth, we need only the knowledge that the paradigm referred to is unmarried, and the further knowledge that if two individuals have the same marital status (across possible worlds), then one is married if and only if the other is. The first bit of knowledge is clearly *a posteriori,* but, according to Donnellan, the second bit of knowledge, unlike the corresponding principles for the case of natural kinds, is *a priori,* perhaps even analytic. The *a posteriority* of the generated necessary truth that whatchamaycallits are unmarried derives only from that of the generating truth that the paradigm is himself unmarried. According to Donnellan, in the case of natural kinds there are not one but two sources of the *a posteriority* of generated necessary generalizations, like the truth that water samples have the chemical composition H_2O. For two of the facts involved in generating the necessary truth that water is H_2O are empirical. The truth that the paradigm liquid sample has the chemical composition H_2O is, of course, *a posteriori.* And, on Donnellan's view, the further required principle concerning what consubstantiality "consists in" is similarly empirical, or in some sense scientific. Donnellan concludes:

> If this is correct, then I think we might say that "Water is H_2O," assuming the correctness of Putnam's account, is doubly exotic. Involved in our knowledge of its truth, even though it is necessarily true, is not only the empirical discovery that the stuff we call "water" has the chemical structure, H_2O, but also the knowledge, if that is the right term, that we have, and the ancients did not have, that two liquids are the same only if they have the same chemical structure. And that also is not *a priori* knowledge (1973b and 1974b).

18. THE *OK*-MECHANISM

18.1. *A Valid Modal Argument*

Donnellan's account of the mechanism employed by Putnam in generating the necessary truth that water is H_2O strongly suggests the use of a certain valid argument, one whose premises include Putnam's suggested ostensive definition of water and whose conclusion is the necessitation of the generalization that water samples have the chemical structure H_2O. Specifically, it suggests the following modal argument:

(13′)   It is necessarily the case that: something is a sample of water if and only if it is a sample of *dthat*(the same substance that *this* is a sample of).

(18′)   *This* (liquid sample) has the chemical structure H_2O.

(19′)   Being a sample of the same substance as something consists in having the same chemical structure.

166

FIVE · *The* K *and* I *Mechanisms*

Therefore

(23′)   It is necessarily the case that: every sample of water has the chemical structure H_2O.

Given that the direct reference theory of the designation of natural kind terms is correct, the conclusion of this argument will be true if and only if the substance water has as an essential property the feature that all of its samples have the chemical structure H_2O. Our main concern here is with the question of whether a statement like (23′) is derivable from the direct reference theory of the designation of general terms *taken together only with premises that are themselves free of any nontrivial essentialist import,* so that the essentialist import of the statement derives only from the theory of reference. The modal argument presented above represents Putnam's proposal, as elaborated by Donnellan, to answer our question affirmatively. That the argument is valid is intuitively verified by the piece of informal reasoning sketched in the previous section. If it can be further shown that each of the premises is either an assertion of the theory of direct reference proper or else entirely free of any nontrivial essentialist import, we can be satisfied that the theory of direct reference does indeed have the nontrivial essentialist import claimed for it by Putnam in his thesis (T9).

18.2. The General Case

The modal argument sketched above (Section 18.1) generalizes to other natural kinds. Making the obvious changes, for instance, one directly obtains the following modal argument generating the necessity of the *a posteriori* truth that tigers are mammals, from an ostensive definition of a tiger:

It is necessarily the case that: something is a *tiger* if and only if it is a member of *dthat*(the same species that *this* is a member of).

This has the biological class property of *being a mammal.*

Being a member of the same species as something consists (in part) in being a member of the same biological class.

Therefore, it is necessarily the case that: all tigers are mammals.

Similarly, the following application of Putnam's mechanism generates the necessary *a posteriori* truth that gold has atomic number 79, from an ostensive definition of gold:

167

It is necessarily the case that: something is a sample of *gold* if an only if it is a sample of *dthat*(the same chemical element that *this* is a sample of).

This has atomic number 79, i.e., this has exactly 79 protons in virtually all of its constituent atoms.

Being a sample of the same chemical element as something consists in having the same atomic number.

Therefore, it is necessarily the case that: every sample of gold has atomic number 79, i.e., has exactly 79 protons in virtually all of its component atoms.

Let us call the mechanism exhibited by each of these arguments *the* OK-*mechanism*—'*O*' for 'ostensive definition' and '*K*' for 'kind'. The *OK*-mechanism may be represented by a valid modal argument schema consisting of three premises and a conclusion. The first premise is an ostensive definition for a common noun ν. The second premise describes the "hidden nature" of the paradigm referred to in the ostensive definition. The final premise asserts what being the same K as something 'consists in," where the common noun ν designates a K-kind. The conclusion asserts the necessity of the generated *truth*. Formally, the *OK*-mechanism is given by the following:

(15′)   It is necessarily the case that: something is a (bit of) ν if and only if it is an instance of *dthat*(the same K-kind that *this* is an instance of).

(25′)   *This* has the Ψ-property of *being* ψ.

(26′)   Being an instance of the same K-kind as something consists, at least in part, in having the same Ψ-property that the given thing has.

(28′)   Therefore, it is necessarily the case that: every (bit of) ν is ψ.

K is a generic natural kind predicate, ψ expresses a "hidden structural property," and Ψ expresses the property of being a hidden structural property *of a certain specified sort*. If all of the premises were *a priori*, then the conclusion would have to be *a priori*. But as Donnellan points out, at least premise (25′) will generally be *a posteriori,* and the conclusion (28′) will generally be *a posteriori* as a consequence. In each case, given that the theory of direct reference is correct, the conclusion will be true if and only if the kind designated by the common noun *ν* has a certain essential property. If it can be shown that each of the premises is either a consequence of the theory of direct reference or free of nontrivial essentialist import, the *OK*-mechanism will be seen to provide a neat apparatus for generating *a posteriori* essentialist assertions from the theory of direct reference *via* ostensive definitions that fix natural kind terms as rigid designators for natural kinds.

19. THE GENERAL *K*-MECHANISM AND THE *I*-MECHANISM

19.1. The General K-Mechanism

The various modal arguments considered thus far can be further generalized. The *OK*-mechanism can be modified to accommodate so-called operational definitions as well as so-called ostensive definitions. The second premise, asserting what the hidden nature of the paradigm is, can be replaced by a less specific premise to the effect that *some* instance of the natural kind mentioned in the definition actually has such-and-such a hidden nature. The third premise remains as before. Thus for instance the necessary truth that water samples have the chemical structure H_2O can also be generated from the following three premises:

> It is necessarily the case that: something is a sample of *water* if and only if it is a sample of *dthat*(the colorless, odorless, tastless, thirst-quenching liquid substance that fills *that* like and *that* ocean) [operational definition].

> Some sample of the colorless, odorless, tasteless, thirst-quenching liquid that fills *that* lake and *that* ocean has the chemical structure H_2O.

> Premise (19′).

Similarly, the necessary truths that tigers are mammals and that gold has the atomic number 79 can also be generated from the corresponding operational definitions. In the general case, the *OK*-mechanism described above may be seen as a special case of the following mechanism, which we may call *the general* K-*mechanism*:

169

(17') It is necessarily the case that: something is a (bit of) ν if and only if it is an instance of *dthat*(the K-kind that has the property of *being* ϕ).

(29') Some instance of the K-kind that has the property of *being* ϕ has the Ψ-property of *being* ψ.

Schema (26'). Therefore (28'),

where ν, K, ϕ, ψ, and Ψ are all as before.

The general K-mechanism employs as its first premise schema the general form of a "definition" for any natural kind common noun ν. It should be noted, however, that strictly speaking the first premise schema of the general K-mechanism need not be instantiated by a genuine *definition* for the term ν, in any customary sense. Thus, assuming that the species of California condors happens to be the only species all of whose extant members are on wildlife preserves, the necessary truth that California condors are birds can be generated by way of the following argument:

> It is necessarily the case that: something is a California condor if and only if it is a member of *dthat*(the unique species all of whose extant members are on wildlife preserves).
>
> Some member of this species has the biological class property of *being a bird*.
>
> Being a member of the same species as something consists, in part, in being a member of the same biological class.
>
> Therefore, it is necessarily the case that: all California condors are birds.

By varying what K, ϕ, ψ, and Ψ are to represent, the general K-mechanism may also be applied to any general term τ in place of ν, whether τ is a common noun, an adjective, or an intransitive verb, and whether it is a natural kind term, an artifact term, or whatever. Thus for instance the necessary truth that pencils are writing utensils may be generated by way of the following argument:

> It is necessarily the case that: something is a pencil if and only if it is a utensil of *dthat*(the same type of utensil that *this* is an instance of).
>
> *This* was designed primarily for the function of writing.

170

Being the same type of utensil as something consists, at least in part, in being designed for the same function.

Therefore, it is necessarily the case that: all pencils are designed primarily for the function of writing.

It should be noted, however, that when the general *K*-mechanism is applied to terms other than natural kind terms, it is generally less plausible that the generated necessary truth (e.g., that pencils are writing utensils) is not also knowable *a priori*. Indeed, as we noted above, it is part of Donnellan's intention (1973b and 1974b) to isolate some of the features of natural kind terms that separate them from other (single word) general terms in just this way.

The general *K*-mechanism is significant for two reasons. First, it has a direct bearing on Donnellan's observations concerning the distinctive features of natural kind terms that account for the special *a posteriori* character of generated necessary truths. As we have seen, on Donnellan's view there are two features of natural kind terms and their definitions that account for the special *a posteriori* character of generated necessary truths: (*i*) that they are *paradigmatic,* in the sense defined above, and (*ii*) that they involve a theoretical cross-world relation *being an instance of the same K*. The general *K*-mechanism indicates that the presence of those two features in the "definition" of a natural kind term, i.e., in the first premise of the *K*-mechanism, is not a crucial component, since as we noted above, in Section 15.2, operational definitions of the form of (16) or (17) do not have either feature, yet it is still possible to generate truths of the form of (28) from operational definitions using the general *K*-mechanism. Indeed, we have just pointed out that premise schema (17) of the general *K*-mechanism need not be instantiated by a *definition* for the term *v*. Nor must instances of (17) be used as a means to *introduce v* into the language. All that is required is that the instance of (17) correctly fix the semantical intension of *v*, i.e., that it be true. It seems, then, that Donnellan has not given a fully adequate account of what it is about natural kind terms that makes for the possibility of necessary *a posteriori* generalizations, such as 'Water is H_2O' and 'Gold has atomic number 79'.[1]

---

[1]This is not to say, of course, that Donnellan is wrong to locate the source of the phenomenon ultimately in the way natural kind terms are typically introduced or "defined," rather than in the sort of kinds they designate. His 'whatchamaycallit' example is no doubt important in this regard. But a modification of this example
(footnote continued on next page)

19.2 The I-Mechanism

The second reason that the general K-mechanism is significant is that it strongly suggests an analogous mechanism for the case of proper names (or indexical singular terms) and individuals. Suppose for instance that 'Woody' is a proper name denoting a particular table in front of us. Consider now the following argument:[2]

(30')   It is necessarily the case that: Woody is *dthat*(the table located *here*).

(31')   The table located *here* was originally constructed from hunk of wood *H*.

(32')   Being the very same table as something consists, at least in part, in having the same original material composition.

Therefore

(34')   It is necessarily the case that: Woody, if it exists, was originally constructed from hunk of wood *H*.

In Section 3.3 we adopted as a criterion for saying that a singular term α is an obstinate designator of an individual i that some sentence of the form

(3) $\Box[\alpha = dthat(\beta)]$

be true, where β is a singular term denoting the individual i. Premise (30') is in just this form. It asserts that the term 'Woody' rigidly

---

indicates that so-called paradigmaticity is not the ultimate source of the phenomenon, but at most only a special case.

It is worth noting in this connection that some descriptional nonnatural kind terms, by being descriptional relative to a natural kind, inherit the feature of natural kind terms that makes for the possibility of necessary *a posteriori* generalizations. It would seem to be analytic (and hence *a priori*) that water hoses have the function of conveying water. Hence it is necessary that they do. (In any case, it is certainly necessary that hoses whose function is to convey water have the function of conveying water.) But if it is necessary and *a posteriori* that water is H_2O, it presumably follows that it is also necessary, even though *a posteriori*, that water hoses have the function of conveying H_2O. Similarly it is necessary, even though *a posteriori*, that gold rings are made of matter having atomic number 79, etc.

[2] Strictly speaking, this argument also requires the further premise, also from the theory of direct reference, that '*H*' is a rigid designator. Without this stipulation, there is no assurance that *being constructed from hunk H* is an original material composition property of the sort required by (32'). Consider what would result, for instance, if the name '*H*' were replaced with the nonrigid description 'the hunk of wood that made up Uncle John's wheelbarrow'.

designates the table located *here,* hence that Woody is the very same table in every possible world. The reasoning behind the argument is precisely analogous to the informal derivation in the case of water having the chemical structure H_2O. By premise (32′), in order for something in another possible world to be the very same table as the one located *here* in the actual world, it must be originally constructed in its possible world from the same matter that this table is constructed from in the actual world. Since by premise (31′) this table actually was constructed originally from hunk of wood H, it follows that in any possible world in which this table exists, it is constructed from hunk H. By premise (30′), this table is none other than Woody in every possible world. Hence, Woody is constructed from hunk H in every possible world in which Woody exists— *Q.E.D.*

Notice that, as in the argument that it is necessary that water is H_2O, each of the three premises is actually used in this piece of reasoning. In particular, the full modal force of the first premise, which fixes the term 'Woody' as a rigid designator of the relevant table, is used. Without the stipulation that this very same table is Woody in every possible world, the two premises (31′) and (32′) no more yield the conclusion (34′) than they yield the obvious falsehood that it is necessary that the table Uncle John built for Aunt Martha, if there is a unique such table, was made from hunk H—even given that the table in front of use was indeed built by Uncle John for Aunt Martha.

Let us call the general mechanism exhibited by this modal argument *the I-mechanism*. The argument schema corresponding to the *I*-mechanism is obtained directly from the argument schema of the general *K*-mechanism, roughly, by taking a singular proper name α in place of the common noun v, and talking about the individual designated by α in place of talking about the natural kind designated by v or instances of the kind. We thus obtain the following general mechanism for the case of individuals:

(3′)   It is necessarily the case that: $\alpha = dthat(\beta)$.

(35′) β has the Ψ-property of being ψ.

(36′)   Being the very same individual (of kind I) as something consists, at least in part, in having the same Ψ-property.

Therefore

(38′)   It is necessarily the case that: α, if it exists, is ψ.

173

Using our criterion for obstinacy from Section 3.3, premises of the form (3′) may be taken as object language assertions to the effect that α obstinately designates whatever β designates. Where α is a proper name, premise schema (3′) may be thought of as a kind of definition for α, one that fixes the reference of α using the singular term β in such a way as to guarantee that α is a rigid designator of whatever it is that β denotes. If β is an indexical like 'this' or 'him', the premise becomes a kind of ostensive definition for the proper name. But β need not be an indexical. It may be a definite description of the form ⌜the individual of kind I having the property ϕ⌝, e.g., 'the table located *here*'. The I-mechanism, then, is a mechanism for generating necessary truths involving individuals, from reference-fixing "definitions" for proper names. Since instances of premise schema (35′) may in general be *a posteriori,* the generated necessary truth may also be *a posteriori.* The I-mechanism is thus a mechanism for generating necessary *a posteriori* truths whose expression involves proper names, precisely analogous to the general K-mechanism for generating necessary *a posteriori* truths whose expression involves natural kind terms.

20. THE PROGRAM

The OK-mechanism represents Donnellan's reconstruction of the justification for Putnam's claim, made in his thesis (T9), that the direct reference theory of the designation of natural kind terms yields the consequence that certain *a posteriori* generalizations involving a natural kind, like those mentioned in Section 8.1, are necessary. We have seeen that if (T9) is true, it follows that this theory of direct reference for natural kind terms yields as further consequences certain forms of essentialism concerning natural kinds. The OK-mechanism is the analytical apparatus with respect to which it is proposed that this program of deriving these essentialist assertions from the direct reference theory of natural kind terms be carried out. Guided by Donnellan's insights into the nuts and bolts of Putnam's program, we have set forth two similar but more versatile mechanisms, the general K-mechanism and the I-mechanism, devised for the purpose of generating essentialist assertions involving kinds and individuals, respectively, from appropriate "definitions" that fix the reference of a nondescriptional rigid designator.

We are concerned here with the question of whether any such proposal for deriving nontrivial essentialism from the theory of direct

174

reference can succeed. Putnam's original proposal concerns only natural kinds, and if it succeeds, we can be satisfied that our question has been solved in the affirmative. But any successful application of either a K-mechanism or the I-mechanism would be sufficient for our purpose. If it can be shown that each of the premises of any of the various modal arguments exhibiting one of these mechanisms is either a consequence of the theory of direct reference or else entirely free of nontrivial essentialist import, Putnam's program of deriving nontrivial essentialism from his theory about language must be seen as a genuine triumph in philosophy.

SIX · *Hidden Essentialism in the* K *and* I *Mechanisms*

In the preceding two chapters we undertook a detailed study of Putnam's special version of the direct reference theory for the case of natural kind terms, together with a Putnam-inspired attempt, as elaborated by Donnellan, to substantiate Putnam's thesis (T9) that this theory yields certain essentialist consequences. Our task in the present chapter is to make some assessment of this bold attempt to derive deeply metaphysical results from a theory whose first concern is with language. Specifically, we must focus our attention on the components of the K-mechanisms and the I-mechanism, and investigate whether each of the premises in any application of one of these mechanisms is either an assertion of the theory of direct reference or else free of any nontrivial essentialist import.

21. THE FIRST TWO PREMISES

We begin with the original modal argument presented in Section 18.1 for the conclusion that necessarily all water is H_2O. Premise (13′) of this argument is our analysis of Putnam's suggested ostensive definition of water, as given in his thesis (T3). We have seen that (13′) may be taken as an object language formulation of the assertion that the term 'water' rigidly designates a certain substance. As such, (13′) may be taken as coming from the theory of direct reference. Premise (18′), the premise asserting that the paradigm sample referred to in the ostensive definition of water has the chemical structure H_2O, conveys a piece of empirically verified information that is obviously free of any nontrivial essentialist import. The first two premises of the argument, then, are perfectly acceptable from our present point of view. In any case, we shall take them to be so. We must turn our attention now to premise (19′), which asserts that consubstantiality "consists in" having identical chemical structure.

22. THE THIRD PREMISE

22.1. *Putnam and Donnellan on the Third Premise*

If Putnam's mechanism is to succeed in substantiating his thesis (T9), premise (19′) must be either itself a consequence of the theory

176

of direct reference or else free of any nontrivial essentialist import. Neither Putnam nor Donnellan explicitly provides much reason to suppose that it is one or the other. Putnam says very little about the theoretical status of (19'), only that its truth is a matter that is relative to one's interests in a given context. Intriguing though this may be, it is of no help in determining that (19') is either a consequence of the direct reference theory or essentialism-free.

Donnellan has more to say about the status of (19'). He sometimes denies outright that (19') is *a priori,* as in the last sentence of the passage quoted in Section 17, but a more cautious statement of his view is that (19') is "the product of scientific discovery, of scientific theories or, perhaps, change in scientific outlook." The suggestion that (19') has some empirical, or in some sense "scientific," import is an interesting one, and it may hint in the direction of claiming that (19') is not strictly a consequence of the theory of direct reference, but is instead a philosophically uncontroversial non-question-begging premise. The issue, however, is not so clear. Essentialist assertions can have *a posteriori* scientific import, as for example the assertion that Hesperus is such that it would be impossible for it not to be Phosphorus. This essentialist assertion seems to convey *a posteriori* information, for it entails that Hesperus and Phosphorus are one, and the latter fact is apparently an empirical, scientific one. (Donnellan's suggestion that (19') may be *a posteriori* and the relation of this suggestion to the present project are discussed further in Appendix II.)

Vagueness in (19') is an additional problem. Donnellan says little that would clarify his use of the phrase 'consists in'. Yet clarification is crucial to our present investigation.

22.2 Formalization

Clarification is often accomplished by formalizing, and the present case is one such instance where formalization is illumination. We shall pursue our investigation into the theoretical status of (19') by seeking a symbolization of the modal argument in which it occurs. Since the argument is intuitively valid, as verified by the informal reasoning in Section 17, there is in addition to the ordinary constraints on symbolization the further constraint of modal validity. In symbolizing and thereby clarifying (19'), we shall be guided by the role (19') plays in the informal reasoning. In effect, Donnellan's vague phrase 'consists in' will be made precise in terms of *whatever is called for* to make the argument a modally valid one. Of course, if the argument is invalid, then the Putnam-inspired program is a failure in any case. Since our aim is to show that the case has not been successfully made, we commit no violation in assuming the opposite of our conclusion. If one likes, our argument against the Putnam-inspired program may be regarded as a *reductio ad absurdum*.

We already have a symbolization for (13′) in

(13) $\Box(x)[\Pi_{water}(x)$

$\leftrightarrow x \in dthat((\imath z)[Substance(z) \wedge (this \in z)])]$.

A symbolization for the conclusion (23′) that necessarily all water is H_2O, is straightforward. Letting 'H_2O' be our symbolization for the predicate 'is chemically composed of two parts hydrogen and one part oxygen', we may symbolize (23′) by

(23) $\Box(x)[\Pi_{water}(x) \rightarrow H_2O(x)]$.

A symbolization for premise (18′) is less straightforward. If we allow ourselves a second-order symbolic language, with second-order quantifiers and predicates for first-order predicates, then (18′) may be symbolized by

(18) $H_2O(this) \wedge Chemical\text{-}structure(H_2O)$,

where '*Chemical-structure*' is used as a second-order predicate meaning something like "is a chemical structure property," and is attachable to predicates like that for the property of *being chemically composed of two parts hydrogen and one part oxygen.*[1]

In attempting to symbolize premise (19′), we must come to terms with its vague phrase 'consists in'. The phrase seems to suggest some

---

[1]The use of second-order formulations facilitates, but is not necessary for, the development of the arguments of this and later sections. Premise (18), for instance, could be recast in a first-order language by positing a property *h* (the property of *being composed mainly of two parts hydrogen and one part oxygen*) as an *individual* such that

$\Box(x)[Has(x,h) \leftrightarrow H_2O(x)]$.

Premise (18) may then be replaced by

$Has(this,h) \wedge Chemical\text{-}structure(h)$

or by

$H_2O(this) \wedge Chemical\text{-}structure(h)$,

where '*Chemical-structure*' is now used as a first-order predicate.

178

notion of a *necessary and sufficient condition* for two samples being consubstantial. (Cf. the second Putnam quotation from Section 16.) One natural and plausible reading of (19′) would render it as an assertion of a metaphysically necessary necessary-and-sufficient condition for consubstantiality thus:

(24) $\Box(x)(y)[(x \in (\imath z)[Substance(z) \wedge y \in z])$

$\leftrightarrow (F)(Chemical\text{-}structure(F) \rightarrow [F(x) \leftrightarrow F(y)])]$.

In English: necessarily, a necessary-and-sufficient condition for two individuals x and y to be consubstantial is that whatever chemical structure one has, so does the other.

Unfortunately, given our assumptions, this simply will not do as a correct analysis of the phrase 'consists in' as it is used by Donnellan. The modal argument of (13), (18), (24), ∴ (23) is simply invalid, though the implicit argument embodied in Putnam's mechanism, as described by Donnellan, is assumed to be valid.

The problem is that premise (24) is not a correct rendering of (19′). It is in one sense too weak, but in another sense it is too strong. It is too strong because it asserts both a necessary and a sufficient condition on consubstantiality. It is clear from the way in which the informal reasoning proceeds, however, that only a statement of some sort of *necessary condition* is required in premise (19′). In order to safeguard against packing more into Donnellan's notion of 'consists in' than is necessary, let us take it to imply only some sort of necessary condition.

Premise (24) does assert a necessary condition on consubstantiality, but only for *intra-world consubstantiality,* consubstantiality *within* a single possible world. It asserts that in order for two samples x and y to be consubstantial within an arbitrary possible world w, they must share the same chemical structure within w. What is needed in premise (19′) is a statement of a necessary condition on *cross-world* consubstantiality, i.e., on consubstantiality across distinct possible worlds. This is the sense in which (24) is simply too weak. Using quantification over possible worlds in possible world discourse, premise (19′) must have at a minimum the force of

(19) $(w_1)(w_2)(x)(y)(Exists_{w_1}(x) \wedge Exists_{w_2}(y)$

$\rightarrow [(x \in_{w_1} (\imath z)[Substance_{w_2}(z) \wedge (y \in_{w_2} z)])$

$\rightarrow (F)(Chemical\text{-}structure(F) \rightarrow [F_{w_1}(x) \leftrightarrow F_{w_2}(y)])])$.

Premise (19) asserts that if x exists in w_1 and y exists in w_2, and if furthermore x is a sample in w_1 of the same substance that y is a sample of in w_2, then whatever chemical structure x has in w_1, y has that same chemical structure in w_2, and vice-versa. Given this premise, in order for some liquid sample x in an arbitrary possible world w to be cross-world consubstantial with the actual paradigm water sample mentioned in the ostensive definition of water, sample x must have the same chemical structure in w that the actual paradigm has in the actual world, namely the chemical structure H_2O.[2] It follows that in every possible world, every sample of water has the chemical structure H_2O. The modal argument (13), (18), (19), $\therefore$ (23) is valid.[3] Sentence (19), then, may be taken as our analysis of premise (19′).

22.3. The K-Mechanisms

Analogously, the third premise needed in the argument concerning tigers and mammals is the following:

[2] By now, the reader can see the need for our lengthy discussion in Chapter Four of cross-world relations and the logical form of Putnam's "ostensive definition" of water.

Premise (19) is stronger than need be for Putnam's purpose. The argument requires only the special instance of (19) where w_2 is the actual world $W_@$, though it is clear that the intended force of (19′) is the full force of (19). Use of the more specific premise mentioning $W_@$ would not affect our main point below, for even this weaker premise has nontrivial essentialist import, and is quite independent of the theory of direct reference. In fact, given the assumption that every possible substance has some sample in the actual world, the stronger and weaker principles become equivalent.

[3] It is assumed here that inferences of the form $\ulcorner \phi \therefore$ Actually, $\phi \urcorner$ are valid. Also, by not subscripting the higher-order predicate '*Chemical-structure*' in (19) with a possible world variable or constant, we implicitly assume that *being a chemical structure* is world-independent or world-invariant. (See Chapter Four, footnote 16.) Put another way, the argument implicitly assumes that any possible thing that *might* be a chemical structure is *essentially* a chemical structure. Thus it is already apparent that some form of essentialism is presupposed in the argument. This essentialist presupposition is roughly analogous to our axiom (*Sub*2) for substances (Section 14.1), and might be regarded as a trivial form of essentialism. Also, in instantiating the higher-order universal quantifier on the predicate variable '*F*' to the particular predicate 'H_2O', we make a tacit assumption, analogous to those mentioned in Chapter Two, footnote 5, that the property of *being composed of two parts hydrogen and one part oxygen* is such that it must be the kind of property that it is, so that the property of *being H_2O* is the same property in every possible world. Without this assumption, the instantiation to 'H_2O' would be analogous to the illegitimate instantiation of a quantifier on an individual variable in a modal context to a nonrigid definite description. Here again, the essentialist assumption might be regarded as entirely trivial. Neither of these essentialist presuppositions has the metaphysical bite that the conclusion (23) has.

180

An individual x is a member in a possible world w_1 of the same species that an individual y is a member of in a possible world w_2 only if whatever biological class x is a member of in w_1, y is also a member of that same biological class in w_2, and vice-versa.

Similarly, the third premise in the case of gold having atomic number 79 is the following:

A sample x is a sample in a possible world w_1 of the same chemical element that a sample y is a sample of in a possible world w_2 only if whatever atomic number x has in w_1, y also has that same atomic number in w_2, and vice-versa.

In the general case, the third premise of any application of the OK-mechanism must have the following form:

(26) $(w_1)(w_2)(x)(y)(Exists_{w_1}(x) \land Exists_{w_2}(y)$

$\rightarrow [(x \in_{w_1} (\imath z)[K_{w_2}(z) \land y \in_{w_2} z])$

$\rightarrow (F)(\Psi(F) \rightarrow [F_{w_1}(x) \leftrightarrow F_{w_2}(y)])]),$

where as before K is a generic natural kind predicate like 'is a species' or 'is a substance', and Ψ expresses the higher-level property of being a first-level property of a certain specified sort. Any premise concerned only with the intra-world *same-K* relation will render the argument invalid. Only an assertion of a necessary condition for the full cross-world *same-K* relation will do.

In Section 19.1, we saw that Donnellan's account of what it is about natural kind terms that makes for the possibility of necessary *a posteriori* generalization was inadequate since, as the general K-mechanism reveals, neither reference to a paradigm nor reference to the cross-world *same-K* relation is required in the first premise of an application of a K-mechanism. On the other hand, it should be noted at this point that the cross-world *same-K* relation does indeed pay a crucial role in the general K-mechanism, even if it need not appear in the first premise of its applications. We have just established that the third premise schema of the OK-mechanism must assert, at a minimum, a necessary condition on the cross-world *same-K* relation. This remains true of the general K-mechanism as well, as the mechanism applied to the "operational definition" of water easily reveals. There again, premise (24) would be inadequate. Nothing less than (19) will do. In the general case, premise (26') of the general K-mechanism must have the full cross-world force of (26).

22.4. The I-Mechanism

The situation is entirely analogous in the case of the I-mechanism. Consider again the argument from Section 19.2 for the conclusion (34'), asserting that necessarily Woody the Table, if it exists, was originally constructed from hunk of wood H. As in the case of the modal argument concerning water, the first premise of the argument concerning Woody, premise (30'), may be thought of as an object language introductory "definition" for the proper name 'Woody', a definition that fixes the name as a rigid designator of the table located before the speaker. As such, premise (30') may be regarded as an assertion of the theory of singular direct reference. On the other hand, the premise (31'), that the table in question was originally constructed from hunk of wood H, conveys only empirically established information, entirely free of any nontrivial essentialist import. Once again, it is only the theoretical status of the third premise, in this case premise (32'), that remains in question. In order to infer the conclusion (34'), we had to assume in our use of premise (32') in the informal derivation that, if a table x in some other possible world is identical with a given table y in the actual world, then the tables x and y must be originally constructed in both possible worlds from the same hunk of matter. That is, we had to assume that sameness of original composition is a necessary condition, not only for the intra-world identity of tables, but for their cross-world identity as well. We were then able to infer that any table that is the very same table in some other possible world that Woody is in the actual world must, like Woody in the actual world, be constructed from hunk of wood H. The corresponding intra-world principle is a truth of (modal) logic: In any possible world, identical tables are originally constructed from the very same matter. It is a special instance of Leibniz's Law, or the Indiscernibility of Identicals. Merely invoking this logical law would not enable one to draw the necessary inference. Premise (32'), asserting that the identity of a table "consists, in part, in" its original composition, must be interpreted as having the force of the following:

(32) $(w_1)(w_2)(x)(y)(Exists_{w_1}(x) \land Exists_{w_2}(y)$

$\rightarrow [(x =_{w_1} (\imath z)[Table_{w_2}(z) \land y =_{w_2} z])$

$\rightarrow (F)(Original\text{-}composition(F) \rightarrow [F_w(x) \leftrightarrow F_{w_2}(y)])])$, i.e., if x exists in possible world w_1 and y exists in possible world w_2, and if furthermore x is the very same table in w_1 that y is in w_2, then whatever original composition x has in w_1, y also has that original composition in w_2, and vice-versa.

In the general case, premise (36') of the *I*-mechanism, asserting what being the same individual of kind *I* "consists in," is to be interpreted as having the force of the following:

$$(36) \qquad (w_1)(w_2)(x)(y)(Exists_{w_1}(x) \wedge Exists_{w_2}(y)$$
$$\rightarrow [(x =_{w_1} (\imath z)[I_{w_2}(z) \wedge y =_{w_2} z])$$
$$\rightarrow (F)(\Psi(\vec{r}) \rightarrow [F_{w_1}(x) \leftrightarrow F_{w_2}(y)])]).$$

A Liebniz's Law intra-world construal of (36') would simply be too weak. As in the case of the *K*-mechanisms, the full cross-world force of (36) is called for.

23. THE FAILURE OF THE PROGRAM

We return to the crucial question: Is it the case that premises of the form of (26) or (36) are either consequences of the theory of direct reference proper or else entirely free of any nontrivial essentialist import?

23.1. The Original Argument

Consider again premise (19') of the original modal argument concerning water, as interpreted by the cross-world assertion (19). Premise (19) is a statement in possible world discourse, unlike its companions (13'), (18'), and (23'), which are statements in modal operator discourse. We argued in Section 14.4 that it is often desirable to rephrase statements made in possible world discourse into equivalent statements in modal operator discourse. It happens that premise (19) does have various translations into modal operator discourse, translations which better reveal the full force of the English (19'). One such modal operator formulation of (19) is given by

$$(22) \qquad \Box(F)\Box(x)[\Diamond Chemical\text{-}structure(F) \wedge \Diamond Substance(z)$$
$$\rightarrow (\Diamond(\exists x)[x \in z \wedge F(x)] \rightarrow \Box(x)[x \in z \rightarrow F(x)])].$$

In English we have

(22′)   Given any possible chemical structure F and any possible substance z, if it is merely *possible* that some sample of substance z have the chemical structure F, then it is *necessary* that every sample of z have the chemical structure F.[4]

This premise is a nontrivial general principle of essentialism concerning liquid substances. It entails that every liquid substance is such that it could not have any chemical structure other than the one that it actually has. Thus in the full exposition of Putnam's mechanism for generating the necessary truth that water is H_2O, we find that the mechanism employs a certain nontrivial general principle of

---

[4]More accurately, the modal operator formulation of (19) would be

(21) $\Box(F)(\Diamond Chemical\text{-}structure(F)$

$\qquad \to \Box(z)[\Diamond(Substance(z) \wedge (\exists x)[x \in z \wedge F(x)])$

$\qquad \to \Box(Substance(z) \to (x)[x \in z \to F(x)])])$.

In English, we have the following:

(21′)   Given any possible chemical structure F and any possible entity z, if it is merely *possible* that z be a substance and that some sample of substance z have the chemical structure F, then it is *necessary* that, if z is a substance, then every sample of substance z has the given chemical structure F.

To be still more precise, (21) is the modal operator formulation of

(20) $(w_1)(w_2)(x)(y)(Exists_{w_1}(x) \wedge Exists_{w_2}(y)$

$\qquad \to [((\imath z)[Substance_{w_1}(z) \wedge x \in_{w_1} z] = (\imath z)[Substance_{w_2}(z) \wedge y \in_{w_2} z])$

$\qquad \to (F)(Chemical\text{-}structure(F) \to [F_{w_1}(x) \leftrightarrow F_{w_2}(y)])])$,

which is an alternative rendering of premise (19′) in possible world discourse, one that is strictly speaking weaker than (19). Assuming as we have the necessations of axioms (*Sub*1) and (*Sub*2) from Section 14.4, (19) and (20) are equivalent. Both (19) and (20) may be taken as asserting that if x and y are cross-world consubstantial across w_1 and w_2, then whatever chemical structure x has in w_1, y has that same chemical structure in w_2, and vice-versa.

The proof that (20) and (21) are equivalent is perfectly straightforward. First, (21) should be recast into possible world discourse thus:

$(F)(Chemical\text{-}structure(F)$

$\qquad \to (z)[(\exists w)(Substance_w(z) \wedge (\exists x)[Exists_w(x) \wedge x \in_w z \wedge F_w(x)])$

$\qquad \to (w)(Substance_w(z) \to (x)[Exists_w(x) \wedge x \in_w z \to F_w(x)])])$.

It is then a simple proof in ordinary second-order quantification theory that this possible world discourse formulation of (21) is equivalent to (20). The proof that the

184

essentialism concerning liquid substances as a crucial premise—a fact which neither Putnam nor Donnellan seem to have recognized.

The full essentialist force of premise (22), which is spelled out in (22′), is all but completely concealed in its vague initial formulation by way of the English (19′). We saw in Section 17 that Donnellan's view is that (19′) is, in some sense, the product of science. Given that the cross-world reading of (19′), as given by (19), is called for, and given the consequent nontrivial essentialist import of (19′), it is not at all clear that the relevant premise is merely a scientific principle. Unmasked in (22′), it looks instead like a principle whose truth is established in good part by conceptual analysis and the reflective methods of the metaphysician. One tests (22′) not by laboratory experiment but by thought experiment. One might reason, for instance, as follows: "Suppose that there were a substance whose chemical structure is different from the actual chemical structure of a given substance, say, water. Could this possible substance be the very same substance, water, nonetheless? No. It must be a different substance, namely, whatever substance *actually* has that particular chemical structure." This line of thought is an activity neither of

---

possible world discourse formulation of (21) entails (20) involves the inference pattern from the logic or definite descriptions mentioned in Chapter Four, footnote 22, an inference pattern that is justified given our assumption that atomic subject-predicate sentences with nondenoting terms are false. The proof of the entailment in the opposite direction involves the assumption of the necesssitation of our axiom (*Sub*1), together with the assumption that in any possible world in which something z is a substance, that thing z exists. (See also the previous footnote concerning an implicit assumption of trivial essentialism concerning chemical structures.) Given the notion of *nontrivial essentialist import* adopted in Chapter Three, footnote 3, it is only the latter entailment that is needed to substantiate the claim that (20) has nontrivial essentialist import.

Allowing ourselves axiom (*Sub*2), (21) may be rewritten more perspicuously as (22) in the text. Appeal to axioms (*Sub*1) and (*Sub*2) can be avoided entirely by simply taking the weaker (21) in place of (19) as our analysis of Donnellan's (19′). If so, the ostensive definition of water should be written for complete precision in its alternative form

$$\Box(x)(\Pi_{water}(x) \leftrightarrow$$

$$(\imath z)[Substance(z) \wedge x \in z] = (\imath z)A[Substance(z) \wedge this \in z]).$$

For purposes of simplicity and perspicuity, and in order to retain symbolizations that are as close to the English 'same substance' locution as possible (see Section 13.3), we focus in the text on possible world formulation (19), and modal operator formulation (22), as our analysis of (19′), in place of (20) and (21). The remarks given below concerning the theoretical status of (22) apply equally to (21).

science nor of philosophy of language. It is metaphysics and nothing else. (This topic is discussed at greater length in Appendix II below.)

More to the point, we have already established that premise (19′) is a crucial part of the original modal argument for a nontrivial essentialist conclusion, yet analysis reveals that the premise in question already has nontrivial essentialist import. As such, it is just the sort of proposition that is the subject of controversy between essentialists and anti-essentialists. Whether (22′) is a product of metaphysics or is instead the product of science, or is in some sense both a product of metaphysics and of science, the program intended to substantiate Putnam's thesis (T9) must be seen as a failure. The result, that the *a posteriori* truth that water is H_2O is also a necessary truth, does depend, in part, on the theory of direct reference, since the modal ostensive definition, which fixes the semantic intension of 'water', is a part of the argument for the necessity of 'Water is H_2O'. But the result also depends crucially on a premise, (19), which is a contestable essentialist principle that does not in any way seem to come from the philosophy of language. Unless it can be shown that this premise is itself a consequence of the theory of direct reference, we have no reason to suppose that a rational and thoroughgoing proponent of the theory of direct reference cannot consistently deny that 'Water is H_2O' expresses a necessary truth. The proponent need only deny (22′), i.e., the proponent may hold that the actual chemical structure of the substance water is only an accidental feature of the substance, and that the very same substance water can have a different chemical structure in different possible worlds. There seems to be nothing in the theory of direct reference to block the anti-essentialist assertion that the substance water might have been the very same entity and yet have had a different chemical structure. The theory of direct reference seems to be perfectly compatible with nontrivial essentialism concerning chemical substances, and also with its negation. What Putnam and Donnellan fail to acknowledge is that it is only when the direct reference theory is taken in conjunction with this apparently independent essentialist point of view that one obtains the result that necessarily water is H_2O. Taken by itself, or taken together only with premises that are free of nontrivial essentialist import, the theory of direct reference, so far, seems metaphysically impotent.

In fact, whatever the epistemological or theoretical status of the essentialist principle (22′)—whether it is *a priori* or *a posteriori*, metaphysical or scientific—once we are allowed to assume it, or its equivalent (19), there is no further need for the theory of direct reference to obtain nontrivial examples of *a posteriori* essentialist theses concerning water. For example, if the modal operators '□' and '*dthat*' are removed from the ostensive definition of water in the original modal argument, the resulting nonmodal ostensive definition,

> Something is a sample of *water* if and only if it is a sample of the same substance as *this* (paradigm),

is something that can be accepted by even the orthodox Fregean theory of meaning, either as an empirical hypothesis or perhaps as a strict synonymy definition of 'water'. In either case, when this nonmodal premise is substituted for the modal ostensive definition of water in the original modal argument, the new set of premises still yields an *a posteriori* essentialist thesis as a consequence:

> Every sample of water is a sample of a substance S which is such that, necessarily, each of its samples has the chemical structure H_2O.

In addition, necessary *a posteriori* truths formally analogous to 'Water is H_2O' (construed as an assertion about the chemical composition of every sample of water) can also be obtained from (22') independently of the theory of direct reference, using the logic of 'actually'. Dispensing entirely with any ostensive definition of water, for instance, the two remaining premises of the original modal argument, (18') and (19'), by themselves yield the consequence that the following *a posteriori* sentence expresses a necessary truth:

> The substance that *this* (paradigm) is actually a sample of (if there is a unique such substance) is H_2O.

Similarly, given (19') and the additional empirical premise, which is quite independent of the theory of direct reference, that some sample of the most abundant liquid substance on earth has the chemical structure H_2O, one may easily derive the consequence that the following *a posteriori* sentence expresses a necessary truth:

> The substance which is *actually* the most abundant liquid on earth (if there is a unique such substance) is H_2O.

More generally, given any property ϕ which is necessarily unique to the substance water (an essence of water) and which is such that it

187

is an *a posteriori* truth that the substance having ϕ is H_2O, one may use (19′), together with the fact that some sample of the substance having ϕ has the chemical composition H_2O, and the further essentialist fact that ϕ is an essence, to derive the nontrivially necessary *a posteriori* truth that every sample of the substance which has ϕ (if a unique such substance exists) has the chemical structure H_2O.[5] This can be seen by inspecting a variant of the application of the general K-mechanism to the case of water, and noticing the exchangeability of the first premise when the argument is made for this slightly different conclusion. Yet the original first premise is the only premise which may be identified as coming from the theory of direct reference. All that is needed to extract necessary *a posteriori* truths concerning water from (19′) is some rigid designator for the substance water. The theory of direct reference asserts that 'water' is such a term, but this is not the only way to find a rigid designator for water. Any reasonable theory of the sentential actuality operator—even an orthodox theory of meaning which accords the operator a Fregean sense—must accommodate the result that a proper definite description of the form ⌜the actual ϕ⌝ is a rigid designator. (See Section 4.1.) And any rigid designator of water satisfying the constraints mentioned above will do the trick. Hence, once we are given (19′), we can easily generate an infinity of nontrivial necessary *a posteriori* generalizations concerning water, and we do so with no apparent help from the theory of direct reference. Clearly, then, it is not the modal ostensive definition of water, but the apparently independent essentialist principle (19′), which is doing the brunt of the work in obtaining such necessary *a posteriori* truths.

In light of this result, it is difficult to see how Putnam's thesis (T9) can be maintained—except, of course, in the trivial sense that the existence of nontrivially necessary *a posteriori* truths concerning water is a consequence of the theory of direct reference *taken in conjunction with* the essentialist principle (19′). This is trivial because the existence of such truths is a consequence of (19′) in conjunction with *any* reasonable theory of meaning, even the orthodox Fregean theory which Putnam so vigorously opposes. (Moreover, in this sense, the consequence is hardly a "startling" one.) The

---

[5]Of course, given any *a posteriori* truth p, the sentence ⌜It is actually the case that p⌝ is a necessary *a posteriori* truth, one obtained solely from the logic of 'actually'. This procedure, however, yields only trivial examples of necessary *a posteriori* truths. The examples of necessary *a posteriori* truth that Putnam claims to find in his theory of natural kind terms are nontrivial. Cf. Sections 8.2 and 8.3 above.

existence of nontrivially necessary *a posteriori* truths concerning water results not from one's choice of a theory of meaning and reference, but from the apparently independent essentialist principle (19′).

23.2. *The* K *and* I *Mechanisms*

Our results from the previous section can be generalized. For example, the third premise of the argument involving the species *Tiger* is equivalent to the following general essentialist principle concerning species:

> Given any possible biological class property F and any possible species z, if it is merely *possible* that some member of species z have the biological class property F, then it is *necessary* that every member of species z have the biological class property F.

Likewise, the third premise of the argument involving gold is equivalent to the following general essentialist principle concerning chemical elements:

> Given any number n and any possible chemical element z, if it is merely *possible* that some sample of element z have exactly n protons in virtually all of its component atoms, then it is *necessary* that every sample of element z have exactly n protons in virtually all of its component atoms.

In other words, the argument involving the species *Tiger* involves a premise to the effect that every species is such that it could not be subsumed under any biological class other than the one that actually subsumes it. And the argument involving gold involves a premise to the effect that every chemical element is such that it could not have any atomic number other than the one it actually has. These are essentialist principles which play a crucial role in the arguments, yet they seem to be quite independent of the theory of direct reference. As in the previous case, formally analogous necessary *a posteriori* truths concerning tigers and gold may be obtained from these essentialist principles independently of the theory of direct reference, as the theory is embodied in the first premise of the relevant modal arguments. These essentialist principles, and not the theory of direct reference, do the brunt of the work in obtaining nontrivially necessary *a posteriori* truths concerning tigers and gold.

In the general case, any application of either the *OK*-mechanism

189

or the general K-mechanism will involve, as an instance of premise (26), a premise that is equivalent to a general essentialist principle of the following form:[6]

(27) $\quad \Box(F)\Box(z) [\Diamond \Psi(F) \wedge \Diamond K(z)$

$\quad\quad\quad\quad \rightarrow (\Diamond(\exists x) [x \in z \wedge F(x)] \rightarrow \Box(x) [x \in z \rightarrow F(x)])]).$

Thus, the essentialism generated by way of the K-mechanisms is in some sense already there in the tools one is using. It is this essentialist premise and not the theory of direct reference, as it is embodied in the first premise of the K-mechanisms, which is primarily responsible for the generated nontrivial necessary *a posteriori* truth.

The result generalizes also to the use of the I-mechanism. Premise (32) of the argument involving Woody the Table—the premise asserting what the cross-world identity of tables "consists, in part, in"—is equivalent to the following general principle of essentialism concerning tables:

(33) $\quad \Box(F)\Box(x) [\Diamond Original\text{-}composition(F) \wedge \Diamond Table(x)$

$\quad\quad\quad\quad \rightarrow (\Diamond[Exists(x) \wedge F(x)] \rightarrow \Box[Exists(x) \rightarrow F(x)])].$

In English we have

(33′)   Given any possible original-composition property F and any possible table x, if it is merely *possible* that table x have original-composition F, then it is necessary that table x, if it exists, has original-composition F.

Principle (33) entails that every table is such that it would be *impossible* for it to have originated from any hunk of matter other than the hunk of matter from which it was actually made. Once we are allowed to assume this essentialist principle, we may easily obtain necessary *a posteriori* truths concerning Woody the Table which are formally analogous to (34) but which do not depend in any way on

---

[6]The proof of the equivalence involves assumptions and inference patterns entirely analogous to those refered to in the previous footnotes. In particular, the proof that (26) entails (27) involves a schematic generalization of (the necessitations of) (*Sub*1) and (*Sp*1):

(K1) $\quad\quad (x)(y)(z)[K(y) \wedge K(z) \wedge x \in y \wedge x \in z \rightarrow y = z].$

Given the notion of *nontrivial essentialist import* adopted in Chapter Three, footnote 3, it is only the entailment of (27) by (26) that is needed to substantiate the claim that (26) is a nontrivial essentialist premise schema.

premise (30) of the theory of direct reference. For example, given the essentialist principle (33) and the further empirical premise that the table Uncle John built for Aunt Martha was built from the hunk of wood that made up Uncle John's wheelbarrow, we easily obtain the result that the following *a posteriori* sentence expresses a necessary truth:

> The table that was actually built by Uncle John for Aunt Martha, if there is a unique such table, was built from the hunk of wood that actually made up Uncle John's wheel-barrow.

It is the essentialist principle (33) which is the primary source of the necessity of *a posteriori* truths like (34). (It will be argued in Appendix I that (33) must be weakened in a certain way. Generated necessary truths like (34) must also be weakened accordingly.)

In the general case, it may be shown that the third premise schema of the *I*-mechanism, premise (36), which asserts a necessary condition on the cross-world *same-I* relation, is equivalent to a certain general principle of essentialism concerning individuals of type *I*. Specifically, instances of premise (36) will be equivalent to a general essentialist principle of the form[7]

(37) $\quad \Box(F)\Box(x)\,[\Diamond\Psi(F) \wedge \Diamond I(x)$

$\rightarrow (\Diamond[Exists(x) \wedge F(x)] \rightarrow \Box[Exists(x) \rightarrow F(x)])].$

---

[7] The proof of this involves the inference pattern from the logic of definite descriptions referred to in Chapter Four, footnote 22. It also involves assumptions analogous to those mentioned in the previous footnotes. In addition, it requires two special assumptions. First, it requires the important principle that individuals are intra-world identical if and only if they are identical in the absolute sense of being one and the same thing. (See Chapter Four, footnote 18.) Second, the proof requires the special assumption that the predicate *I* designates an *essential* property in the sense that

$$\Box(x)(\Diamond I(x) \rightarrow \Box[Exists(x) \rightarrow I(x)]).$$

This assumption may seem unwarranted, but it is less than crucial. For most purposes, the predicate position occupied by *I* may be deleted entirely from the *I*-mechanism, either by absorbing its predicate instances into ϕ or by dropping the predicate instances entirely. Thus instead of saying that x is the same *table* in w_1 that y is in w_2, we may say simply that x is the same *thing* in w_1 that y is in w_2: $x =_{w_1} (\imath z)[y =_{w_2} z]$. This eliminates the need for any special essentialist assumptions. In any case, it is only the entailment of (37) by (36) that is needed to substantiate the claim that (36) has nontrivial essentialist import. This entailment requires no special essentialist assumptions about *I*.

191

Thus any application of the *I*-mechanism, like applications of the *K*-mechanisms, crucially involves a certain general principle of essentialism, one that seems to be a principle from metaphysics and that seems to be, in particular, quite independent of the theory of direct reference. This general principle of essentialism can also be made to yield necessary *a posteriori* truths formally analogous to those obtained by means of the *I*-mechanism, but without any reliance on the mechanism's first premise. It is this general principle of essentialism, then, which does the brunt of the work in obtaining the relevant necessary *a posteriori* truths.

Our conclusion: Neither Putnam nor Donnellan have succeeded in making the case that nontrivial forms of essentialism are, in any significant sense, derivable from the theory of direct reference, taken together only with premises that are, unlike (19′) and (32′), free of any nontrivial essentialist import. There is no reason to suppose that there are mechanisms which provide a means for generating nontrivial essentialism, or equivalently, for generating nontrivially necessary *a posteriori* truths like 'Water is H_2O', from the theory of direct reference.[8]

[8]Here is an exercise for the reader. Consider the following application of the *I*-mechanism (Section 19.2). Let α be the name 'Hesperus', and let β be the definite description 'the heavenly body ordinarily visible in *that* location in the sky from *this* vantage point at dusk'. Let ψ be the predicate 'is Phosphorus'. Let Ψ be the second-order predicate 'is an haecceity', where the phrase $\ulcorner F$ is an haecceity$\urcorner$ is formally defined with a second-order identity predicate by the following:

$$(\exists y)[F = \lambda x(x = y)],$$

i.e., F is the property of *being y*, for some individual y. What necessary yet apparently *a posteriori* truth is thereby generated? The second premise of the modal argument asserts that Hesperus has the haecceity of *being Phosphorus*. The content of this premise has two parts: (*a*) that Hesperus is Phosphorus, and (*b*) that *being Phosphorus* is an haecceity. Part (*a*) is an astronomical fact. What is involved in our knowledge of (*b*)? [Hint: The property of *being the heavenly body ordinarily visible in such-and-such location in the sky from so-and-so vantage point at dawn* is not an haecceity, nor is it any sort of essential property.] Translate the third premise of the argument (the essentialist premise) into modal operator discourse. [Hint: Use (37).] Use a principle of λ-conversion and the logical law that identity is world-invariant (see Chapter Four, footnotes 16, 18) to show that this premise is a valid truth of modal logic. Since this essentialist premise is a truth of logic, it may be omitted entirely as a premise to the argument. Hence, this special application of the *I*-mechanism genuinely succeeds in generating a necessary yet apparently *a posteriori* truth from the theory of direct reference without relying on any special essentialist premise! How does this compare with our findings in Section 8.2?

SEVEN · *Arguments for the Essentiality of Origin*

24. KRIPKE AND THE PUTNAM PROGRAM

So far we have concentrated on the views of Donnellan and Putnam concerning the relation between the theory of direct reference and certain *a posteriori* essentialist statements. In stating his thesis (T9), Putnam writes:

> What Kripke was the first to observe is that this theory of the meaning (or "use," or whatever) of the word 'water' (and other natural-kind terms as well) has startling consequences for the theory of necessary truth.
>
> . . . it is conceivable that water isn't H_2O. It is conceivable but it isn't possible!
>
> . . . a statement can be (metaphysically) necessary and epistemically contingent (1973b, pp. 708–709).

Putnam asserts not only that the existence of necessary *a posteriori* truths like 'Water is H_2O' is a consequence of the theory of direct reference, but also that Kripke was the first to observe that this is so.

Kripke does not explicitly propose any "mechanisms" for generating nontrivial *a posteriori* essentialist theses from the theory of reference. Nevertheless, much of what he says may seem to suggest the formal apparatus of the K and I mechanisms. Indeed, some of Kripke's remarks seem to accord with Donnellan's concerning the role of science in the K-mechanisms; for instance, he says: "present scientific theory is such that it is part of the nature of gold as we have it to be an element with atomic number 79. It will therefore be necessary and not contingent that gold be an element with atomic number 79" (1972a, p. 125). Again, later he says: "Whether science can discover empirically that certain properties are *necessary* of cows, or of tigers, is [a] question, which I answer affirmatively" (p. 128).

One must be careful, however, not to misread these remarks. Kripke also says things which strongly suggest, contrary to Donnel-

193

lan, that the crucial essentialist principles of the form of (27) involved in the *K*-mechanisms are not *a posteriori,* but rather *a priori.* Thus he says: " 'Cats are animals' *has* turned out to be a necessary truth. Indeed of many such statements, especially those subsuming one species under another, we know *a priori* that, if they are true at all, they are necessarily true" (1972a, p. 138). And in an addendum he writes:

> The peculiar character of mathematical propositions (like Goldbach's conjecture) is that one knows (*a priori*) that they cannot be contingently true; a mathematical statement, if true, is necessary.
>
> All the cases of the necessary *a posteriori* advocated in the text have the special character attributed to mathematical statements: Philosophical analysis tells us that they cannot be contingently true, so any empirical knowledge of their truth is automatically empirical knowledge that they are necessary. This characterization applies, in particular, to the cases of identity statements and of essence. It *may* give a clue to a general characterization of *a posteriori* knowledge of necessary truths (1972a, p. 159).

This last passage is intended to apply not only to the examples from Section 8.1 involving natural kinds but also to the examples involving individuals. Indeed, in an earlier work Kripke says something very similar in discussing how one arrives at the *a posteriori* knowledge that a particular table necessarily originates from a certain hunk of wood and not from a block of ice:

> . . . if *P* is the statement that [a particular table] is not made of ice, one knows by a priori philosophical analysis, some conditional of the form "if *P*, then necessarily *P*." If the table is not made of ice, it is necessarily not made of ice. On the other hand, then, we know by empirical investigation that *P*, the antecedent of the conditional, is true—that this table is not made of ice. We can conclude by *modus ponens:*
>
> $$P \supset \Box P$$
> $$\frac{P}{\Box P}$$

The conclusion—'$\Box P$'—is that it is necessary that the table not be made of ice, and this conclusion is known a posteriori, since one of the premises on which it is based is a posteriori (1971, p. 153).

If we take these passages together, Kripke's view of the matter seems to be this: We know *a priori* that if a biological kind (e.g., a species) *k* is subsumed under a higher-level biological kind (e.g., a genus, class, kingdom, etc.) *k'*, then it is necessary that *k* is subsumed under *k'*. We also know by the direct reference theory of the designation of natural kind terms that such terms as 'cat', 'tiger', 'mammal', and 'animal' are rigid designators of natural kinds. Putting these two together, we know *a priori,* by "philosophical analysis," that if all cats are animals, then it is necessary that all cats are animals, and that if all tigers are mammals, then it is necessary that all tigers are mammals, etc. Science discovers empirically that cats are in fact animals, and that tigers are in fact mammals. Combining these scientific discoveries with what we know *a priori* by philosophical analysis, we infer that it is necessary, even though *a posteriori*, that cats are animals and that tigers are mammals. Given what we know by philosophical analysis—the theory of direct reference plus the *a priori* essentialist fact that every biological kind *k* is such that it could not fail to be subsumed under any of the higher level biological kinds *k'* that in fact subsume it—any empirical discovery that cats are in fact animals, or that tigers are in fact mammals, is indirectly but automatically an empirical discovery that it is *necessary* that cats are animals, or that tigers are mammals. But involved in the latter empirical discovery is the *a priori* philosophical knowledge of certain essentialist principles concerning biological kinds. Thus Kripke might be seen as employing a mechanism very similar to the *K*-mechanisms.

The last of the passages quoted above suggests that Kripke might also be interpreted as using a mechanism similar to the *I*-mechanism in generating necessary *a posteriori* truths ascribing nontrivially essential properties to individuals such as people and tables. Specifically, Kripke might be seen as generating the necessary *a posteriori* truth that *this* very table was originally constructed from hunk of wood *H*, precisely by way of some such mechanism. We have seen in Section 23.2 that the use of this mechanism to generate this necessary *a posteriori* truth involves a nontrivial general principle of essentialism concerning tables and their origins. This is principle (33'). Indeed, as the passage indicates, Kripke also seems to hold the view that this general essentialist principle (or instances of one very much like it) is knowable *a priori*.

The important point is that Kripke seems to take the position that the general essentialist principles of the form of (27) or (37) involved in the *K* and *I* mechanisms are knowable by *a priori* "philosophical analysis."[1] Although Kripke might be seen as employing mechanisms similar to the Putnam-inspired *K* and *I* mechanisms for generating necessary *a posteriori* truths, it would be a serious mistake to interpret his use of these modal arguments as an endorsement of the Putnam-inspired program, elaborated by Donnellan and set forth in Chapter Five above. That program uses the *K* and *I* mechanisms in an attempt to substantiate the claim that the theory of direct reference has the consequence that there are certain nontrivial examples of *a posteriori* truths which are nevertheless necessary, and hence, by the theory, essentialist. We have seen that this program is flawed in that it employs as a crucial premise a principle which appears to be quite independent of the theory of direct reference, and which can be made to yield the desired consequence without further help from the theory of direct reference, though neither Donnellan nor Putnam seemed to have recognized this. Kripke, on the other hand, explicitly recognizes the essentialist import of the major premise in his modal arguments generating necessary *a posteriori* truths. Given this explicit and conscious use of essentialist principles in these modal arguments, one should not interpret Kripke to be offering these modal arguments as substantiation for the claim that nontrivial forms of essentialism are derivable as consequences from the theory of direct reference.

25. Kripke's "Proof" of the Essentiality of Origin

Though Kripke cannot be interpreted as endorsing Putnam's attempt, as elaborated by Donnellan, to substantiate the claim that nontrivial essentialism is derivable from the theory of direct reference, Kripke does say things that have been interpreted by some philosophers (by myself-from-1973-to-1979, and by others as well) as an endorsement of the claim, with a separate attempt to substantiate it.

25.1. Kripke's Formulation of the Argument

The Putnam-inspired program relied on the use of certain general essentialist principles for its major premise—principles of the form of (27) concerning natural kinds for applications of the *K*-mechanisms, and principles of the form of (37) concerning individuals for applica-

---

[1]This interpretation of Kripke is supported by Albert Cassulo (1977, pp. 152–154).

tions of the *I*-mechanism. What is left wanting, however, is an argument to show that these principles are themselves consequences of the theory of direct reference. Of course, if a sound argument to this effect can be formed, then this argument alone would substantiate the claim that nontrivial essentialism is derivable from the theory of direct reference, and the *K* and *I* mechanisms could be dispensed with. But this seems a dubious prospect.

Kripke also endorses some or all of the crucial essentialist principles employed in the Putnam-inspired program. He says little about how one arrives at the general essentialist principles concerning natural kinds other than that they are knowable by *a priori* "philosophical analysis." He does, however, say a great deal more about how one may arrive at essentialist principles like the principle (33′) involved in the application of the *I*-mechanism to the case of a particular wooden table and its original composition. In fact, in a footnote, Kripke attempts to show that (33′), or something very close to it, can be given something like a demonstration using the direct reference theory of the reference of proper names:

A principle suggested by [my] examples is: *If a material object has its origin from a certain hunk of matter, it could not have had its origin in any other matter.* Some qualifications might have to be stated (for example, the vagueness of the notion of hunk of matter leads to some problems), but in a large class of cases the principle is perhaps susceptible of something like proof, using the principle of the necessity of identity for particulars. Let '*B*' be a name (rigid designator) of a table, let '*A*' name the piece of wood from which it actually came. Let '*C*' name another piece of wood. Then suppose *B* were made from *A*, as in the actual world, but also another table *D* were simultaneously made from *C*. (We assume that there is no relation between *A* and *C* which makes the possibility of making a table from one dependent on the possibility of making a table from the other.) Now in this situation $B \neq D$; hence, even if *D* were made by itself, and no table were made from *A*, *D* would not be *B*. Strictly speaking, the 'proof' uses the necessity of distinctness, not of identity. The same types of considerations that can be used to establish the latter, can, however, be used to establish the former.... In any event, the argument applies only if the making of *D* from *C* does not affect the possibility of making *B* from *A*, and vice-versa (1972a, p. 114, n. 56).

197

This passage appears to provide just the sort of argument we have been seeking. For it apparently "proves" a nontrivial essentialist conclusion, using nothing in addition to the theory of direct reference but an innocuous premise asserting that if there is a wooden table *B* and a separate hunk of wood *C*, then table *B* could have been made just as it actually is, from the same matter, while a new table *D* is independently made from the second hunk *C*. What could be less controversial, or freer of nontrivial essentialist import, than this premise?

25.2 Some Initial Considerations

A few points should be clarified before we attempt an analysis of this argument. Kripke's use of the phrase 'something like proof' clearly suggests that he regards the argument as falling somewhat short of a genuine proof of his essentialist thesis. This does not mean, however, that he believes the reasoning to be fallacious or the argument inconclusive. He asserts the argument. He wants to establish the truth of a version of the essentialist thesis (33′), and he clearly intends that the argument be taken as doing just that. One reason he might well balk at calling the argument a *proof* is that, strictly speaking, it is a derivation from certain assumptions taken as premises, whereas a proof is not. A proof is a derivation from axioms and theorems perhaps, but not from premises. The assumption of the necessity of distinctness might be taken as a theorem of the theory of direct reference, and it might be taken as a premise. (See Chapter One, footnote 35.) For present purposes, let us take it to be a theorem. Even then, we are left with the assumption concerning the possibility of constructing two tables simultaneously from distinct hunks of wood. Though this assumption may be trivial and philosophically uncontroversial, it is not part of a theory of reference. Strictly speaking, it is an independent premise from which the derivation proceeds.

Let us consider what the argument is supposed to show. Kripke intends to derive a special instance of the general essentialist principle mentioned at the beginning of the quoted passage. Specifically, he intends to show that *if a wooden table has its origin from a certain hunk of wood, it could not have had its origin in any other hunk of wood.* He begins his argument by supposing that we have an arbitrary table *B* in the actual world constructed from a hunk of wood *A*. Theoretically, however, there is no reason to restrict our initial assumptions to an *actual* table and *actual* hunks of wood.

198

Indeed, it is clear that if Kripke's argument is successful, one can obtain an even stronger conclusion simply by beginning with an arbitrary possible world w_1, letting A be the original component material in w_1 of some table B, whatever kind of material that may happen to be, and letting C be any distinct hunk of matter. Thus we might allow that A be a hunk of wood in w_1 whereas C is, say, a sample of water hardened into ice. It must be assumed that A and C are distinct hunks of matter, but they may or may not be hunks of the same *kind* of matter. If Kripke's specific argument is successful, these more general initial assumptions should yield the stronger conclusion that *if a table might have had its origin from a certain hunk of matter, it could not have had its origin in any other hunk of matter*. That is, assuming that Kripke's argument is successful, we may similarly derive the strong essentialist thesis that if it is merely *possible* for a given table to originate from a certain hunk of matter, then it is *necessary* that the table originate from that hunk of matter and no other. This, of course, is a version of principle (33′).

Kripke's argument is perfectly general. Similar considerations can be raised with regard to objects other than tables: other artifacts such as walls and bridges, natural inanimate objects such as mountains and rocks, and even natural organisms such as people. In fact, the argument seems to apply to virtually any sort of object that may be said to have a physical origin and composition. Instead of speaking about the original material from which a given table was made, we may speak of the original gametes from which a given person sprang, and so on. In this way, if Kripke's argument is successful, variants of it may be used to establish several strong essentialist theses concerning the origin and composition of a variety of both animate and inanimate objects. Indeed, as we shall see shortly, a similar argument may even be offered in support of essentialist theses concerning chemical substances, like thesis (22′) and analogues of (22′) for the special case of chemical elements. For substances may also be said to be composed of more primary or fundamental substances or particulars, namely, component elements in the case of compounds, and atoms having a certain number of protons in the case of elements.

One further point of clarification should be made before we turn to the argument. We shall assume for the sake of simplicity that when Kripke says that a table x was originally made from a hunk of matter y, he means that table x was originally constructed *entirely* from *all of* hunk y, i.e., that no (original) part of table x did not come from hunk y, and furthermore that no part of hunk y did not contribute to forming part of table x. It follows from this, presumably, that it is impossible for the same table to be originally constructed from two distinct hunks of matter. In fact, given the appropriate axioms, the supposition that a single table is originally constructed entirely from all of each of two distinct hunks of matter should be a provable contradiction. In any event, we shall take this assumption to be philosophically uncontroversial wherever it is useful to Kripke's argument. That is, we shall take ourselves to be given the following:

(I)   It is impossible for the same table x to be originally constructed from a hunk of matter y and in addition to be originally constructed from a *distinct* hunk of matter y'.[2]

25.3. The Compossibility Premise

In attempting an analysis of the argument, we have a problem at the outset concerning the special assumption about the possibility of constructing two tables simultaneously. Kripke's remarks leave it unclear precisely what this premise is. In one place he says that we must assume that the possibility of constructing a table from hunk A is not dependent on not simultaneously constructing a table from hunk C, and vice-versa. In another place he says that the argument assumes that constructing the very table D from hunk C does not affect the possibility of simultaneously constructing the very table B from hunk A, and vice-versa. (I have altered the wording slightly to make the formulations more perspicuous.) These are quite different assumptions. They are both what might be called *compossibility assumptions,* asserting that two separately possible states of affairs are jointly possible, but the second one is specific in a way that the first is not. The first assumption says only that *some table or other* is to be constructed from each of hunks A and C, whereas the second assumption tells us furthermore exactly which tables are to be constructed from the two hunks. More precisely, the first assumption Kripke mentions is that if it is possible for some table or other to be

---

[2]We also assume that the phrase 'hunk of matter' is used in roughly the same sense as 'portion of matter', 'sample of matter', 'bit of matter', etc. The fact that a table is not identical with the hunk of matter that constitutes it is established by the familiar argument that a severe blow with a sledgehammer will destroy the table but not the matter. Also, as a single table becomes chipped and scraped, and as its dents and chips are filled with putty, etc., different (albeit largely overlapping) portions of matter constitute the same table at different times. (For more on our use of the phrase 'hunk of matter', see Appendix I, footnote 8.)

constructed from hunk A, and it is also possible for some table or other to be constructed from hunk C, then it is yet a third possibility that some table or other be constructed from hunk A and in addition some table or other be constructed from hunk C. And the second assumption Kripke mentions is that if it is possible for the very table B to be constructed from hunk A, and it is also possible for the very table D to be constructed from hunk C, then it is yet a third possibility that the very table B be constructed from hunk A and in addition the very table D be constructed from hunk C.

Whichever assumption the argument actually employs, it must be seen as placing certain restrictions on admissable choices for hunk C. One trivial restriction, of course, is that it must be possible to construct a table from hunk C. A less trivial restriction is that there not be any matter in common between hunk A and hunk C. If hunk C were, for instance, a proper part of hunk A, say its bottom half or an interior portion, the compossibility assumptions may not be satisfied despite the fact that hunk A and its bottom half are distinct hunks of matter. It may be that this restriction simply reduces to a requirement that A and C be *nonoverlapping* hunks of matter, in the sense that they can have no parts in common throughout their existence. In order to avoid additional complications, let us suppose that it does reduce in this way. Then we may state the two compossibility assumptions Kripke mentions as follows:

(II)   For any possible hunks of matter y and y', if it is possible for *a table* (meaning *some table or other*) to be originally constructed from hunk y while hunk y' does not overlap with hunk y, and it is also possible for *a table* (meaning *some table or other*) to be originally constructed from hunk y', then it is also possible that *a table* be originally constructed from hunk y and in addition *a table* be originally constructed from hunk y'.

(III)   For any possible tables x and x' and any possible hunks of matter y and y', if it is possible for table x to be originally constructed from hunk y while hunk y' does not overlap with hunk y, and it is also possible for table x' to be originally constructed from hunk y', then it is also possible that table x be originally constructed from hunk y and in addition table x' be originally constructed from hunk y'.

Now, then, which compossibility principle does the argument actually assume? The argument begins by letting 'B' be a name of an

201

arbitrary possible table in an arbitrary possible world w_1. We also let 'A' name the hunk of matter from which table B is originally constructed in w_1, and we let 'C' name some distinct hunk of matter that also exists in w_1. We want to show that it is impossible for table B to originate from hunk C, i.e., that there is no possible world in which table B is originally constructed from hunk C. At this point in his presentation of the argument Kripke invokes the relevant compossibility principle. He writes:

> Then suppose B were made from A, as in the actual world, but also another table D were simultaneously made from C. . . . Now in this situation, $B \neq D$.

If we change the description 'the actual world' to 'the world w_1' to accommodate our more general initial assumption, it would appear that what Kripke infers from the existence of the first possible world w_1 is that there is an expanded possible world, call it w_2, in which B is still a table originally constructed from hunk A, but in which a second table, which Kripke calls 'D', is now constructed from hunk C in such a way that it follows by (I) that the tables B and D are distinct. The operative premise in this inference is neither (II) or (III), but something between the two. Unlike (II), it is specific concerning which table is to be constructed from hunk A. But at the point the premise is invoked, there is not yet any particular table which is already constructed from hunk C and which is to be reconstructed in w_2. Consequently, unlike (III), the operative premise is nonspecific concerning the second table in w_2. Thus, given the way in which Kripke's presentation of the argument proceeds, it would appear that the premise actually used asserts that if it is possible for table B to be constructed from hunk A, then it is also possible that table B be constructed from hunk A and in addition hunk C be made into a table, some table or other. Given this premise, we simply apply *modus ponens* to infer the existence of a possible world w_2 in which table B is constructed from hunk A and in which a second, and by (I) distinct, table is constructed from hunk C. Once this inference is drawn, we may then name the second table in w_2 'D'.[3]

---

[3]Actually, there is already a problem in supposing that we may give a name to a merely possible table constructed from hunk C, for in order to name something we must first single it out in some way (by description, ostension, etc.). To suppose that we have singled out one particular possible table from all the rest simply by noting that it is (possibly) constructed from hunk C is to presuppose that there is only one possible

The main strategy contained in this compossibility premise is to expand the original possible world w_1 into a world w_2 by adding to it a new entity, in this case a table. Let us call any such argument for essentialism, i.e., an argument based on a strategy of expanding a possible world into a new world with an additional entity, an *expansion* or *addition argument*. And let us call the particular, partially nonspecific, addition argument for Kripke's essentialist thesis concerning tables *the Nonspecific Expansion Argument for Tables*, or *the Neat Argument*, for short.

More precisely, the compossibility premise of the Neat Argument is the following:

(IV)   For any possible table x and any possible hunks of matter y and y', if it is possible for table x to be originally constructed from hunk y while hunk y' does not overlap with hunk y, and it is also possible for a table to be constructed from hunk y', then it is also possible that table x be originally constructed from hunk y and in addition some table or other x' be originally constructed from hunk y'.

This proposition seems trivial and uncontroversial enough for the purposes at hand, even if it is not something that is entailed by the theory of direct reference. Perhaps some further qualifications must be added (e.g., perhaps hunks y and y' must be assumed to be contemporaneous), but surely some version of (IV) is correct. Moreover, (IV) seems to be true independently of any theory about the essential properties of tables and their constitutive matter.

Given this premise, instead of letting C be any hunk of matter distinct from A, we must add the further stipulation that C does not overlap with A. The conclusion of the argument will not be that a table could not originate from any hunk of matter distinct from its actual (or possible) original matter, but only that a table could not

---

table that *could be* constructed from hunk C; i.e., it is to presuppose the principle that we shall call (V) below. (See Chapter One, footnote 41.) This difficulty in naming merely possible objects is a pragmatic difficulty, not a logical difficulty. In fact, instead of taking the letter 'D' as a name, we may take it along with the other letters 'A', 'B', and 'C' as *free variables* that occurs within a derivation by way of instantiation. This point does not affect the validity of the argument, since free variables are also rigid (under an assignment of values to variables; see Sections 3.1 and 3.2).

originate from any nonoverlapping hunk of matter. This weaker conclusion does not diminish the significance of the argument for our present inquiry, for even this assertion represents a substantive nontrivial essentialist thesis. Surely, if such a thesis can be obtained from the theory of direct reference, then the claim that nontrivial forms of essentialism are derivable from the direct reference theory is vindicated.

25.4. *The Unfinished Argument*

The conclusion that Kripke needs to derive is that table *B* could not originate from hunk *C*, i.e., that there is no possible world in which table *B* is originally constructed from hunk *C*. Since *B* is an arbitrary table in an arbitrary possible world w_1 and *C* is an arbitrary hunk of matter that does not overlap with hunk *A* (*B*'s original constitutive matter in w_1), it will follow from this that if it is possible for a given table to originate from a certain hunk of matter, then it is necessary that the given table originate from that very hunk of matter, or at least from no entirely distinct hunk of matter. The proposition that Kripke actually derives, however, is not that table *B* could not originate from hunk *C*, but rather the assertion that "even if *D* were made by itself, and no table were made from *A*, *D* would not be *B*." That is, what Kripke explicitly derives is the assertion that there is no possible world in which table *D* is identical with table *B*, not even a possible world where table *D* is made by itself and no table is made from hunk *A*. Although this assertion certainly does follow from the principle of the necessity of distinctness together with (I) and the compossibility premise (IV), it is not yet the desired conclusion. So far we have shown only that in any possible world in which table *D* is constructed, *D* still is not the same table as *B*. What we need to show is that in any possible world in which *a table* (meaning *any* table) is made from hunk *C*, *that very table* made from hunk *C* still is not table *B*.

The situation can easily be represented formally. Let '$T(x,y)$' mean "*x* is a table that was originally constructed entirely from all of hunk *y*." We want to show, using only principles from the theory of reference and essentialism-free premises such as (IV), that it is impossible for table *B* to be constructed from hunk *C*:

(*C*1) $\sim\!\Diamond T(B,C)$.

What we have so far succeeded in showing is that in any possible world in which table D is constructed from hunk C, the tables D and B are still distinct:

$(C2)$ $\Box[T(D,C) \rightarrow D \neq B]$.

The desired conclusion $(C1)$ is, of course, trivially equivalent to the assertion that in any possible world in which some table is constructed from hunk C (and hence in any possible world in which some table is constructed from hunk C and table B is not constructed from hunk A), the table constructed from hunk C still is not table B:

$(C3)$ $\Box(x)\,[T(x,C) \rightarrow x \neq B]$.

Conclusion $(C3)$ is formally very similar to our present conclusion $(C2)$. Indeed, it would seem that Kripke's reasoning is aimed in the general direction of something like $(C3)$, since it is equivalent to the desired conclusion $(C1)$. Instead he apparently derives $(C2)$. The issue, however, is not whether table B could be identical with table D, but whether table B could be originally constructed from hunk C instead of from hunk A. Unless there is some way of moving from our present conclusion to the desired conclusion using only premises that are either entailed by the theory of direct reference or free of nontrivial essentialist import, our ambitious attempt to derive essentialism from the theory of reference is unsuccessful. It would be sufficient to be able to infer $(C3)$ from our present conclusion $(C2)$, since $(C3)$ is equivalent to the desired conclusion $(C1)$. But simply ending the derivation with $(C2)$ is not enough.

The fact of the matter is that $(C3)$, though formally very similar to our present conclusion $(C2)$, simply does not follow from it, not even given all of the direct reference theory. Insofar as the Neat Argument for Kripke's essentialist thesis appeals only to principles from the theory of reference together with premises (I) and (IV), it is simply a *non sequitur*. If the Neat Argument is going to live up to its acronym, it must rely on some further premise that has not yet been made explicit. This additional premise must for our purposes be free of any nontrivial essentialist import.

25.5. *A Principle of Cross-World Identification*

How then might we argue from the present premises to the desired conclusion $(C1)$, or $(C3)$? One way would be to make the additional assumption that if it is possible for table D to originate from hunk C, then it is necessary that D originate from hunk C. It would then seem to follow that table B does not originate from hunk C in any possible world, since it is table D that originates from hunk C in every possible world, and since B and D are necessarily distinct.[4] But given the arbitrary way in which hunk C and table D were selected, this additional assumption is tantamount to the assumption that if it is possible for a given table to originate from a certain hunk of matter, then it is necessary that the given table originate from that hunk of matter. Since this assertion is precisely what the Neat Argument was designed to "prove," it obviously cannot be taken as a further premise to the argument. If this were the missing premise, our neat "proof" of essentialism would not only be a failure; it would be a howler.

What Kripke does appear to assume is that in any possible world, any table originating from hunk C is the very table D and no other. More precisely, Kripke appears to assume the following principle as a tacit premise:

(V)   If it is possible for a table x to be originally constructed from a hunk of matter y, then necessarily, any table originally constructed from hunk y is the very table x and no other.

This principle may be symbolized thus:

$$\Box(x)\Box(y)[\Diamond T(x,y) \rightarrow \Box(z)(T(z,y) \rightarrow z = x)].$$

One can easily verify that premises (I), (IV), and (V), together with the principle of the necessity of identity and distinctness, yield Kripke's essentialist conclusion that if it is possible for a given table to originate from a certain hunk of matter, then it is necessary that the given table does not originate from any nonoverlapping hunk of matter:

$$\Box(x)\Box(y)\Box(y')[\Diamond(T(x,y) \wedge$$

$$y \text{ does not overlap with } y') \rightarrow \Box \sim T(x,y')].$$

We may mimic Kripke's apparent reasoning as follows. Let w_1 be some possible world in which an arbitrary table B originates from

---

[4]It is assumed here that only one table can originate from a single hunk of matter within a single possible world. We shall see below that this assumption is probably false. It should also be pointed out that what must be assumed here is that table D originates from hunk C in *every* possible world, including worlds in which D is never constructed at all and does not even exist.

some hunk of matter A. Let C be any hunk of matter that does not overlap with A in w_1. We wish to show that there is no possible world in which table B originates from hunk C. Now either it is possible to construct a table from hunk C or it is not. Suppose first that it is not. (Hunk C is absolutely unmalleable, or whatever.) Then it follows directly that there is no possible world in which table B is originally constructed from hunk C. Suppose now that it is possible to construct a table from hunk C. Then by premise (IV), there is an expanded possible world w_2 in which table B originates from hunk A, just as in w_1, but also in which a second table, which we shall call 'D', originates from hunk C. By premise (I), tables B and D are distinct in w_1. It follows by the necessity of identity and distinctness that tables B and D are distinct in every possible world. (Since B and D are distinct in w_2, they must also be distinct in the actual world. Otherwise, by the necessity of identity, they would be identical in every possible world, including w_2. Since B and D are distinct in the actual world, it follows, by the necessity of distinctness, that B and D are distinct in every possible world.) Now consider an arbitrary possible world w_3 in which some table is constructed from hunk C. Could that table be the very table B from w_1? Given premise (V), it cannot. For by premise (V), the table in question in w_3 is none other than table D, and B and D are distinct entities in every possible world, including w_3. Therefore, there is no possible world in which table B originates from hunk C—$Q.E.D.$

Principle (V) is a crucial component in this piece of reasoning. It tells us that in any possible world, any table originating from hunk C must be D and not B. Without some such additional information, there is no reason to suppose that the table in question in w_3 could not be B. Thus the Neat Argument uses origin as a (necessarily) sufficient condition for being *this very table* in order to prove that origin is also a (necessarily) necessary condition.[5]

---

[5]Recalling a point made in footnote 3, one can see that the theory of direct reference, insofar as it is a theory of *closed* expressions (proper names, natural kind terms, indexicals, perhaps referentially used definite descriptions, etc.) and not a theory of free individual variables, is entirely inessential to the argument. (Cf. Section 23.) The argument requires only (I), (IV), (V), and the principle of the necessity of identity and distinctness taken in the form

$$\Box(x)\Box(y)[\Diamond(x = y) \rightarrow \Box(x = y)],$$

i.e., as a law of modal logic, not as a special assertion of the direct reference theory of proper names. Our point may thus be put as follows. If the argument from (I), (IV),

(*footnote continued on next page*)

The identification principle (V) is quite compelling. In fact, for many of us, (V) or some weakened version of it may be so fundamental to our point of view that it might easily have escaped our notice at first that the reasoning in the informal presentation of the Neat Argument crucially depends on it. But there is a clear sense in which, given our purposes, any reliance on this additional principle simply begs the question of whether nontrivial essentialism is derivable from the theory of direct reference. For premise (V) is a strong essentialist principle concerning tables and their origins. It asserts that if a given table *x* is such that it *might have* originated from a certain hunk of matter *y*, then the given table *x* has as an *essential* property the feature that no table distinct from it originates from hunk *y*. Looked at in another way, it asserts a nontrivial essential property of any hunk of matter *y*, namely, that if any table is constructed from it, it is always the *same* table, or that hunk *y* has, so to speak, only one potential table "in" it.[6] This additional premise is not something that can be obtained from the theory of direct reference unbolstered by any nontrivial metaphysical theory of essentialism. Since in the end the Neat Argument falls back on a hidden essentialist premise that is quite independent of the theory of direct reference, the argument, taken as an attempt to derive essentialism from the direct reference theory, simply does not succeed.[7]

---

and the direct reference theory of proper names to Kripke's essentialist conclusion is valid without the help of (V), then a similar argument for the same conclusion using only (I), (IV), and the logical law mentioned above is equally valid. (The derivation is the same, except that the letters '*A*', '*B*', '*C*', and '*D*' are introduced not as proper names but as free variables obtained by universal and existential instantiation.) But it can be proved model theoretically that the latter argument without (V) is invalid. Therefore, the argument using proper names is also invalid without (V).

[6]More accurately, assuming that intra-world identicals are identical in the absolute, world-independent sense, the principle is simply tantamount to the assertion that any possible table that might have originated from a certain hunk of matter *y* is in fact the *only* possible table that *could* originate from hunk *y*.

[7]Cf. Strawson's remarks concerning the possibility of a different original composition for buildings and ships:

[A particular building]—the Old Bodleian, say—might have been built of (composed of) stone from quarry A instead of being built, as it was, of stone from quarry B.

Will someone say: then it would not have been *this* building, but another just like it? The retort seems insufficiently motivated. Before the building existed, there existed a plan: a plan for a building on *this* site, for *this* purpose, to be constructed of such-and-such type-materials according to such-and-such archetectural specifications. . . . If someone said: 'The *QE II*, you know, might have been built of quite a

It is instructive to compare this argument with a similar addition argument given by Colin McGinn concerning persons and their origins:

> . . . it seems essential that you come from the gametes you actually come from, as the following train of thought makes plain. Suppose, with a view to *reductio,* that I come from Nixon's actual gametes, i.e., consider a world in which this occurs. Now, what is surely com-possible with the first supposition, add my actual gametes to the aforementioned world and suppose they develop into an adult. Which of these individuals has the stronger title to be me? My intuitions seem decisively to favor the latter individual. And the same verdict seems delivered if the counterfactual gametes are similar to mine (1976, p. 132).

McGinn's exposition is informal, but it would seem that his argument is merely a permutation of the sort of addition argument we have been considering (though McGinn's formulation in terms of something's having a "stronger title" to be identical with something is highly suggestive of a certain theory to be criticized in Appendix I). McGinn is explicit in his reliance on a certain intuition concerning the identification of persons across possible worlds, namely, the intuition that in any possible world, any person who springs from the actual gametes of a given individual x is the person x himself or herself. This general principle is the analogue of (V) for the case of persons. It is an exceedingly plausible principle. But it is a general

---

different lot of steel from that which it was actually built of'—and gave his reasons—would it not be absurd to reply: 'In that case it wouldn't have been the *QE II* at all—the *QE II* wouldn't have existed—it would have been a different ship of that name'? (1979, p. 235).

Strawson is concerned here primarily with an epistemic 'might have been', but I have many times heard a similar position taken regarding the *metaphysical* possibility of a different original composition for certain elaborate or artistic human constructions made according to a pre-determined plan and with certain intentions, etc. The view is often coupled with a rival version of essentialism concerning such objects which locates their essence in their Aristotelian formal, efficient, and/or final causes, rather than in their material cause or in the conjunction of the material cause with one or more of the others. (See, e.g., Wiggins, 1980, p. 125.) Our point is that a proponent of this general position, whether it is coupled with a competing version of essentialism or part of a broader anti-essentialism that denies any nontrivial essence to complex things, will almost certainly want to deny such principles as (V) and its analogues. The theory of direct reference *per se* is quite independent of these issues.

principle of essentialism nonetheless, and would certainly be rejected by any anti-essentialist. It asserts of any person other than McGinn that he or she could not originate from McGinn's actual gametes. This thesis, of course, is entirely separate from the theory of direct reference.

Although Kripke never discusses in print how one might establish general essentialist principles of the form of (27) concerning natural kinds, such as (22') and its analogues, it is easy to see how one might construct an addition argument for the principle that, if a substance S might have had a chemical structure C, then substance S is such that it could not have any chemical structure other than C. We assume the following two premises:

> If it is possible for a substance S to have a chemical structure C, and C' is any chemical structure distinct from C, then it is also possible for substance S to have chemical structure C whereas some *other* substance S' has chemical structure C'.

> If it is possible for a substance S' to have a chemical structure C', then it is necessary that any substance having the chemical structure C' is substance S' and no other.

Given these two premises, we reason exactly as before to the desired conclusion. Though it may indeed be by way of this addition argument that one arrives at general essentialist principles concerning natural kinds, the same remarks made above concerning premise (V) of the original Neat Argument apply with equal force to the second premise of this addition argument concerning substances. Like (V), this premise is a nontrivial essentialist principle concerning substances. It is philosophically controversial to the extent that any thoroughgoing anti-essentialist would certainly reject it. Moreover, it is logically quite independent of the theory of direct reference.

As it is stated, (V) (and its analogues) may be too strong. Principle (V) asserts that any table z that originates from the actual constitutive matter of a given table x must be the very table x. It does not require that the table z be constructed *in the same way* that x is actually constructed, following the same design, or anything of the sort. All it requires is that the table z be constructed from the same matter. It is not at all clear, however, that this is sufficient. Suppose that, in some other possible world w, the constitutive matter of a given table x is shaped into a table that is radically different from x

in design and structure. Suppose, for instance, that the portion of matter that actually makes up the top surface of x goes instead to make up the legs of the table in w, and so on. Would the table in w nevertheless be one and the same entity as the original table x, since it is constructed in w from the same matter that x is actually constructed from?[8] Principle (V) may be replaced with the following, considerably weaker, assertion:

(V')   If it is possible for a given table x to be originally constructed from a certain hunk of matter y *according to a certain plan P,* then necessarily any table originally constructed from hunk y *according to precisely the same plan P* is the very table x and no other.

(One may wish to weaken this principle even further by making reference not only to the configuration of the matter of table x but also to such factors as the artisan who constructs x, the artisan's reasons for constructing x, the time and place of the construction, and so on.) Principle (V') together with (I) and a correspondingly strengthened version of the original premise (IV) still yield the intended essentialist conclusion concerning tables and their origins.[9]

Principle (V') is exceedingly plausible, almost to the point of being indubitable. If two tables in two different possible worlds are constructed from the very same stuff in precisely the same way and, let us assume, with exactly the same structure atom for atom, how can they fail to be the very same table? What more could one ask? What more is there to being *this very table*? The fact remains, however, that even the weaker (V') is a substantive metaphysical principle that is not entailed by the theory of direct reference. It is supported by a set of intuitions that are entirely separable from our intuitions concerning reference and intensionality.

[8]Similar questions can be raised with regard to McGinn's principle concerning persons and their origins. Intuitions may differ in the two cases.

[9]The strengthened version of (IV) that is needed is the following:

> For any possible table x, any possible hunks of matter y and y', *and any plan P,* if it is possible for table x to be originally constructed from hunk y while hunk y' does not overlap with y, and it is also possible for a table to be constructed from hunk y' *according to plan P,* then it is also possible that table x be originally constructed from hunk y and in addition some table x' be originally constructed from hunk y' *according to plan P.*

If premise (V') is weakened by including reference to the table's artisan, time, and place, then premise (IV) must be strengthened accordingly.

25.6. An Alternative Argument

We extracted the Neat Argument from the passage from Kripke quoted in Section 25.1 above. But this is not the only addition argument that can be extracted from Kripke's presentation of the derivation of his essentialist thesis. Let us consider again the relevant passage, but this time we shall take certain liberties, indicated by brackets, in quoting the argument:

> Let '*B*' be a name (rigid designator) of a table, let '*A*' name the piece of wood from which it actually came. Let '*C*' name another piece of wood. [Suppose a table *D* were made from *C* and no table were made from *A*.] Then suppose *B* were made from *A*, as in the actual world, but also [the other] table *D* were simultaneously made from *C* [as in the second world]. . . . Now in this situation *B* ≠ *D*; hence even [where] *D* [was] made by itself, and no table [was] made from *A*, *D* [is not] *B*.

This is a slightly different argument from the Neat Argument. It starts out the same: We begin by assuming the existence of a possible world w_1 (or the actual world) in which a table *B* is constructed from a hunk of matter *A*, and *C* is an entirely distinct, nonoverlapping hunk of matter. We wish to show that there is no possible world *w* in which table *B* is constructed from hunk *C*, i.e., conclusion (*C*1). At this point the reasoning diverges from the Neat Argument. We derive (*C*1) not by immediately applying a compossibility premise to our assumption of w_1, but by first making an additional assumption in order to derive (*C*1)'s equivalent (*C*2), i.e., that in any possible world *w* in which a table is constructed from hunk *C*, that table is not the very same table as *B*, but a different table. Assume an arbitrary possible world *w* in which an arbitrary table *D* is constructed from hunk *C*. We need only show that *D* ≠ *B* in *w*, and we are done. To do this, we invoke a compossibility premise like (IV) to construct an expanded possible world w_2 containing both table *B*, constructed from hunk *A* as in w_1, and table *D*, constructed from hunk *C* as in *w*. By (I), *B* ≠ *D* in w_2. It follows by the necessity of identity and distinctness that *B* ≠ *D* in *w*—Q.E.D.

This argument is an addition argument, but unlike the Neat Argument, it does not employ the cross-world identification principle (V), or anything as strong, as a premise. It makes do with (I), the necessity of identity and distinctness, and a compossibility premise analogous to (IV). In the Neat Argument, (IV) is used to swell the ranks of the tables in the initial world w_1 by constructing a new, nonspecific table from hunk *C*. In the present argument, the addition strategy is more specific. In addition to the world w_1, we assume a second, arbitrary world *w* containing a table constructed from hunk *C*. It is only after this second assumption is made that compossibility is invoked, creating a more table-filled world not merely by nonspecific expansion of w_1, but by *fusing* both of the initial worlds w_1 and *w*, with their particular tables *B* and *D*, into an expanded world w_2. This higher degree of specificity in constructing the expanded world w_2 makes further reliance on the essentialist (V) unnecessary.

Let us call addition arguments employing this more specific addition strategy *fusion arguments*. Let us call the particular addition argument just presented *the Fusion Argument for Tables*, or *the Fat Argument*, for short.

We have already encountered the compossibility premise operative in the Fat Argument. It is none other than

(III)   For any possible tables *x* and *x'*, and any possible hunks of matter *y* and *y'*, if it is possible for table *x* to be originally constructed from hunk *y* while hunk *y'* does not overlap with hunk *y*, and it is also possible for table *x'* to be originally constructed from hunk *y'*, then it is also possible that table *x* be originally constructed from hunk *y* and in addition table *x'* be originally constructed from hunk *y'*.

If this compossibility premise is free of nontrivial essentialist import in the way that (IV) is (or is itself a consequence of the theory of direct reference), then the Fat Argument succeeds, for our purposes, where the Neat Argument failed. For the Fat Argument generates the same essentialist conclusion as the Neat Argument without invoking the latter argument's extra essentialist premise (V).

Unfortunately (III), unlike (IV), is nontrivially essentialist, in our sense, though perhaps not obviously so. Principle (III) trivially entails, by letting *x* and *x'* be the same, that if it is merely possible for a given table *x* to originate from a certain hunk of matter *y*, then it is in fact necessary that the given table *x* does not originate from any nonoverlapping hunk of matter *y'*, *provided that* it is impossible for the given table *x* to be constructed entirely from all of hunk *y* and in addition entirely from all of the distinct hunk *y'*. In fact, this special instance of (III), with *x* and *x'* the same, is the only instance actually needed in the Fat Argument. Although this premise is slightly weaker than Kripke's essentialist thesis without the additional proviso, it hardly has any less essentialist import. (See Chapter Three, footnote 3.)[10] Moreover, it is fairly obvious that this premise is no mere consequence of the theory of direct reference.

There are at least two reasons why premise (III), although nontrivially essentialist, appears at first glance to be no more objectionable than the less specific compossibility premise (IV). One reason is that the bound variables '*x*' and '*x*'' occurring in the statement of (III) are distinct, and consequently the reader immediately thinks of instances where these two variables take on distinct entities as values. For *distinct* tables *x* and *x*', principle (III) is quite plausible, and indeed quite free of any nontrivial essentialist import.

The other reason that (III), though essentialist, might appear metaphysically hollow at first blush is that (III), and (IV) as well, are reminiscent of, and easily confused with, (II), the least specific of the three compossibility principles. Principle (II) is a perfectly trivial and uncontroversial truth, but by the same token, like (IV), it is too weak to take us from (I) and the necessity of identity and distinctness to nontrivial essentialism.

26. COMPOSSIBILITY PRINCIPLES AND CROSS-WORLD IDENTIFICATION PRINCIPLES

Loosely speaking, all that separates (III) and (IV) from their nonspecific counterpart (II) is the Neat Argument's premise (V), the principle that sameness of original constitutive matter is a sufficient condition for the cross-world identification of tables. Principle (II) together with (V) entail both (III) and (IV). In fact, what I want to

---

[10]See also footnote 5 above, which applies *mutatis mutandis* to the Fat Argument. The argument yields nontrivial essentialism using only (I), the special instance of (III), and the necessity of identity and distinctness taken as a logical law. We are granting that (I) is philosophically uncontroversial. The essentialist import of the logical law is only trivial haecceity essentialism. The nontrivial, substantive essentialism comes entirely from (III).

Kripke has informed me in discussion of these issues that it was in fact the Fat Argument, not the Neat Argument, that he had in mind when he wrote his footnote—though he acknowledges that the footnote is so compressed as to admit an interpretation resulting in the Neat Argument. (He did not use these names, of course. See Salmon, 1979b and the first page of the preface of the book edition of *Naming and Necessity,* especially its second footnote.) It should be noted again here that Kripke has also informed me that it was probably not part of his intention in his footnote to derive a nontrivial version of essentialism without relying on anything essentialist beyond the theory of direct reference. See Chapter Three, footnote 11.

suggest, roughly, is that nonspecific compossibility principles like (II) are typically the source of specific compossibility principles like (III). Whatever plausibility there is to (III) rests largely on the obviousness of (II). If we believe (III), we do so in some sense *because* we believe (II), and we are prone to make cross-world identifications of the sort licensed by (V) or (V'). Of course, one may believe (III) for other reasons, without basing it on (II) and (V'), but the intuitive obviousness of (II) together with a deep-seated inclination to reason in accordance with (V') provide a natural and compelling basis for (III). The idea is something like this: In some sense, we first recognize the obvious truth of (II). Then, making the cross-world identifications, we also assent to the more specific principles (III) and (IV). Thus, (III) and (IV) are, as it were, the epistemic progeny of (II) and (V). Both (III) and (IV) closely resemble their parent (II), but (III) remains nonessentialist like (II), whereas (IV) is essentialist, inheriting its essentialist import from (V).

Of course, the anti-essentialist who rejects (V) and (V') may still accept (IV) on its own hook, so to speak, or on the basis of some very general anti-essentialist principle, e.g., that anything not provably contradictory is possible (assuming that, given the appropriate axioms, the supposition that the same table is originally constructed entirely from all of each of two distinct hunks of matter is a provable contradiction). But what I am suggesting is that, for many of us, the identification principle embodied in (V') plays some role in our acceptance of at least (III), if not (IV) as well. Such cross-world identification principles, though typically not explicit, are fundamental to a very common point of view—perhaps the *ordinary* point of view—concerning what would remain true if a certain portion of matter were made into an object such as a table. These identification principles are so central to the common point of view, so deeply internalized, that it may often completely escape our notice when our modal thinking—as in the informal Neat Argument, and if my speculations are correct, in the Fat Argument as well—depends crucially on just such identifications.[11]

This is not to say that all such cross-world identification principles are categorically true, or to forget their nontrivial essentialist import. It is only to suggest that they play a basic structural or organizational role in our modal thinking, or at least in the standard modal

---

[11]See also Chapter Two, footnote 5.

thinking of many of us. The anti-essentialist philosopher may still consistently deny these principles. In so doing, the anti-essentialist may go against the grain of the way many of us organize our thought about certain counterfactual situations, but so far, it would seem that acceptance of the theory of direct reference *per se* presents no obstacle whatsoever to the anti-essentialist position. The two positions are perfectly compatible. (Cross-world identification principles like (V′) are discussed and scrutinized in Appendix I below.)

Conclusion

The case has not been successfully made that nontrivial forms of essentialism concerning natural kinds or concrete individuals, such as artifacts or organisms, are genuine (modal logical) consequences of the theory of direct reference supplemented only by premises themselves philosophically uncontroversial and free of nontrivial essentialist import. Each of the arguments that appear to derive nontrivial forms of essentialism from the philosophy of language involve in the end some hidden nontrivial essentialist premise or other that cannot be shown—or at the very least, *has not* been shown—to be itself completely reducible in some way to the philosophy of language. Our essentialist intuitions aside, the theory of direct reference seems perfectly compatible with the claim that examples such as 'Water is H_2O', 'Tigers are mammals', and 'This very table originated from hunk of wood H' presented in Section 8.1 are contingent *a posteriori* rather than necessary *a posteriori*. No conclusive reason has yet been given to suppose that the essentialist principles entailing the necessitations of these statements are anything but what they appear to be: theses stemming from an irreducibly metaphysical, and philosophically controversial, theory of essentialism, a theory that is no mere consequence of the philosophy of language.

The theory of direct reference bears directly on several important issues in philosophical semantics. We have seen, for instance, that it entails that proper names are rigid designators, and hence it entails the existence of certain necessary but apparently *a posteriori* truths, e.g., that Hesperus is identical with Phosphorus. The theory might also entail the existence of certain contingent but *a priori* truths, e.g., that Neptune is a planet causing perturbations in the orbit of Uranus (*a priori* for Leverrier). We have seen that the theory even entails a certain trivial form of essentialism, e.g., that Hesperus is such that it could not fail to have the property of *being Phosphorus,* and hence

217

also such properties as that of *being a planet if Phosphorus is*. But one must be careful not to let the banners fly too high, and take the theory to solve difficult philosophical problems that are in fact beyond its scope. It is indeed a powerful and interesting theory, but it is not the philosophical panacea that it is sometimes thought to be.*

*As we mentioned in the Introduction, Kripke has brought his theory of direct reference to bear on classical philosophical issues in the philosophy of mind, specifically the mind-body identity theory. Using rigid designator theory, Kripke challenges the identity theorists to provide a plausible account for the prevailing intuition that any connection between mental events, such as sensations, and physical events taking place in the central nervous system is contingent, and that events of one kind could occur even in the absence of events of the other kind. Kripke's arguments have been vigorously criticized on the grounds that they rely heavily on a contention that anything which is in fact a pain sensation is such that it *must* have its actual characteristic phenomenological quality, and could not have the feel of a tickle—an essentialist thesis that would certainly be denied by any mind-body identity theorist. See for instance Feldman, 1973; Lycan, 1974, p. 684; and Rorty, 1973; see also Rorty, 1979, p. 111n. Kripke's critics generally take it for granted that essentialist theses concerning sensations are fundamentally metaphysical in nature, and quite independent of the theory of direct reference. Kripke anticipates this objection, and defends his challenge to the identity theorist by appealing to intuition:

> Can any case of essence be more obvious than the fact that *being a pain* is a necessary property of each pain? . . . Consider a particular pain, or other sensation, that you once had. Do you find it at all plausible that *that very sensation* could have existed without being a sensation, the way a certain inventor (Franklin) could have existed without being an inventor? (1972a, p. 146).

Kripke seems to acknowledge that his challenge to the identity theory relies on certain essentialist intuitions that may be completely independent of the theory of reference, but others have taken Kripke's arguments to constitute a refutation of mind-body identity, one that relies primarily on theses from the philosophy of language. To these philosophers the point made by Kripke's critics is a sound one. The theory of direct reference taken by itself says nothing either for or against mind-body identity.

We have investigated the more fundamental question of whether nontrivial forms of essentialism are genuine consequences of the theory of direct reference. We are driven to the conclusion that they are not. The theory of direct reference, in combination with purely empirically verifiable or otherwise philosophically uncontroversial premises, says nothing either for or against nontrivial Aristotelian essentialism. The theory of direct reference can no more solve the difficult problems of essentialism (which properties of a thing are essential properties?) than it can solve the mind-body problem.

APPENDIX I · *Principles of Cross-World Identification*

27. CROSS-WORLD IDENTIFICATION PRINCIPLES AND THE SHIP OF THESEUS

27.1. An Argument for Contingent Identity

In Chapter Seven it was suggested that essentialist cross-world identification principles along the lines of (V)—the principle that if it is possible for a table x to be made from certain matter, then it is necessary that any table made from that matter is x—may represent fundamental features of the ordinary way of thinking about certain counterfactural situations. What is especially interesting is that principle (V), and even the weaker principle (V')—that if it is possible for a table x to be originally constructed (by a certain artisan in a certain place at a certain time) from certain matter according to a certain plan, then it is necessary that any table originally constructed (by that artisan in that place at that time) from that matter according to that plan is the table x—conflict with certain plausible views regarding identity and the possibility of change in the physical composition of an object. This fact becomes apparent if we consider an argument given by Hugh Chandler (1975) against the theory of direct reference.[1] Following Hobbes' depiction from *De Corpore* of the story of the Ship of Theseus, Chandler describes two possible worlds, let us call them 'W' and 'W'', in which the component planks of a certain ship a are very gradually removed one by one beginning at time t_1, each plank set aside for later use. In W each plank removed from a is immediately replaced by a new and different plank, so that at the end of this process of removal and replacement at time t_2, there stands a ship c composed of entirely different materials in the place where a once stood. Some time later at time t_3, the wood removed plank by plank from the original ship a is reshaped following the original plan into a

---

[1] A similar argument is given by Allan Gibbard (1975).

ship *b* distinct from c.[2] Following Chandler, we may diagram *W* as in figure 1.

Chandler claims that it would be reasonable to describe this situation by saying that, taken individually, both *b* and *c* have a *prima facie* claim to being the same ship as *a*, though for different reasons. Ship *b* is made at t_3 of the very same wood as ship *a* at t_1. Ship *c*, on the other hand, is linked to the original ship *a* by a special sort of spatiotemporal continuity. Taken together, Chandler wishes to maintain that being made of the same matter provides only a *recessive claim* for being the original ship *a*, whereas the special spatiotemporal continuity provides a *dominant claim*. Thus ship *c* wins out over ship *b*; in this situation, *a* and *c* are one and the same ship, whereas *b* is simply a new ship assembled from *a*'s original planks.[3]

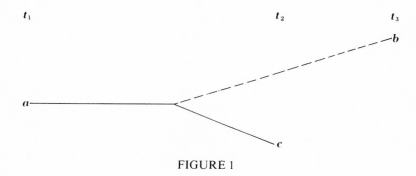

FIGURE 1

[2]Chandler lets $t_2 = t_3$, but his argument is made slightly more plausible if ship *b* is constructed sometime after ship *c*.

Here and throughout this appendix I shall not distinguish sharply between a plank of wood and its matter, or its "hunk" of wood, though no doubt there is a distinction, since the wood that constitutes the plank can presumably survive the destruction of the plank and since different, albeit overlapping, portions of matter constitute the same plank at different times. See Chapter Seven, footnote 2. I blur this distinction out of necessity of exposition, since the problem of the Ship of Theseus is best formulated in terms of planks (constituent parts), though the relation between the ship and its matter is no less relevant to the problem, as we shall see. The conflation is not a serious defect here. Generally speaking, as far as this discussion of the problem is concerned, what is true of the constituent parts is true of the constitutive matter, and vice-versa. Nevertheless, I shall maintain a sharp distinction between the ship itself and its matter (or planks), for this distinction is indeed crucial to the discussion.

[3]Cf. the quote from McGinn in Section 25.5 above. See also Hirsch, 1976, pp. 27–28.

It is not clear that the identification of ship *a* with ship *c* is universally correct. Suppose, for instance, that *a* is an historically important ship, say Columbus's *Nina,* and that some unscrupulous philosopher had been commissioned to disassemble this ship, transport its disassembled parts to the Smithsonian Institution in Washington, D.C., and reassemble it there, all over a very long period of time. Suppose further that, intending to perpetrate a hoax on the authorities, this scoundrel carefully replaces each plank by a new one before removing the next. He then smugly transports the original planks to Washington, for reassembly, believing that the real *Nina* remains standing in his garage. If the authorities discovered what had been done, they would be quite content to let this foolish rascal keep the ship standing in his garage. For it is nothing more than a *replica* of the genuine *Nina,* which is now disassembled, though its parts are safe and sound in Washington awaiting reassembly.[4]

There are other cases, however, which seem to go the other way. If, for instance, my dead body cells over a period of several years were collected, revived, and fused together to form a living human being, it is quite clear that this cloned individual would not be me, even though in many respects he would be more like my former self than I am. And it is equally clear that even if my dead body cells were fused into a human body, I would still have the same body now that I have always had, so that my clone must have a different body than the body I used to have (and still have). The case of Chandler's possible world *W* is not so clear-cut as either of these two cases. Let us simply assume, for the sake of argument, that Chandler is correct and that in this situation *a* is the same ship as *c*.

Chandler describes the second possible world *W'* by stipulating that in *W'*, "... *a*'s planks [are] removed one by one *without being replaced. b* is then constructed as in [*W*]. In this case *a* and *b* are the same ship. What it comes to is that [a ship] is transported from one place to another by being disassembled and then reassembled." Chandler diagrams *W'* as in figure 2.

In this situation, on Chandler's view, *b*'s recessive claim to being the same ship as *a* stands unchallenged, in view of the absence of any rival claimants. Thus, in this world *a* is identical with *b*. Chandler draws conclusions from this that are clearly incompatible with the theory of direct reference. The ships *a* and *b*, according to Chandler, are identical in *W'* but distinct in *W*. Hence it seems that some

---

[4] I owe the example to David Kaplan. A similar example has been given by Kripke in lectures, and another by Wiggins (1980, pp. 93–94).

FIGURE 2

identities are contingent. Furthermore, if '*b*' is a proper name, then it is a nonrigid proper name. For with respect to *W'* it denotes the ship *a*, but with respect to *W* it denotes instead a new and different ship. Hence it also seems that some proper names are nonrigid.

27.2. *A Fallacy*

From the point of view of the theory of direct reference, Chandler's argument involves a fundamental mistake. The mistake occurs when he uses the letter '*b*' to name two objects in different possible worlds without first settling the question of whether they are indeed the same object. It is true that a possible world may be given, as it were, "by stipulation." We say "Consider a possible world in which so and so exists, and has such and such properties. . . ," where we mean by this "Suppose that so and so had such and such properties. . . ." It is perfectly legitimate, therefore, for Chandler to begin with the hypothesis that the ship *a* exists in both *W* and *W'*, and that its planks are gradually removed, with replacement in *W* and without replacement in *W'*, and that its original planks are later reassembled in both worlds. But once certain stipulations have been made, one is automatically barred from making further stipulations that are not

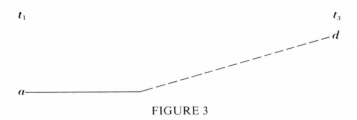

FIGURE 3

compossible with the initial stipulations, on pain of "stipulating" an *impossible* state of affairs. In Chandler's example, once the ship constructed at t_3 in W has been christened 'b', it is illegitimate to refer to the ship constructed in W' at t_3 by the very same name. According to the theory of direct reference, to do so is to presuppose that the two ships are one and the same. To guard against such "overstipulation," the ship constructed at t_3 in W' should be given a neutral name, say 'd'. W' would then be diagrammed as in figure 3.

With this correction made, we can now raise the question of whether d is b and can, therefore, be given the same name. Given some of Chandler's assumptions about identity through time, one can actually *prove* from the point of view of the theory of direct reference that b and d are in fact distinct entities. For, by hypothesis, $a = d$ but $a \neq b$. Hence $d \neq b$. This proof presupposes one version of haecceitism, viz., the view that it makes sense to identify, in an *absolute* sense, individuals in different possible worlds. The proof also presupposes the principle that objects identical *within* a possible world are identical in the absolute sense of being numerically one and the very same object, and vice-versa. These are presuppositions of the theory of direct reference. It is important to notice, however, that Chandler himself seems to be working within a haecceitist framework, since his initial hypothesis is that a certain ship a exists in two different possible worlds, W and W'. Moreover, he also seems to rely on the assumption that intra-world identicals are identical in the absolute sense.[5] This is indicated by his conclusion that the name 'b'

---

[5]In fact, we have seen that there is a certain sense in which these two assumptions go hand in hand. See Chapter Four, footnote 18. It should be noted, however, that Chandler shows some sympathy for the view that objects that are intra-world identical are not *ipso facto* identical in an absolute sense. Gibbard's argument, which is similar in thrust to Chandler's, is coupled with an explicit and emphatic rejection of haecceitism.

223

denotes ship *a* with respect to *W'*. We may grant that '*b*' denotes *b* with respect to *W'*, and according to Chandler, ship *b* is identical with ship *a within W'*. But it does not follow directly that '*b*' also denotes *a* with respect *W'* unless *a* is identical with *b* in the absolute sense of being one and the very same thing.[6] From the point of view of the theory of direct reference, Chandler's argument that some proper names are nonrigid commits a fallacy of equivocation. It depends crucially on the illegitimate use of a single expression as a name for what are, following his own view, two distinct objects.[7]

27.3. *A Better Theory*

We conclude then that it is incorrect to describe the relationship between Chandler's two possible worlds by saying that there is a single thing, *b*, composed in both worlds at t_3 of ship *a*'s original planks and having a recessive claim to be the same ship as *a*. As Chandler notes, the theory of dominant and recessive rival identity claims is incompatible with the principle of the necessity of identity and distinctness. For if a thing *x* can have a "recessive claim" to be the same thing as *y*, then in those worlds where there is no rival claimant *x* = *y*, but in those worlds where a dominant rival is present, $x \neq y$. Hence, as we have just shown, the theory is also incompatible with the view that intra-world identity is genuine identity, that *x* and *y* are identical in a world *w* if and only if *x* and *y* are, in an absolute

---

[6] The necessitation, or intra-world version, of Leibniz's Law, $x =_w y \rightarrow [F_w(x) \leftrightarrow F_w(y)]$, applies only to intra-world attributes *F*. The notion of denotation involved here is not intra-world denotation *within W'*, but extra-world denotation *with respect to W'*. See Sections 3.2 and 13.2

[7] The basic criticism of Chandler given thus far has been given in one form or another in Cook, 1979; Del Carril, 1978; King, 1978; Wiggins, 1980, pp. 95, 207–209; and by myself in Salmon, 1979b. The other authors mentioned here are not concerned in their criticism with the bearing of the problem on addition arguments for essentialism.

In fairness to Chandler, it should be noted that his discussion leaves some reason to believe that he may be using the letter '*b*' as an abbreviation for some nonrigid definite description, such as 'the ship constructed at t_3 from such-and-such planks'. Insofar as Chandler's argument depends on the premise that proper names are sometimes synonymous with descriptions, it is not so much an *argument* against the theory of direct reference as it is merely its denial.

I am not interested here in trying to settle the issues that separate the direct reference theorists from Chandler and Gibbard, but rather in pointing out an erstwhile unnoticed connection between the theory of direct reference and such cross-world identification principles as (V) and (V').

sense, one and the very same thing. (See Chapter Four, footnote 18). Of course, one may maintain the principle that intra-world identicals are absolutely identical and retain the jargon of "dominant" and "recessive" identity claims, but these terms then lose their *raison d'être*. Given the principle, 'dominant' becomes just another word for 'true', and 'recessive' just another word for 'false'. For what is this thing *x* having only a "recessive claim" to be identical with *y*? Not *y* itself, since *y* surely has a dominant claim to be *y*. Therefore it must be something else, and its claim to be *y* is a lie. The only object having a "dominant claim" to be *y* is *y* itself, and any object having only a "recessive claim" is an imposter. Recessiveness collapses into absolute distinctness.

At this point the reader may have the uneasy feeling that there may be a baby somewhere in the bath water—and well you should. There must be *something* to the theory of recessive identity claims, some kernel of truth that it is trying to capture. For given that we may be inclined to distinguish the ships *a* and *b* in *W* but to identify the ships *a* and *d* in *W'*, there is some sense in which the presence of ship *c* at t_2 in *W* makes all the difference in the world. Were it not for the process of replenishment that results in ship *c*, it would have been true that the ship constructed from *a*'s original planks at t_3 is none other than the ship *a* reassembled. *Something* about ship *b*, some aspect of it, is recessive with respect to the corresponding aspect of ship *c*, which is dominant. What is it, if not its haecceity or its "claim" or "title" to be identical with ship *a*?

The answer is *its matter*. Let us call the hunk of matter that makes up the ship *a* at t_1 in *W* and *W'* '*a'*'. Let us also call the hunk of matter that makes up the ship *b* at t_3 in *W* '*b'*', and let us call the hunk of matter that makes up ship *c* at t_2 in *W* '*c'*'. Then with hunks of matter differentiated appropriately, there are the following salient facts concerning these hunks: (*i*) $a' = b'$; (*ii*) $a' \neq c'$, but *c'* is linked to *a'* from t_1 to t_3 in *W* by a special sort of spatiotemporal continuity; and (*iii*) ship *d* is made from hunk *b'* at t_3 in *W'*.[8] Fact (*i*), together

---

[8] These facts illustrate how the phrase 'hunk of matter' is being used throughout our discussion here and in Chapter Seven. One might insist that, in the usual or ordinary sense of the phrase, if the hunks of matter *a'* and *c'* are linked by an appropriate sort of spatiotemporal continuity, then they are one and the same hunk of matter. Perhaps some other phrase, e.g., 'portion of matter', would better serve our purpose. There is *something* salient that ship *a* has at t_1 in common with ship *b* at t_3 but not with ship *c* at

with the fact that hunk b' is in the same configuration at time t_3 and is shaped with the same purpose and function (viz., that of *a ship*) as hunk a' at time t_1, give hunk b'—not ship b itself, but its constitutive matter—a claim in W to *constitute* at t_3 the same ship a that hunk a' *constitutes* at t_1. This claim of hunk b' is a recessive one. Fact (*ii*), together with the fact that hunk c' retains at time t_3 the same configuration, constituting something of the same purpose and function, as hunk a' at time t_1, give hunk c' a dominant claim in W to constitute the same ship as hunk a'. Hence, in the world W, hunk c' wins out over hunk b', and the ship it constitutes at t_3 is identical with the ship constituted by hunk a' at t_1, i.e., $a = c$. Hunk b' also constitutes a ship at t_3 in the world W', just as it does in W. But in W' there is no rival claimant dominating over hunk b', which by fact (*i*), again, has a claim in W', albeit a recessive one, to constitute the same ship at t_3 that hunk a' constitutes at t_1. Therefore, lacking a challenger in W', hunk b' constitutes the same ship at t_3 that hunk a' constitutes at t_1. By fact (*iii*), this ship is none other than ship d, i.e., $a = d$ (not b, but d). Thus there does seem to be some playoff between dominant and recessive forces present in the first possible world but absent in the second. In W, hunk b' does not constitute the same ship at t_3 that hunk a' constitutes at t_1, because of the presence at t_3 of a rival hunk of matter with a stronger title to constitute ship a. In W', on the other hand, hunk b' does constitute the same ship at t_3 that hunk a constitutes at t_1, as it were, by forfeit.

Let us call the theory embodied in this alternative account of the two worlds *the theory of dominant and recessive rival constitution claims*. This theory has all of the charm and appeal of the theory of dominant and recessive rival identity claims, but none of the serious drawbacks. It provides a perfectly coherent account of the situation Chandler describes, preserving the intuitive element of truth in the recessive identity account. The major difference between the two accounts is in the contingencies they impute. The theory of dominant and recessive identity claims makes certain identities contingent. The

---

t_2, some aspect in which a and b coincide across time in a way that a and c do not. Though ship a is distinct from ship b, b is made at t_3 of *the very same matter* that ship a was made of at t_1. We use 'b'' to name *the very matter* that makes up ship b at t_3, and we use 'c'' to name *the very matter* that makes up ship c at t_2. We call these, perhaps incorrectly or unconventionally, 'hunks of matter'. I believe that this use of the phrase coincides with that of Kripke, from whom our discussion took the phrase. See Chapter Seven, footnote 2.

only contingencies ascribed by the recessive constitution account are matters of which concrete artifact is constituted by a certain portion of matter at a certain time, or whether portions of matter x' and y' constitute the same or a different artifact at different times—and not even all of these facts need come out contingent. In Chandler's example, hunk b' has a recessive, and therefore only contingent, claim to constitute the ship a at t_3. In some worlds ship a is made of hunk b' at t_3, and in other worlds where both a and b' exist, a is not made of b' at t_3. Similarly, hunk c' is only contingently linked to hunk a' by the relevant sort of spatiotemporal continuity. In some worlds ship a is made of hunk c' at t_2, and in other worlds where both a and c' exist, perhaps even W', a is not made of c' at t_2. Even so, the theory can accommodate Kripke's form of essentialism concerning artifacts, by allowing that in every possible world in which ship a exists it *first* comes into existence made (substantially) of hunk a' $[= b']$. All that need be contingent is the fact of which matter constitutes ship a at times later than a's original construction. Unlike the recessive identity account, all of the identities asserted by the recessive constitution account may be taken to be necessary truths, asserting a relation of absolute numerical identity. Ship a is one and the very same ship as ship c, but hunk a' is absolutely distinct from hunk c'. Hunk a' is hunk b', although ship a is distinct from ship b. These facts are necessary facts. In particular, it is contingent whether hunk b' constitutes ship a at t_3, but it is necessary that $b \neq a$.[9]

Assuming that the theory of dominant and recessive constitution claims yields the correct account of Chandler's two worlds, we might say that the mistake in the theory of dominant and recessive identity claims is traceable to the common confusion between the 'is' of identity and what Wiggins (1980, pp. 30–35) calls the 'is' of constitution. Hunk b' has a recessive claim to be (constitutive of) the same thing that hunk a' is (constitutive of). But ship b has no *real* claim, recessive or otherwise, to be (identical with) the same thing that ship a is (identical with).

---

[9]There may be some temptation to say that $d = a$ in W' *because* there is no rival hunk of matter in W' dominating over d's constitutive matter b' at t_3, or that the fact in W' that hunk b' constitutes the same ship at t_3 that hunk a' constitutes at t_1 *determines* that $d = a$ in W'. But these assertions are mistaken, since they make a necessary fact dependent on a contingent fact. What these contingent facts determine is not that $d = a$ but the further contingent fact that the ship made at t_3 of hunk $b' = a$, i.e., that hunk b' constitutes ship a at t_3.

One reason that it is tempting to use the same expression as a name for each of the two ships constructed at t_3 in W and W' is that they are made of the same matter, and we may forget that we are christening the ship itself rather than naming its matter. More likely, we may fail to distinguish sharply between the ship and its matter. Another reason, perhaps closely related to those just mentioned, is that the two ships are constructed from the same matter, and, as argued in Section 25.7, we are strongly inclined to think in accordance with cross-world identification principles like (V').[10] One must be careful here not to confuse cross-world identity with cross-time identity. Chandler's example is unusually complex in that it involves elements of both. An analogue of (V') for the case of ships would assert that any two ships constructed from the very same matter *in different possible worlds,* according to precisely the same plan, must be the very same ship. This is a *modal* principle. It would identify the two ships b and d across W and W'. It would also identify the ships a and b within W, though that may be less obvious. A corresponding *temporal* principle for the case of ships would identify any two ships at different times *within a single possible world* provided only that they were made of the same matter. Such a principle would also identify a and b within W, but it would not identify b and d across W and W'. In adopting a certain point of view concerning cross-time identity and spatiotemporal continuity, Chandler has rejected any such naive principle of identity through time. What I want to suggest is that the modal principle may still be operant within us even after we have rejected the corresponding temporal principle. Unconscious and uncritical thinking in accordance with a modal principle like (V') would lead us to identify b and d across possible worlds, and consequently to give them the same name. We may be prone to make this identification even in philosophically sophisticated contexts in which our sensititivty to issues involving identity and change is considerably heightened. The fact is, however, that given our assumptions about identity, principles such as (V') are incompatible with the plausible view that a given object can maintain its identity through time by an appropriate sort of spatiotemporal continuity

[10]The preceding discussion may suggest that principles like (V') may themselves be traceable to the principle of the necessity of identity and distinctness and a "confusion," or perhaps an *assimilation,* of the 'is' of identity with the 'is' of constitution. The question of how this idea might be developed may be worthy of further research.

though its matter is frequently replenished. Insofar as there are possible situations structurally similar to *W* in which this view concerning identity through time is correct, principles like (V') which allow for cross-world identification of individuals by way of more fundamental particulars are in need of further refinement. Addition arguments for essentialism that rely on principles like (V') must make do with even weaker versions if they are going to hold up under careful scrutiny.

Principles like (V') can be reformulated to handle difficulties like that raised by Chandler and still yield Kripke's essentialist conclusion when taken together with (I) and a correspondingly strengthened version of (IV), or their analogues for objects other than tables. Perhaps all that is required to repair principle (V') is some restriction clause that rules out cases of replenishment or reassembly. For instance, we might replace (V') with the weaker principle that if it is possible for a table *x* to be *the only table* originally constructed (by a certain artisan in a certain place at a certain time) from a certain hunk of matter *y* according to a certain plan *P*, then necessarily, any table that is *the only table* to be originally constructed (by the very same artisan in the very same place at the very same time) from the very same hunk *y* according to the very same plan *P* is the very same table *x* and no other. Call this principle '(V'')'. There are two essentialist conclusions that can be derived from this weakened version of (V'), together with (I) and a correspondingly strengthened version of (IV), though both are slightly weaker than Kripke's original thesis. One conclusion is that if it is possible for a table *x* to be *the only table* originally constructed from a hunk of matter *y*, then table *x* could not have been originally constructed from any nonoverlapping hunk *y'*. The other conclusion is that if it is possible for a table *x* to be originally constructed from a hunk of matter *y*, then table *x* could not have been *the only table* originally constructed from any nonoverlapping hunk *y'*. These formulations sidestep the difficulties raised by Chandler.

28. THE FOUR WORLDS PARADOX

There is a serious and delicate problem that arises in connection with even the weaker (V''), a problem which does not involve disassembly, reassembly, or replenishment, and which applies equally to the original (V) and (V'). Ironically, this problem, or one very much like

229

it, is raised by Chandler himself in another paper (1976). I shall call our variant of this problem *the Four Worlds Paradox.*[11]

28.1. The Argument

In order to make out this paradox we must assume that some concrete object of a certain sort (table, ship, etc.) is such that it could have originated from matter which differs only in part from the actual original matter. That is, we need to assume that some concrete physical object of a certain sort, say, some ship, could have originated with slightly different parts, as long as some, or perhaps most, of the parts are the same. We do not have to specify exactly how much of the actual original material can be different before one gets a different ship. We need only admit that *some* difference, even if only slight, is allowable. If Kripke's type of essentialism is correct, then no one ship could have originated from *entirely* different matter. It seems then, given our assumption, that there must be some *threshold,* some point at which one more change from the actual original matter must result in a different ship altogether.[12] The difficulty encountered by cross-world identification principles like (V′) and (V″) is easily exhibited in an example which is completely representative of the general case. Consider a possible world w_1 in which a ship *a* consists of exactly 100 planks of wood. Suppose for the sake of argument that any ship of this particular plan and structure is such that it *could have* originated from a different set of planks as long as 98% of them are the same, and only 2% are different, but that a change of 3% or more in the original material must yield a distinct ship. That is, suppose that the threshold point for allowable variation

[11]See Chandler, 1976, p. 108. Chandler credits Robert Stalnaker in connection with the discovery of the particular problem he considers. A similar problem is also noticed by Roderick Chisholm (1973, pp. 584–586, and 1976, appendix B, pp. 148–149). The version of the problem that we shall consider (first presented in Salmon, 1979b) involves a special difficulty not present in Chandler's problem, namely that it is not settled by hypothesis that the two qualitatively indiscernible worlds differ in their accessibility relations. This feature of the problem will be discussed in Section 28.3. Graeme Forbes brought it to my attention that the general problem qualifies as a philosophical paradox.

[12]The assumption of a sharp cutoff point between what the ship definitely could and what it definitely could not have been made from is not necessary to the paradox, thought it greatly facilitates the exposition. Weakening of this assumption is discussed in Section 28.4.

in original matter is 2%. It is important to notice here that we do not assume that in *any* possible world, any ship constructed from 98% or more of the same matter as ship a in w_1 and only 2% or less different matter is a itself. This assumption is somewhat stronger than the analogue of (V'') for ships. We make only the weaker assumption that there are *some* possible worlds in which ship a is constructed from matter as much as 2% different from that in w_1. At present, we leave open the question of whether there might also be other possible worlds in which a different ship, distinct from a, is made from 98% of the same matter as a in w_1. What we shall show, on our assumptions, is that there must be other such worlds. Let us call the planks that constitute ship a in w_1 'P_1', 'P_2', and so on, up to 'P_{100}'. Now surely there is a possible world w_2 in which a ship b is constructed according to the very same plan from planks $P_1, P_2, \ldots, P_{97}, P_{101}, P_{102}$, and P_{103}, where P_{101}, P_{102}, and P_{103} are any three planks that are qualitatively identical with P_{98}, P_{99}, and P_{100}, respectively, but do not even overlap with any of ship a's original planks in w_1. Ship b does not have enough planks in w_2 in common with ship a in w_1 to be ship a itself. It must, therefore, be a numerically distinct ship. Now either of these ships a and b could have originated from a different set of planks as long as 98 of them are the same. Thus there is a possible world w_3 in which ship a is constructed according to the same plan from planks $P_1, P_2, \ldots, P_{97}, P_{98}, P_{102}$, and P_{103}, since the first 98 of these planks are the same as those in w_1. But there is also a possible world w_4 in which ship b is also constructed according to the very same plan from the very same planks, since all but one of them, namely plank P_{98}, are the same as those in w_2. We may diagram the situation as in figure 4.

$$
\begin{array}{ccc}
w_1 & & w_2 \\
\langle\langle P_1, P_2, \ldots, P_{97}, P_{98}, P_{99}, P_{100}\rangle\rangle & & \langle\langle P_1, P_2, \ldots, P_{97}, P_{101}, P_{102}, P_{103}\rangle\rangle \\
a & \neq & b \\
\| & & \| \\
a & \neq & b \\
\langle\langle P_1, P_2, \ldots, P_{97}, P_{98}, P_{102}, P_{103}\rangle\rangle & & \langle\langle P_1, P_2, \ldots, P_{97}, P_{98}, P_{102}, P_{103}\rangle\rangle \\
w_3 & & w_4
\end{array}
$$

FIGURE 4

Hence we have two ships, a and b, in two different worlds, w_3 and w_4, such that both are constructed in their respective worlds (by the very same artisan in the very same place at the very same time) from the very same planks according to the very same plan; nevertheless they are distinct entities.

Here, then, we seem to have a situation that gives the lie to cross-world identification principles like (V″) and its analogues. For what the argument seems to show is that ships solely constructed from the very same hunk of matter in different possible worlds, and according to the very same plan, cannot always be identified. This conclusion is very surprising in itself, but that is not all. There is nothing in the argument that requires that the two worlds w_3 and w_4 should differ in any way, purely qualitatively or even in the totality of matter they contain, with its exact configuration through time, atom for atom, quark for quark. Nor does the argument require that the entities constituted by the various portions of matter in each world be different, except in the single case of the two ships *a* and *b*. And it is difficult to see why variations extraneous to the ships would be called for in any case, since the two worlds are, as it were, minor variants on the initial two worlds w_1 and w_2, and these two worlds may be as alike as one pleases, within the constraint that the two ships differ by three qualitatively identical planks. Thus, for all that the argument requires, we seem to have two possible worlds, w_3 and w_4, that are exactly alike purely qualitatively and even in the very matter they contain with its exact configuration through time, differing only gratuitously over the fact of which ship is constituted by a certain hunk of matter. This is quite paradoxical. How can these two ships, having the very same original matter and structure, not be one and the same ship? After all, it would seem that a ship is nothing *over and above* its parts put together in a certain way, and these two ships, and even the entire possible worlds in which they reside, do not differ in any way qualitatively or structurally. Nevertheless, the correct conclusion seems to be that they differ in their haecceities; the first ship is *this* ship, the second ship is *that* ship, they are different ships, and that is all there is to it. As unpalatable as this may sound, the conclusion seems to follow if we assume that an object might have originated with *some* different parts, but not all. This is a paradox.[13]

28.2. *One Solution*

I have found that a common reaction to the Four Worlds Paradox is to resist its conclusion by holding that the worlds w_3 and w_4 are really

[13]A more precise formulation of the argument for the general case is provided in Salmon, 1979b, pp. 724–725, n. 22.

one and the same possible world, and that we are simply calling a single ship by two names, '*a*' and '*b*'. Chandler, for instance, flirts with this idea in his discussion of (a variant of) the problem (1976, p. 108)—although he explicitly recognizes that his account affords an alternative solution, one that I accept. The idea that w_3 and w_4 are really identical can take various forms, and has been embedded within various accounts that make an effort to accommodate the initial assumption that artifacts might have been originally made from slightly different matter. The basic idea of these accounts is as follows. Strictly speaking, it is not true that there is a possible world in which the ship that we have called '*a*' in w_1—that very entity—is originally constructed from any matter (planks) other than the very same matter (planks) from which it is originally constructed in w_1, even if the difference is ever so slight. In the strict and absolute (haecceitist) sense of 'identical', it is not true that the ship in w_3 that we have called '*a*' is identical with the original ship a in w_1; it is not the case that ship a of w_3 is numerically one and the very same thing as the ship a of w_1. Rather, the two ships are, as it were, near misses, not quite numerically identical, but the next best thing. They are proxies or "counterparts" of one another. It is only in virtue of this special connection between the two ships—which is not a strict and genuine identity—that we call the ships by the same name; our doing so should not be construed as a strict identification. We should not say that ship a of w_1 *is* ship a of w_3—or if we do, we must not use the 'is' of strict *numerical* identity but an 'is' with some looser sense (the 'is' of counterparthood?). Similarly for the two ships called '*b*' in w_2 and w_4.

This general account may or may not be coupled with a sweeping anti-haecceitism with respect to complex physical objects, restricting the applicability of genuine numerical (haecceitist) identity to more basic entities, e.g., planks of wood, or atoms, etc., or perhaps hunks of matter. In response to the sort of problem posed by the Four Worlds Paradox, Roderick Chisholm, Graeme Forbes, and Kripke have all proposed or suggested one version or another of the basic theory embodied in this account.[14]

[14]See Chisholm 1973, 1975, and 1976, appendix B, pp. 145–158. Strictly speaking, Chisholm is concerned primarily with wholes and their constituent parts, though he would probably wish to extend the view to wholes and their constitutive matter. (In this connection see footnote 2 above. See also Hirsch, 1976, p. 55, n. 9.) Kripke (1972a, p. 51, n. 18) suggests a version of the counterpart theory (also concerned primarily with the part-whole relation) in response to problems in this same cluster,

Whatever particular form this account takes, it flies in the face of a straightforward, literal construal of the initial, plausible assumption that some artifact is such that it might have been originally made of slightly different matter. Suppose I point to a particular ship or table and say "Of course, *this very artifact* might have been originally made of mostly the very same wood, with only an atom or two different here and there." I make no reference—explicit or implicit, literal or metaphorical, direct or allusive—to any ship or table other than the one I am pointing to. I am saying something about it—that very artifact—and not about any of a range of imposters. Things might be different if I were to use a nonrigid definite description like 'the unique artifact most like this one'. But I do not, and I do not whisper it either. I use a demonstrative, an obstinately rigid designator, and I point to a particular actual artifact to say something—something true—about it and it alone.[15] I do not mean "There might have been an artifact here, not really this very artifact, but a reasonable facsimile made from mostly the same

---

although he does not explicitly advocate the theory, and says that the particular version he considers seems utopian in its assumption that there is some ultimate or basic kind of entity out of which complex physical objects are made and for which cross-world identity is unproblematic. (More on Kripke in Section 28.4 below.) This version of the theory, or something closely akin to it, is defended and worked out in detail by Forbes (1981b), where the theory is explicitly put forward as a solution to the Four Worlds Paradox. See also Wiggins, 1980, pp. 97–98. Chisholm (1975, pp. 92, 96–97) traces the essentials of the theory to Bishop Butler, David Hume, and Thomas Reid. It goes without saying that David Lewis—the founder of contemporary counterpart theory—advocates a version of the theory sketched in the text, though Lewis, of course, goes much further than the other authors mentioned here. See, e.g., Lewis, 1968. It is not a necessary part of the theory sketched in the text that a ship exists in only one possible world. Nor does the theory require that a ship can exist in distinct possible worlds. It requires only that a ship have the same original matter wherever it exists. Further requirements yield proper extensions of the theory.

[15]Cf. Kripke, 1972a, pp. 43–47. Kripke recognizes the tension between these considerations and his footnote 18, and he attempts a sort of reconciliation at pages 50–53. I believe that the tension is greater than Kripke acknowledges here, as I will try to show in Section 28.4 below. Kripke writes: "Although we can try to describe the world in terms of molecules, there is no impropriety in describing it in terms of grosser entities: the statement that *this table* might have been placed in another room is perfectly proper, in and of itself. We *need* not use the description in terms of molecules, or even grosser parts of the table, though we *may*" (p. 51). Similarly the statement that *this table* might have been made from mostly, but not exactly, the same matter is perfectly proper, in and of itself, and as Kripke seems to argue (p. 45, n. 13), it is a statement about the very table demonstrated, not about various of its imposter "counterparts."

wood that this was actually originally made of." If that were what I meant, that is what I would have said.[16] But if for some reason I am wrong about this, and what I said does mean what the counterpart theorist says it means, then let him or her tell me how to say what I meant to say, and I will construct a new Four Worlds Paradox. Better yet, interpret the above formulation of the argument for the paradox in the way that it was intended; then the idea that $w_3 = w_4$ is quite definitely mistaken.

[16]Hazen (1979, pp. 320–322) objects to arguments of this sort on the grounds that they confuse pronouncements of ordinary subjunctive discourse, pronouncements about which we may have firm modal intuitions, with the counterpart theory's proposed analysis into possible world discourse using the technical notion of *counterpart,* where this analysis "is not a sentence that we, qua speakers of our particular natural language, are entitled to have intuitions about." I do not find Hazen's objections convincing, though there is not the space here to develop a full response. In any case, taken as an objection to the argument given in the text, it misses the point: Intuitively the modal operator sentences 'It might have been the case that: *this* be made from hunk H' and 'It might have been the case that: something (most and sufficiently) resembling *this* in certain (such-and-such) respects be made from something (most and sufficiently) resembling H in certain (such-and-such) respects' differ in their truth-conditions. The latter assertion is considerably weaker than the former, if not entirely independent of it. (The latter assertion can only be spelled out further insofar as the relevant notion of *counterpart* is fully and adequately explained in terms of resemblance, and counterpart theorists do not always agree in their explanations. Perhaps it would be better to replace the assertion with one explicitly involving the relevant notion of *counterpart:* 'It might have been the case that: a counterpart of *this* be made from a counterpart of H'. However the relevant notion of *counterpart* is plausibly explained short of strict identity, this assertion is, intuitively, considerably weaker than the first assertion, if not entirely independent of it. Moreover, I know of no plausible grounds for prohibiting the *counterpart* notion from modal operator discourse.) Yet the counterpart theory assigns both (all) assertions the same truth-conditions that standard possible-world semantics, supplemented if need be with the relevant notion of *counterpart,* assigns only to the latter. (I assume here Lewis's principle that any possible object is its own sole counterpart in its own world, or minimally that all of a possible object's existing counterparts in a given world are counterparts in that world of anything that the object is itself a counterpart of in that world. Forbes's original treatment in 1981b preserves the latter principle, and it is difficult to imagine a philosophical motivation for counterpart theory which plausibly rejects the principle on independent grounds.) Counterpart theory fails to distinguish the truth-conditions of the two assertions, and thereby misrepresents the full force of the first assertion. The intended force of the first assertion is something much stronger than (or at any rate, different from) the counterpart theory's surrogate, and something that the theory must reject as false. Contra Hazen, this makes the theory an extreme form of essentialism, despite the deceptive fact that the theory can accommodate the first modal operator sentence, which ostensibly belies extreme essentialism.

235

The fact is that the counterpart theory sketched above is, at bottom, just a particularly inflexible brand of essentialism. By denying that there is a possible state of affairs in which the very ship a from w_1 is made from ever so slightly different matter, the counterpart theorist holds, even if only tacitly, that in a strict sense it is absolutely impossible for the very ship a, rather than some other ship, to have been made from matter even only an atom different. The counterpart theorist can mouth the words 'Ship a might have been made from slightly different matter', but any such pronouncement by the counterpart theorist in modal operator discourse is a verbal camouflage that merely postpones the inevitable. What matters is what the counterpart theorist *means* by these words, and more importantly, what is *not meant* by these words. (Cf. Plantinga, 1974, pp. 114–119.) To use an analogy suggested by Kripke, the phenomenalist can *say* 'There is a table in the room', but this does not alter the fact that he or she believes in neither the table nor the room. According to the counterpart theory, *strictly speaking,* if in another possible state of affairs we are ever to have the one and only, one and the very same ship a from w_1—that very entity and no other—it must be made in that state of affairs from the *very same* matter, atom for atom, quark for quark, no exceptions. Otherwise, *strictly speaking,* we get a new and different ship. The theory does not *identify* the worlds w_3 and w_4 so much as it denies their existence (or their possibility). It replaces the two of them with a single world containing neither ship a nor ship b, but some new ship.[17] The theory

[17]Forbes (1980, pp. 359–360, and 1981a, p. 81) discusses a close analogue of the problem posed by the Four Worlds Paradox for the special case of organisms and the gametes from which they sprang. In these papers he urges certain addition arguments for essentialism and puts forward a variant of the Four Worlds problem as part of a *reductio ad absurdum* argument which, if it worked, could be generalized (as Forbes apparently intends) to establish the particularly inflexible brand of essentialism concerning artifacts inherent in the counterpart theory. To couch his discussion in terms of our example, Forbes implicitly identifies (I would say *confuses*) the two worlds w_3 and w_4 and concludes that the initial assumption that there is such a world, where the very individual from another world has a partly different original composition, has the "unacceptable consequence" that the individual (in our case, ship) in the third world (the schizophrenic w_3/w_4 world) is the same thing as a and distinct from b from the point of view of w_1, but is just the reverse from the point of view of w_2, thus making the "identity" (haecceity) of the individual (ship) in the third world "change according as w_1 or w_2 is supposed to be actual" (1980). But this, whatever it means, is not a consequence of the view in question. Nor does the view contradict any version of the necessity of identity, as Forbes claims (1981a). Forbes's discussion suffers from a

then does its best to accommodate our plausible modal pronouncements concerning the two original ships *a* and *b* without reintroducing the paradox by reinterpreting these pronouncements in terms of the single replacement world. But the reinterpretation is a misinterpretation, and it is uncharitable to those of us who, on reflection and in full command of our faculty of modal intuition, reject any inflexible brand of essentialism that cannot accommodate a possible scenario in which the very ship *a* from w_1 is made from ever so slightly different matter. Still, the argument of the Four Worlds Paradox appears to show that this inflexible brand of essentialism is the price one must pay for cross-world identification principles like (V″), in conjunction with the plausible view that the very same artifact could not have been originally made from entirely different matter.

In fact, the temptation to identity w_3 and w_4, despite the contortions that this identification requires, might be traced in part to the organizational role that identification principles like (V″) play in our way of looking at things. (See Section 26.) It might be traced even further to a possibly more fundamental and more general principle of modal thought. This is the "reductionist" principle that physical objects are "nothing over and above" their matter and structure, in the sense that a complete accounting of what matter there is in a genuinely possible world, with its causal interconnections and exact configuration through time, atom for atom, quark for quark, must completely and uniquely determine whatever physical facts there are about each of the physical objects such as tables and ships present in the world, including such facts as that a particular hunk of matter a' constitutes a particular ship *a* at time *t*. This principle would require that any two genuinely possible worlds exactly alike at the level of

flaw analogous to the one we uncovered in Chandler's discussion of his two Ship of Theseus worlds: In deriving the unacceptable "consequence," Forbes illegitimately uses a single expression ('O_2', and the same is true of his use of 'O_3') as a name for what, on the view in question, are distinct individuals originating from the same matter in different (and perhaps mutually inaccessible) worlds. This makes the view seem incoherent when it is not. In fact the view is perfectly tenable, and in the case of ships and tables it is even true. (Caution: Comparison of Forbes's *reductio* argument and our formulation of the Four Worlds Paradox is complicated by the fact that Forbes calls the worlds playing the roles of our w_1 and w_2, 'w_1' and 'w_4', respectively. The situation is complicated still further by the fact that Forbes considers not one but two additional worlds, which he calls 'w_2' and 'w_3', each of which involves a conflation of the distinct roles played by w_3 and w_4 in our example.)

matter and structure must also be exactly alike at least in all their physical-object facts.[18] Assuming as a plausible principle the identity of factually indiscernible possible worlds (worlds in which the very same facts obtain), and given that the worlds w_3 and w_4 are exactly alike in all their non-purely-physical facts, we seem to have that $w_3 = w_4$. If the "reductionist" principle is extended also to self-contained *portions* of full-blown possible worlds, so that a complete accounting of all the causal relations and the exact configuration of a *particular* hunk of matter through time completely determines all the physical facts about the object, if any, so constituted, then we obtain (V″) and its analogues.

28.3. A Better Solution

Despite appearances, the conclusion of the argument of the Four Worlds Paradox does not conflict with this reductionist principle, nor does it conflict with cross-world identification principles like (V″). To see this we must turn to Chandler's own example (1976). Chandler's main concern is to argue that the accessibility relation between possible worlds (*w* is *possible relative to w′*) is not transitive. Considerations similar to those that generate the Four Worlds Paradox seem to yield this result. Given the existence of possible world w_3 in the example, there is by hypothesis yet another world w_5, possible relative to w_3, in which the same ship *a* is originally constructed by changing one more of its original planks, say P_{98} to P_{101}, so that ship *a* is now constructed in precisely the same way as the distinct ship *b* in w_2. But even though w_5 is possible relative to w_3, and w_3 is possible relative to w_1, w_5 is, by hypothesis, not possible relative to w_1. Ship *a* has exchanged one too many planks. We can put the point as follows. Suppose that w_1 is the actual world, or the way things actually are. Then ship *a* is in fact constructed from planks P_1 through P_{100}. It is possible for the same ship *a* to have been constructed from the planks in w_3, since this involves only a change of two planks, but it is impossible for the very same ship *a* to have been constructed from the planks in w_5, since this would involve a change of three planks from its actual original composition. But, if ship *a* *had been* originally constructed from the planks in w_3, i.e., if it *had been* constructed with only two different planks, then it would have

---

[18]The principle is explicitly mentioned by Kripke (1972a, p. 50). The principle, or one very much like it, is also explicitly mentioned and endorsed by Forbes (1980, pp. 353–355, and 1981a, p. 79).

been possible for the very ship *a* to have been originally constructed from the planks in w_5, since this only involves changing one plank from w_3. It *would have been* possible, but it is not *actually* possible! From the point of view of the way things actually are, a scenario or state of affairs in which ship *a* is originally constructed from the planks in w_5 is not a real possibility concerning ship *a*. World w_5 is an impossible world—an impossibility as far as w_1 is concerned. World w_3, on the other hand, is a genuine possibility concerning ship *a*, and if w_3 had been the case, some *new* possibilities concerning the very ship *a* would arise—possibilities as far as w_3 is concerned. In particular, the scenario or state of affairs w_5 would then become a genuine possibility concerning ship *a*. Only a narrow-minded form of modal ethnocentrism would deny this. If it is possible in the actual state of affairs w_1 to have altered slightly ship *a*'s origin, then surely it is also possible in the state of affairs w_3 to have altered *a*'s origin *as it is there*. Although w_5 is an impossible state of affairs from the point of view of the actual state of affairs w_1, it is only *contingently* impossible. (Cf. Fine, 1977a, especially p. 139.) It is what might be called *possible in the second degree,* i.e., possibly possible. Even from the point of view of w_1 it might have been a possibility concerning ship *a*, and indeed it would have been a possibility if only *a* had had a different plank or two.[19]

In our presentation of the argument for the Four Worlds Paradox, we are given that the worlds w_2 and w_3 are possible relative to the initial world w_1, and that w_4 is possible relative to w_2. But we are not given any reason to suppose that w_4 is also possible relative to either w_1 or w_3. Nor are we given that w_4 is impossible relative to either w_1 or w_3. Thus, what the argument of the Four Worlds Paradox shows is that there are pairs of qualitatively indiscernible worlds w_3 and w_4, each of which contains only one of two distinct artifacts *a* and *b* made in their respective worlds from the very same matter, and such that w_3 is possible relative to a given world w_1 (e.g., the actual world) and w_4 is possible relative to an intermediate world w_2 possible relative to w_1. The question remains open whether w_4 is possible or impossible relative to the given world w_1, and whether w_3 and w_4 are possible or impossible relative to each other. This result need not be taken as a threat to cross-world identification principles like (V″) or to the

---

[19]As with the argument of the Four Worlds Paradox, the general argument for intransitivity does not require the assumption of a sharp threshold between what is possible and what is not possible in the construction of a particular artifact. Weakening of this assumption is discussed in the next section.

general "reductionist" principle mentioned in the preceding section, unless some further argument can be given to show that w_4 is also possible relative to w_1 (or that w_3 and w_4 are possible relative to each other).

On the contrary, such principles might be taken as *showing* that w_4 cannot be possible relative to w_1. This would resolve the paradox. Indeed, this is (more or less) the position I wish to take with respect to the paradox.[20] Suppose that there is a world w in which a table is the only table made from the very matter that originally made up an actual table T, and it is made following the same plan, atom for atom. Is this table the same table T? If we are given that w is a way things genuinely might have been, i.e., a world possible relative to the actual world, then the answer seems to be 'yes'. But given that w is a way things could not have been, and is possible in the nth degree for some $n > 1$, i.e., possibly, possibly, . . . , possible, who knows? Certainly our belief in (V″) *per se* does not yield any continuing inclination to answer our question affirmatively.

Thus principles like (V″) are rescued from the Four Worlds Paradox.

28.4. *Vagueness and the Paradox*

By considering a succession of 51 worlds beginning with w_1, one can eventually construct ship a of entirely different matter than that used in w_1, though on the account just sketched the 51st world in this sequence is a far-removed impossible world from the point of view of w_1, possible only in the 50th degree. This is a sorites construction.[21] Sorites arguments are notorious for playing havoc with the phenomenon of vagueness. In constructing the argument of the Four Worlds Paradox, as well as the argument for intransitivity of modal accessibility, we assumed that there is a sharp threshold or cutoff point between what matter could and what matter could not originally constitute a particular ship a. But this assumption is philosophically unsubtle, and seems too crude and vulgar to be true. Shouldn't we recognize an interval of vagueness between these two extremes, rather than a sharp cutoff point? Any ordinary artifact such as a ship

[20]I am indebted to Penelope Mackie for helping me see my way to this position, though I do not know whether it is her position.

[21]It is very reminiscent of arguments given by Chisholm (1967; 1973, pp. 584–586; and 1976, appendix B, pp. 148–149)—though Chisholm draws an inflexible essentialism as his conclusion rather than the intransitivity of modal accessibility. See also Wilson, 1959.

is such that it might have been made from a different hunk of matter as long as it is very nearly the same matter, with only a few tiny replacements here and there. Furthermore, any ship made from a hunk of matter substantially different from the actual matter of an ordinary ship must be a different ship. Between these two extremes it would seem that there is an interval of vagueness, a region of indeterminacy. For hunks of matter in this region—involving a significant amount of overlap with the original ship's actual matter, but also involving a significant amount of new and different matter—it apparently becomes vague or indeterminate (neither true nor false, there is no objective fact of the matter) as to whether a ship made from that very matter in just the same way could be the same ship as the actual ship with which we began. If this is so, any argument that leads to a paradoxical conclusion by ignoring this element of vagueness may be playing havoc with vagueness in just the manner of a sorites argument. Is that what is going on in the Four Worlds Paradox and in Chandler's argument for intransitivity of modal accessibility?

Yes and no. Certainly these considerations of vagueness are relevant to the general problem, but they do not yield a better solution, only something of a better understanding of the general phenomenon. To see this, let us begin by raising a question: Wherein does the vagueness reside? Which terms or concepts involved in the arguments are vague or indeterminate?

Kripke's suggestion of a version of the counterpart theory as part of a possible response to these problems is predicated on the idea that in some instances "the identity relation is vague." He says that

> perhaps, . . . given certain counterfactual vicissitudes in the history of the molecules of a table, T, one may ask whether T would exist, in that situation, or whether a certain bunch of molecules, which in that situation would constitute a table, constitute the very same table T . . . . in concrete cases we may be able to answer whether a certain bunch of molecules would still constitute T, though in some cases the answer may be indeterminate (1972a, pp. 50–51).

In a footnote to this passage, Kripke writes:

> There is some vagueness here. If a chip, or molecule, of a given table had been replaced by another one, we would be content to say that we have the same table. But if too many chips were different,

241

we would seem to have a different one. . . . Where the identity
relation is vague, it may seem intransitive; a [chain] of apparent
[identities] may yield an apparent nonidentity. Some sort of
'counterpart' notion . . . may have some utility here. . . . Logicians
have not developed a logic of vagueness (n. 18; brackets indicate
Kripke's corrections of the original printing).

It is only for cases "where identity is vague" that Kripke proposes
that the counterpart theory might be called into active duty, for lack
of a logic of vagueness (at least, for lack of a logic of vagueness to
Kripke's knowledge circa 1970). But what is such a case? As we
noted above, it would seem that for any actual table T there is a
region of indeterminacy concerning the table's potential for having
had a different origin. For any hunk of matter in this region of
indeterminacy, being significantly different from table T's actual
matter but also involving just enough overlap, there is no definitive
answer to the question of whether a table T' made from that very
matter is the same table T or a different table. The sort of cases that
concern Kripke, and prompt him to say that identity is vague, are
precisely such cases in which we are given a possible world w, with let
us suppose a complete accounting of what matter it contains and its
exact configuration through time, in which a table T' is constructed
with significantly different matter from that of an actual table T, but
just enough of the same matter so that there does not appear to be
any definitive answer to the question of whether it is the same
table.[22]

One must be careful not to be misled by this description of the
situation. As described, it is very much like instructing someone to
suppose an arbitrary possible world w in which a communist x is
elected president of the United States, and then being asked "But
who is x, this lousy would-be spy for the KGB?"—questions of the
sort that Kripke rightfully rejects (e.g., in 1972a, pp. 42–47). There
are some worlds in which Angela Davis is elected president as a

---

[22]Derek Parfit (1971) apparently urges a version of the theory of vague or
indeterminate identity—one which he regards as entirely uncontroversial for certain
sorts of things—as a solution to the problem cases of personal identity. He writes: "No
one thinks [that the question of whether a thing x is identical with a thing y must have
a true answer] about, say, nations or machines. Our criteria for the identity of these do
not cover certain cases. No one thinks that in these cases the questions 'Is it the same
nation?' or 'Is it the same machine?' must have answers" (p. 3).

communist, and there are other worlds in which Milton Friedman is elected president as a communist. (If Friedman is essentially noncommunist, then these latter worlds are impossible ones.) There is no answer to the question 'Who is x?', not because identity is vague, but because 'x' is a variable with a range of values. Our description of w did not pin down a particular possible world, with a particular person x, but a *class* of worlds with different persons x. There is an important difference between this sort of case and the table case that interests Kripke. There is no reason to suppose that there is only one person who might have been elected president as a communist, and consequently there is no reason to suppose that we have singled out a unique person x. But in the case of the tables T and T', a believer in (V'') or in the reductionist principle mentioned in Section 28.2 has a reason to believe that there is only one possible table that might have been (the only table) constructed from the relevant matter.[23] On this assumption, we have singled out a unique possible table T', and the question of whether this table T' is the actual table T is meaningful. If the relevant hunk of matter in w differed more extensively from the actual matter of table T, then we could safely say that T' cannot be the same table as T. If the matter in w overlapped more extensively with the actual matter of table T, then we could safely say that T' must be the same table as T. But in the situation described, no such answer is forthcoming; there is no objective fact of the matter as to whether T is T'. So it seems that the 'is' of identity is not defined for this case.

There are serious problems with this way of looking at the situation. Insofar as I understand the idea that identity is sometimes vague, it is provably mistaken. For suppose that there is a pair of entities x and y (e.g., Kripke's tables T and T', or the original ship of Theseus a and the modified ship of Theseus c, etc.) such that it is vague (neither true nor false, indeterminate, there is no objective fact of the matter) whether they are one and the very same thing. Then this pair $\langle x,y \rangle$ is quite definitely *not* the same pair as $\langle x,x \rangle$, since it is determinately true that x is one and the very same thing as itself. It follows that x and y must be distinct. But then it is not vague whether they are identical or distinct.

---

[23]Kripke's discussion (1972a, pp. 50–51) is in some sense contingent on the assumption of the reductionist principle, though it is unclear to what extent Kripke intends to endorse the principle. See also Chapter One, footnote 41.

This argument is brief, but it is telling.[24] It might be replied that the argument shows no more than that, for any entity x for which there is a y such that the English 'is' of identity is undefined for the pair $\langle x,y \rangle$, the 'is' of identity must also be undefined for the reflexive pair of x and x itself, so that x lies entirely outside of the category of

[24]An argument similar to the one just presented is given in Evans (1978), though the argument had occurred to me independently. It is, I believe, an argument that is straightforwardly demanded by the correct conception of identity as the stark relation between every object and *itself* (as opposed to richer relations like *being constituted by substantially the same matter*).

I have encountered a number of objections to the argument, but none that are convincing. Perhaps the most frequent objection is the idea that if we take vagueness and indeterminacy seriously, it is fallacious to infer that $\langle x,y \rangle \neq \langle x,x \rangle$ from the assumption that it is indeterminate or vague whether the first pair of objects stand in the identity relation, whereas it is fully determinate and settled that the second pair of objects so stand. The objection is usually based on the notion that where a term is applied to objects for which the term's applicability may be vague or indeterminate, classically valid inference patterns are no longer legitimate. But the inference drawn here is from a conjunction consisting of an *assumption*—something we are taking to be determinately the case for the sake of argument—together with something that is quite definitely the case. The inference pattern need only be valid, i.e., truth-preserving. There is nothing more to require of it. Analogously, the term 'bald' may be vague in the sense that there are individuals for whom it is indeterminate whether the term correctly applies, or individuals of whom the term is neither true nor false, and yet the inference pattern $\ulcorner \alpha$ has a full head of hair $\therefore \alpha$ is not bald$\urcorner$ is perfectly valid. The validity of this inference pattern ensures that in order to settle the question of whether it is true, false, or indeterminate that Harry is bald, it is *sufficient* to take note of the fact that Harry's head is very hairy.

For those who may be concerned that the argument against vague identity—which is essentially a metatheoretic argument about the English 'is' of identity—ignores the well-known strictures against conflating object language and metalanguage, it should be noted that the argument could be reformulated entirely within any second language adequate as a metalanguage for English. Alternatively, the formulation of the argument can be left intact, but applied only to an impoverished fragment of English, as object language, which consists only of quantificational idioms and the 'is' of identity. The argument, unlike the suspect arguments of the Liar and the other semantic paradoxes, is a semantical argument about a *nonsemantical* predicate. The crucial assumption is only the modest metatheoretic assumption that the 'is' of identity is determinately true of any object and itself, and determinately false of any pair of distinct objects.

Of course, it might in some cases be "vague" in an epistemological sense (e.g., in principle unknowable) whether a given entity x is identical with a given entity y, but that is a separate matter from the issue before us, and need not entail that there is no objective (albeit unknowable) fact of the matter, or that the 'is' of identity is undefined for the pair $\langle x,y \rangle$. One of the virtues of Kripke's discussion is that he sharply distinguishes metaphysical from epistemological issues, and makes it clear that he is discussing a metaphysical problem about cross-world identity.

meaningful application of 'is'. (Otherwise, by the above argument, x and y would be discernible, hence distinct, and hence the 'is' of identity would be determinately false of them.) But this reply is odious. For the theory of vague identity, and the problems on which the theory is brought to bear, would require that for nearly *any* physical object (ship, table, etc.) x, there will be an object y (in another possible world or at another time) such that it is indeterminate whether $x = y$, and hence, according to this reply, it will also be indeterminate whether $x = x$! More significantly, the reply is ineffective. For suppose that there are entities x for which there is a y such that the English 'is' of identity is neither determinately true nor determinately false of the pair $\langle x,y \rangle$; hence according to the reply, the 'is' of identity is also undefined for the reflexive pair $\langle x,x \rangle$. Now consider the following prophetic argument:

> I shall introduce an artificial relation called 'schmidentity' (not a word of English) which I now stipulate to hold between [*every*] object and itself. Now then . . . the same problems will hold for this [predicate] as were thought in the case of the original [predicate]. . . . If anyone thinks about this seriously, I think that he will see that therefore probably his original account of [vague] identity was not necessary, and probably not possible, for the problems it was originally meant to solve, and that therefore it should be dropped, and identity should just be taken to be the relation between [*anything*] and itself. This sort of device can be used for a number of philosophical problems (Kripke, 1972a, p. 108, taken with gross liberties and out of context).

The assertion that identity is vague is only so much barking up the wrong tree. The 'is' of identity is not vague in the way that an inexact or fuzzy term like 'bald' (in the sense of 'nearly absolutely bald') is vague. Insofar as principles like (V″) or the reductionist principle mentioned above lead to the consequence that identity is vague, we should refuse the principle rather than swallow its consequence. In the case that concerns us, we appear to have a specific and definite table T' that cannot properly be said either to be the same or to be a different table from the table T. But T is an *actual* table, and surely the 'is' of identity is defined for it, determinately true of the pair $\langle T,T \rangle$. Insofar as there is a definite possible table T' such that, for whatever reason, the 'is' of identity is not defined for the pair $\langle T,T' \rangle$, T' simply is not one and the very same thing as T, it is not "schmidentical" with T. There is an objective fact of the matter. On the other hand, if our complete description of the configuration of matter in *w* does not single out a unique and definite possible table *T'*, but only a class of worlds with various tables *T'*, then the question 'Is *T'* identical with *T*?' is as illegitimate as the question 'Who is this would-be spy for the KGB?' In either case, vague identity is not the problem, nor the solution.

Still, the general phenomenon of vagueness seems to play a role in the Four Worlds Paradox, and in Chandler's argument for intransitivity of modal accessibility. For it does seem that, in at least most cases, there simply is no sharp threshold or cutoff point, as the two arguments assume, between what variation in the original matter is possible and what variation is impossible in the construction of a given ship or table. It seems only crude to deny that for any ordinary table *T* there must be a region of indeterminacy such that it is vague or indeterminate whether it is possible for *T* to have been constructed from a certain hunk of matter involving some overlap and some nonoverlap with the actual matter of *T*. For hunks of matter in the region of indeterminacy, there does seem to be no objective fact of the matter as to whether it is possible for the actual table *T* to have been constructed from that very matter, even though it is definitely possible for that very matter to have been made into a table *T'*. Wherein does the vagueness or indeterminacy reside if not in the identity or nonidentity of *T* and *T'*?

One place to look is to the predicate 'constitutes', or the 'is' of constitution. Perhaps in a possible world *w* in which a hunk of matter in the region of indeterminacy for table *T* is made into a table, what is indeterminate is whether that very matter constitutes the very table *T* in *w*. But take notice of what we have just said. For if the relevant matter is formed into a table in *w*, then there is a possible table *T'* in *w* that is constituted in *w* by the relevant matter. Now *T'* cannot be the same table as *T*, for we are given that it is determinately true, and an objective fact, that the relevant matter constitutes table *T'* in *w*, but we are supposing that it is indeterminate, and that there is no objective fact, as to whether that very matter constitutes table *T* in *w*. For this to be the case, it would seem that it must be in some sense a "live option," not ruled out by the objective facts, that the relevant matter should originally constitute both tables *T* and *T'* simultaneously, even though the tables are distinct. If this were ruled out by the objective facts of the matter, then contrary to our hypothesis, it would be determinately *false* that table *T* is constructed from the relevant matter in *w*. But for this to be a live option, not ruled out by the facts, it cannot be the case that it is impossible to construct two *distinct* but ordinary tables T and T' at *the very same time,* each *entirely* from *all* of a single hunk of matter. Yet this seems plainly impossible. At the very least, the prospect is every bit as paradoxical as the prospect of a pair of *mutually* possible worlds otherwise related in the same way as w_3 and w_4 in the Four Worlds Paradox. For here we would have a single world w related to *itself* in just this way. And if we consider possible tables T'' distinct from T' made from matter in the region of indeterminacy for T', presumably we should have that it is not determinately impossible that in constructing a table T' from the matter in w, we thereby construct three distinct but ordinary tables—T, T', and T''—with exactly the same matter in exactly the same place at exactly the same time. Do we not want to say that this is determinately impossible? I do.[25]

Kripke appears to include toward the view that it is of the *essence*—necessarily necessary-and-sufficient condition—of a table T that it be a table originally made from *substantially* such-and-such matter (in *substantially* such-and-such a configuration, etc.). This is a vague property. In some cases it is indeterminate whether a possible table has this property. Hence, if the property is an essence, it is a vague essence. The view that a table T has this vague essence would seem to require that for any possible world w (possible from the point of view of the actual world), and any possible table T' in w, $T' = T$ if and only if T' has this vague property in w.

Suppose we are given a world w in which some table T' is such that it is indeterminate whether T' has the property in question, i.e., suppose T' is made from matter in the region of indeterminacy of table T. It need not follow that it is vague whether $T = T'$. T' may or may not be the same table as T; we have not yet been given enough information concerning w. In fact, w represents a *class* of different worlds, with different tables T'. (Cf. the communist president case.) If we are given further that $T' = T$, then what we might infer is that the world w is not *definitely possible* from the point of view of the actual world.[26] Perhaps it is an impossible world with respect to the actual world, but perhaps it is indeterminate whether w is possible or

[25]But see Unger, 1980.

[26]Precisely what does follow from the biconditional depends on the details of the logic of vagueness. Insofar as the view that an entity has a vague essence leads to the consequence that identity is vague, we should again refuse the view rather than swallow its consequence.

impossible with respect to the actual world. More simply, if it is an essential property of a table *T* that it is originally constructed from *substantially* such-and-such matter, in the (weak) sense that *T* definitely has this vague property in every definitely possible world in which *T* exists, and *H* is a hunk of matter in the region of indeterminacy, then if we are given a world *w* which is not definitely impossible and in which the very table *T* is constructed from hunk *H*, then we may infer that it is indeterminate whether *w* is possible from the point of view of the actual world. This would be to acknowledge an element of vagueness. The vagueness is located not in the 'is' of identity, nor in the 'is' of constitution, but in phrases like 'substantial overlap', and hence, by way of vague essential properties, in the modal idioms themselves: 'possibly', 'could not have', etc., and the accessibility predicate of possible world discourse. If *H* is a hunk of matter differing only very slightly from the actual matter of a table *T*, then it is definitely possible for table *T* to be constructed from hunk *H*. But if *H* is a hunk of matter in the region of indeterminacy, involving an "in between" amount of overlap with the actual matter of table *T*, then it is vague whether it is possible for table *T* to have been constructed from hunk *H*. This is just to say that there is no world determinately possible (relative to the actual world) in which table *T* is constructed from hunk *H*, though there are worlds *w* in which table *T* is constructed from hunk *H*, and for which it is vague whether *w* is possible (relative to the actual world).[27]

[27]See Kripke, 1972a, p. 115, n. 57, point (3). On the account proposed here, it may be vague whether *not being constructed from hunk H* is an "essential property" of table *T*. *T* has this property in every definitely possible world in which it exists, but there are worlds which are not definitely impossible and in which table *T* exists but lacks this property.

The following definitions are hereby proposed: A proposition *p* is *definitely* or *determinately necessary* iff *p* is true in every determinately possible world and in every indeterminate world; *p* is *determinately unnecessary* iff in some determinately possible world *p* is not true; *p* is *determinately possible* iff *p* is true in some determinately possible world; *p* is *determinately impossible* iff *p* is true in no determinately possible world and in no indeterminate world; *p* is *determinately contingent* iff *p* is determinately possible but determinately unnecessary; *p* is *determinately noncontingent* iff *p* is either determinately necessary or determinately impossible. (Exercise: Prove that (*i*) if *p* is indeterminate with respect to necessity [neither determinately necessary nor determinately unnecessary], then *p* is determinately possible; (*ii*) if *p* is indeterminate with respect to possibility [neither determinately possible nor determinately impossible], then *p* is determinately unnecessary; and (*iii*) *p* is indeterminate with respect to contingency [neither determinately contingent nor

How does this account deal with Kripke's problem that the theory of vague identity was meant to solve? If *H* is an ordinary hunk of matter in the region of indeterminacy for an actual table *T*, then it is definitely possible for hunk *H* to have been made into a table. That is, there is a world *w′* which is definitely possible from the point of view of the actual world, and in which a table *T′* is constructed from hunk *H*. Is *T′* the same table as *T*? On this account, the answer must be 'no'. For we are given that *w′* is *definitely* possible with respect to the actual world, but by hypothesis there is no *definitely* possible world in which table *T* is constructed from hunk *H*.[28] On the other hand, if we are given only that there is a world *w′* which is *not definitely impossible* from the point of view of the actual world, and in which a table *T′* is constructed from hunk *H*, then there is no answer to the question 'Is *T′* the same table as *T*?' This is not

---

determinately noncontingent] iff *p* is either indeterminate with respect to necessity or indeterminate with respect to possibility.)

On the modal logic determined by these definitions, it is vague (neither true nor false) whether it is necessary that table *T*, if it exists, is not constructed from hunk *H*.

[28]This account suggests a denial of (V″). For there is a genuinely possible world *w′* in which a table *T′* distinct from *T* is the only table constructed from hunk *H* according to a certain plan. If (V″) is true, it seems to follow that it is impossible for table *T* to be the only table originally constructed from hunk *H* according to that plan, and hence that any world *w* in which table *T* is the only table originally constructed from hunk *H* according to that plan is determinately impossible. Yet on the account proposed here, there is a world *w* in which table *T* is the only table originally constructed from hunk *H* according to that plan, but which is not determinately impossible. Whether the account conflicts with (V″) depends on the logic of vagueness. What surely does follow from (V″) is that if there is a possible world (possible relative to the actual world) in which a table *x* is the only table originally constructed from hunk *H* according to the same plan, then *x* must be *T′*. The world *w* need not be taken as a counterinstance since it is not a determinately possible world. On the definitions proposed in the previous footnote, however, *w* is to be taken as a counterinstance, at least in the sense that it renders (V″) not true. Though (V″) comes out untrue on these definitions, it can still be maintained that necessarily, if a table *x* is the only table originally constructed from a certain hunk of matter according to a certain plan, then necessarily, any table that is the only table originally constructed from that hunk of matter according to that plan is the table *x* and no other:

$$\Box(x)\Box(y)\Box(P)\Box[x = (1z')(T(z', y) \text{ according to plan } P)$$

$$\rightarrow \Box(z)(z = (1z')[T(z', y) \text{ according to plan } P] \rightarrow z = x)].$$

This formulation would require only that the two worlds *w* and *w′* be mutually determinately impossible relative to each other, and allows that *w* may be indeterminate with respect to possibility relative to the actual world.

because identity is vague. We have not been given a single table T', but a class of worlds w' with different tables T'. In some of these worlds, though only in ones that are not definitely possible, the table constructed from hunk H is indeed the same table as T. In others, the table constructed from hunk H is not the same table as T.[29]

We have looked at three candidates for the locus of vagueness in the arguments for the Four Worlds Paradox and the intransitivity of modal accessibility—identity, constitution, and modality. We have argued that locating an element of vagueness in the last of the three appears to afford the most reasonable account. The original arguments made the assumption that there is a sharp threshold or cutoff between what matter could and what matter could not constitute a given artifact. The account just sketched in terms of regions of indeterminacy, and worlds neither determinately possible nor determinately impossible relative to one another, belies this assumption. But it does not block either of the arguments. In both cases, the general argument can easily accommodate regions of indeterminacy and vague accessibility between worlds. In the general argument for intransitivity of modal accessibility, we need only construct a sequence of worlds beginning with w_1 such that each world in the sequence is determinately possible relative to its immediate predecessor but involves some further change in the original constitution of ship a, always keeping within the limits of definitely allowable variation. Eventually we will reach a world w_n in which the original matter of ship a differs so extensively from the original matter in the initial world w_1 that w_n is determinately impossible relative to w_1. Somewhere between the two extreme worlds w_1 and w_n there may be worlds neither determinately possible nor determinately impossible relative to the initial world w_1, but that makes no difference to the argument. For we still have $w_1 \, R \, w_2 \, R \ldots R \, w_n$ but not $w_1 \, R \, w_n$. This means a failure of transitivity of R, modal accessibility, even if only

[29]A similar situation arises in connection with the subjunctive conditional 'If a table had been constructed from hunk H, it would (would not) have been the very table T'. (See Lewis, 1973.) On the account proposed here, for any determinately possible world w' in which a table T' is constructed from hunk H, there corresponds a nearly perfect duplicate world w which is not determinately impossible, and in which table T is constructed from hunk H, and which is, in any ordinary sense, at least as "similar" to the actual world as is w'. Whether the subjunctive conditional is true, false, or neither depends on the details of a logic of counterfactuals supplemented with a logic of vagueness.

via a region of indeterminacy.[30] Similarly, in constructing a less crude version of the Four Worlds Paradox, one can start with a pair of mutually possible worlds w_1 and w_2, each containing artifacts differing from each other in their original matter (planks) by a difference within the limits of determinately excessive (*not* allowable) variation, so that the two artifacts must be distinct. We may then work the matter of these two artifacts back toward each other, staying within the limits of determinately allowable variation, to obtain a pair of worlds w_3 and w_4 differing only in the haecceities of their respective artifacts made from the very same matter according to the very same plan.[31] But, as before, we still have no reason to

---

[30]It should be emphasized that Chandler's argument for intransitivity is no parlor trick. Any philosopher seriously concerned with the metaphysics of modality must come to terms with it. The argument appears to show that modal accessibility is intransitive, or more accurately, that on the usual and standard construal of '$\square$', there are propositions p, e.g., that a certain table is not made originally of a certain portion of matter, such that $\ulcorner \square p \urcorner$ is true, but something of the form $\ulcorner \square \ldots \square p \urcorner$ is false. I believe that it does show this. But even if the argument contains a subtle and serious flaw, there should be *something* interesting and important to be learned by exposing the error.

We have already considered, in the present section and in Section 28.2, two proposals that would block the argument for intransitivity—the inflexible essentialism of the Chisholm-Forbes counterpart theory, and Kripke's idea of vague identity—and we argued that both of these are incorrect. For two other attempts to answer Chandler's argument see Fumerton, 1978, and Odegard, 1976, p. 202. Odegard argues by replacing the inflexible essentialism of the counterpart solution with a brand of anti-essentialism concerning artifacts and their matter, whereas Fumerton seems to attack the haecceitist presupposition of the argument. It should be evident by now that I do not find either of these proposals satisfactory.

A universal $S5$ possible worlds framework has been tacitly presupposed for reasons of simplicity in a number of formulations throughout the present book, particularly in some of the modal operator discourse formalizations in Chapter Seven. However, in no instance is the main line of argument seriously affected by these considerations favoring a (vague) relational possible worlds framework.

[31]In fact, this way in which the argument can accommodate regions of indeterminacy can already be illustrated in our original example involving ship a in world w_1. We assumed that a ship of this design and structure was such that it could have been constructed from a hunk of matter differing by no more than 2% from the matter in w_1, but that a change of 3% or more must result in a different ship. It is perfectly compatible with this assumption that the interval between 2% and 3% is a region of indeterminacy. Alternatively, one can start with a pair of mutually determinately possible worlds w_1 and w_2, containing artifacts a and b, respectively, differing in their original matter by a difference just barely outside the limits of determinately allowable variation. Since the two worlds are determinately possible relative to each

251

suppose that w_3 and w_4 are possible relative to the initial world w_1, or to one another, and principles like (V″) might be invoked to argue that they are at least not both determinately possible relative to w_1 or to each other. (See footnote 28.) Thus it seems that the main elements of the Four Worlds Paradox, and its solution, are relatively undisturbed by the presence of vagueness and indeterminacies.

other, artifact b must be distinct from artifact a even if b is made in w_2 from matter in the region of indeterminacy for a in w_1; otherwise it would be at most indeterminate whether w_2 is possible relative to w_1. The argument then proceeds as before. This version of the argument exploits the fact that the infusion of vagueness does not, in the appropriate sense, remove the boundary lines, but introduces new ones.

The general arguments for the Four Worlds Paradox and the failure of transitivity of modal accessibility require the assumption that some alteration in the original matter of a particular artifact, even if only extremely slight (e.g., one atom), is definitely possible, while some more sweeping alteration, even if only total alteration, is definitely impossible. We need not say where the boundaries are between definitely allowable variation and indeterminacy, or between indeterminacy and definitely excessive variation, only that there are nonempty regions of determinately allowable and determinately excessive variation. In addition, the first version of the general argument of the Four Worlds Paradox depends on the further assumption that the region of indeterminacy is smaller than the region of definitely allowable variation. If the region of indeterminacy is as large as or larger than the region of definitely allowable alteration, one must resort to a sorites-type construction as in the argument for failure of transitivity. It is worth noting in this connection that in the central cases of vagueness that come readily to mind (bald vs. not bald, red vs. red-orange, embryo vs. fetus, etc.), the region of indeterminacy is relatively small when compared with the region of definiteness. In any case, the alternative version of the argument does not require the further assumption.

APPENDIX II · *The Essentialist Principles in the* K *and* I *Mechanisms*

29. DONNELLAN VS. KRIPKE

Donnellan and Kripke disagree concerning the theoretical status of the general essentialist principles of the form of (27) involved in the *K*-mechanisms, principles which assert the essentiality of certain structural or subsumption properties of natural kinds. Donnellan discusses these principles only in the form of (26'), asserting what being an individual of the relevant kind "consists in." He suggests that such principles are knowable only *a posteriori,* or that in any case they are "the product of scientific discovery, of scientific theories, or, perhaps, change in scientific outlook." Kripke, who discusses these principles as overt essentialist principles, contends that they, and even certain principles of the form of (37) asserting the essentiality of certain original structural properties of individuals, are knowable by *a priori* "philosophical analysis." The question of the theoretical status of these principles—the question of whether they are the product of *a posteriori* science or of *a priori* philosophical analysis—is of some importance to the investigation in Part II above. For if they can be conclusively established on solely empirical, scientific grounds, then the anti-essentialism of some philosophers must be branded as *unscientific.* If, on the other hand, these essentialist principles are supported by premises not subject to direct scientific or empirical confirmation or disconfirmation, but knowable only by recourse to philosophical analysis, then since, as we have argued, they are not reducible to the philosophy of language, it would seem that these principles have at least some purely metaphysical import.

30. A PROBLEM IN THE EPISTEMOLOGY OF MODALITY

There is a familiar argument that no general essentialist principle like (22') can be known directly by empirical observation, and in general that no modal truth of the form ⌜It is necessarily the case that

253

$\ulcorner\phi\urcorner$ can be known directly by observation.[1] Modal statements involving the necessity operator make an assertion not only about the actual world but about *every* possible world. In possible world discourse, such statements involve universal quantification over possible worlds. But empirical investigation is a process occurring *within* a single possible world. In particular, empirical investigation conducted in the actual world directly yields information only about the actual world, not about other possible worlds. To put the point another way, empirical investigation directly yields knowledge only about what is actually the case, not about what must be the case. Echoing a recurrent theme in Hume, we cannot "see" necessity. Metaphysical necessity is, in this sense, *invisible*. Consequently, it seems that any statement of the form $\ulcorner$It is necessarily the case that $\phi\urcorner$ cannot be purely empirically verifiable.

This argument is not part of a general skepticism concerning the possibility of verifying universal generalizations, or even the possibility of verifying universal generalizations involving an infinite domain over which the variables range. When empirically verifying the universal generalization that crows are black, one examines a number of crows. If they are all found to be black, and if the examined sample is sufficiently large and sufficiently representative of the totality of crows, one then draws the inductive inference that *all* crows are black, including the unexamined ones. Hume raised doubts about whether such inductive inferences from the examined to the unexamined are ever rationally justified, but we are not calling into doubt here all such inductive inferences. Ordinarily, any information obtained by means of cautious induction is regarded as genuine knowledge, and in fact as genuinely empirical knowledge.

The situation is quite different with respect to the belief that such-and-such is necessary. If one inductively inferred from direct observation of what is *actually* the case to a belief about what *must be* the case, one would be grounding one's belief on no more than a single observed instance. One would be passing from the knowledge that such-and-such is in fact the case, things being the way they are, to a belief that such-and-such would still be the case even if things had been different in any one of countless other ways. One would be basing an induction concerning all of an infinite totality of possible worlds simply on the evidence provided by a single possible world, the

---

[1]The essentials of the argument can be found in Whewell, 1840, pp. 59–61. The idea that necessity is not observable, of course, traces back at least as far as Hume.

actual world. The so-called argument from analogy for the existence of other minds has been vigorously criticized on the grounds that, taken as an inductive argument, it would be a terribly weak analogy based on only a single instance.[2] But at least an inference that other human bodies are inhabited by conscious minds is an inference about a manageable number of entities, human bodies, that are similar in a great many important and relevant respects to the single instance on which the inference is based, one's own human body. Similarly, when scientists claim to have verified some general nomological statement about what is the case in every *nomologically* possible world (or in every world *nomologically possible relative to* such-and-such a possible world, etc.), they are passing from empirical knowledge about what is the case in the actual world to a proposition about what is the case in every possible world similar in many important and relevant respects to the actual world. One might well raise doubts about the legitimacy of passing from knowledge of a single observed instance to a belief about a great many relevantly similar but unexamined instances. But we are concerned here with something much worse. In passing from empirical knowledge about what is the ✗ case in the actual world to a belief about what is the case in *every* possible world, one seems to be conjecturing, on the basis of a single instance, about the nature of each and every one of a colossal number of possible worlds, a great many of which have absolutely nothing in common with the single examined instance, the actual world, save only that both are possible. Perhaps such a move is in many cases a perfectly legitimate means for obtaining genuine knowledge about what must be the case. The point is that it is in no way a permissible inductive inference. Any belief based on such reckless "reasoning" should no more count as knowledge than does a belief formed by gazing into a crystal ball. Knowledge of what must be the case, like our knowledge that there are other minds, may indeed be based on no more than a single instance, but if so, it is not knowledge obtained by induction from observed evidence.

31. THE NONMODAL CONSEQUENCES

At most then, what this argument shows is that truths about what must be the case are not verified directly by empirical observation,

[2]See for instance Wittgenstein, 1953, part I, §§283–303, especially §293, pp. 97–102.

nor by induction from direct observation. It does not show that such truths are not *a posteriori*, in the usual sense. The latter is not a consequence of the former. Consider for instance the statement 'It is necessary that Hesperus is Phosphorus'. We have seen in Section 7.2 that the theory of direct reference genuinely yields the consequence that this statement is true provided only that its immediate component 'Hesperus is Phosphorus' is true. But our knowledge that it is necessary that Hesperus is identical with Phosphorus is apparently not *a priori*, i.e., obtainable without recourse to experience. For if one could know *a priori* that it is necessary that Hesperus is identical with Phosphorus, then by drawing a simple logical inference one could also know *a priori* that Hesperus is *in fact* identical with Phosphorus. Any logical consequence of an *a priori* truth is itself an *a priori* truth, since it can be known simply by reasoning from something known *a priori*. But the knowledge that Hesperus is identical with Phosphorus is apparently *a posteriori* knowledge. This is not to say that we have *directly observed* that it is necessary that Hesperus is identical with Phosphorus, nor is it to say that we have inductively inferred the necessary identity of Hesperus and Phosphorus from what we have directly observed. For we have done neither of these things. We have *deductively* inferred the necessary identity of Hesperus and Phosphorus on the basis of the fact that Hesperus is in fact identical with Phosphorus, taken together with certain linguistic knowledge (the theory of direct reference plus some elementary semantics). Involved in our knowledge that Hesperus is necessarily identical with Phosphorus is the apparently empirical fact that Hesperus is identical with Phosphorus, and the further fact that if this is so, then it is necessarily so. Similarly, if the K-mechanisms more or less accurately represent the way one generates necessary *a posteriori* truths involving natural kind terms, then involved in our knowledge that water is necessarily H_2O is the empirical fact that (some) water is H_2O, and the further fact that if this is so, then it is necessary that (all) water is H_2O.

The issue that concerns us here is the theoretical status of essentialist principles like those involved in the K-mechanisms. In particular, we should like to know whether these principles are the *a posteriori* product of science proper, as Donnellan sometimes seems to suggest. We have just seen that some truths involving the notion of *necessity*, namely certain necessitated identity statements, are apparently *a posteriori* since the logical consequence obtained by deleting the occurrence of the modal operator is itself apparently *a posteriori*. Similarly we might consider the epistemological status of the statements that result upon deletion of the modal operators occurring in (22′) and its analogues, for these nonmodal principles are themselves logical consequences of the modal principles. If they are *a posteriori,* then so too are the modal principles required in the *K*-mechanisms.

The nonmodal consequences of (22′) and its analogues may be stated thus:

> If some sample of a given substance z has a certain chemical structure F, then every sample of substance z has chemical structure F.

> If some member of a given species z is a member of a certain biological class, then species z is completely subsumed under that biological class.

> If some sample of a given chemical element z has exactly n protons in its component atoms, then every sample of element z has exactly n protons in its component atoms.

Are any of these nonmodal principles *a posteriori?* In no case is the answer obvious.

The first principle asserts, in effect, that each substance has a unique chemical structure. If the word 'substance' is understood in such a way as to make this true—say in the sense of 'chemical element or compound'—then there is some inclination to say that this is not an empirical discovery of science, but perhaps some sort of *presupposition,* maybe even an *a priori* presupposition, within which chemical theory progresses. One may even be tempted to say that if the word 'substance' is understood in a sense that makes this principle true, then it is also understood in a sense that makes the principle in question *analytic*.

A similar situation obtains in the case of the second nonmodal principle. This principle asserts, in effect, that the relation between biological species and biological classes is such that a species is always entirely subsumed by any class it overlaps. According to this principle, there never occurs a situation in which there are two animals that are of the same species but nevertheless belong to distinct biological classes. Here again there is some temptation, although perhaps less so than in the case of substances, to say that

257

this principle is not a discovery of science but rather a presupposition, perhaps *a priori,* of biological taxonomic theory. The very notions of *species, genus, class,* and so on, seem to require that principles such as this be true. Thomason, for instance, writes that

> taxonomic systems are characterized by a property which is not in general possessed by semi-lattices:
>
> (D)   No natural kinds a and b of a taxonomic system overlap unless a [is subsumed under] b or b [is subsumed under] a.

The principle D of disjointness holds because the natural kinds of a system of classification may be conceived of as obtained by a process of division. The universe is first divided into disjoint sorts (e.g., *animal, vegetable,* and *mineral*), then these are further divided into disjoint sorts, and so forth (1969, p. 98).

We are considering here a special instance of Thomason's principle D of disjointness. His remarks about why this principle holds seem to suggest that the principle is knowable *a priori,* by the very nature of the process of classification in taxonomy.

The situation is different in the case of the third nonmodal principle mentioned above. This principle asserts, in effect, that chemical elements are substances composed only of atoms having the same number of protons in their nuclei. There is much less temptation to say that this principle is anything but a genuine empirical discovery of science. The original concept of an *element* was that of a substance whose samples cannot be "separated" or decomposed into different substances. With 'element' so defined, it seems clear that the principle in question represents an empirical scientific discovery, if anything does. Still, the term 'element' is a technical term of science, and with the advent of modern atomic theory there is at least the possibility that the term is now defined in such a way that the principle in question is ultimately analytic. Even if the principle is not analytic, it is not entirely implausible that the current concepts of *atom, proton,* and *element* are such that it is in some sense *conceptually necessary* (i.e., inconceivable that it is not the case) that elements are composed only of atoms all having exactly the same number of protons. Perhaps all three of these principles are synthetic but conceptually necessary.

On the other side of the coin, it is not entirely implausible to suppose that each of these nonmodal principles is ultimately subject to empirical verification or falsification.[3] Consider the principle concerning species. Can we imagine a situation in which scientists might claim to have discovered two conspecific animals which nevertheless are not to be classified as belonging to the same biological class? Suppose for instance that scientists discovered an interbreeding population of organisms that looked and behaved completely alike, in a communal manner, and so on, but that upon dissection it was found that despite extraordinary surface similarity and resemblance, and despite a capacity for fruitful interbreeding, some of these organisms were definitely mammals whereas others were definitely not mammals. Would this constitute an empirical discovery that there is a species that overlaps with, but is not subsumed under, the class *Mammalia?* It is difficult to guess what scientists would claim about such a discovery. If more and more discoveries of this type were made, perhaps such notions as *mammal, reptile,* and so on, would be radically altered. If things got bad enough, taxonomists might simply scrap the old system of classification and start all over with new biological "kinds." Or perhaps scientists would retain the old system and abandon Thomason's principle D of disjointness.[4]

A similar situation obtains with respect to the other two principles, concerning chemical compounds and elements. Suppose for instance that scientists were to discover empirically that there are very special physical properties which are characteristic of distinct substances but which are scientifically more "fundamental" to substances than is their component structure of elements and atoms of like atomic number. Suppose for instance that these fundamental physical properties concern things at the subatomic level. (For all that I know, such a discovery *has* been made.) Suppose further that two substance samples were discovered on Neptune, or artificially created in the laboratory, which shared just such a fundamental property but which differed in chemical composition or atomic number. Would this constitute an empirical discovery that substances are not character-

---

[3] I am indebted here to separate discussions in 1977 with Donnellan and Kaplan. Donnellan has since informed me that he has developed an argument which bears on this issue and which is slated to appear in a collection of his philosophical papers (forthcoming, Oxford University Press), though I do not know to what extent his argument is similar to the considerations raised here.

[4] In this regard see Wiggins, 1980, pp. 201–204, n. 2.09.

ized by unique chemical structures, or that elements are not characterized by unique atomic numbers?

32. CONNECTING STATEMENTS

32.1. *The Need for Connecting Statements*

Even if the case can be made that one or more of these nonmodal principles is *a posteriori,* one still has not shown that certain nontrivial forms of essentialism concerning substances and species are, in the relevant sense, a "product of science." It is true that if the nonmodal principles concerning substances and species are *a posteriori,* then so too are the modal principles of the form of (27) involved in the K-mechanisms. But if the claim is to be substantiated that certain nontrivial forms of essentialism concerning natural kinds are, in the relevant sense, a product of empirical science, then the case must first be made that the truth of the essentialist principles involved in the K-mechanisms can be established in some manner that does not ultimately rely on some empirically unverifiable, and consequently controversial, metaphysical theory.

We have seen an argument intended to show that the immediate data of empirical investigation does not directly yield information about necessary states of affairs. How can this be reconciled with the fact that certain modal statements, perhaps 'It is necessary that Hesperus is Phosphorus', is *a posteriori?* Involved in our knowledge of the necessary identity of Hesperus and Phosphorus are two epistemically prior facts. The knowledge that Hesperus is necessarily identical with Phosphorus is apparently *a posteriori* knowledge, but it is also *derivative* knowledge. It is based on the prior knowledge that Hesperus is in fact identical with Phosphorus, together with certain linguistic knowledge from semantics and the philosophy of language, all of which yields the result that if Hesperus is in fact identical with Phosphorus, then it is necessary that Hesperus is identical with Phosphorus. Similarly, Kripke points out in the quotation from Section 24 above that the essentialist fact that a particular table necessarily does not originate from a hunk of ice is knowable *a posteriori* because it is derived in part from the *a posteriori* fact that the table *actually* originated from a hunk of wood. This purely empirically verified fact is taken together with a further bit of information that "connects" the table's original composition in the actual world with a general fact about the table's original composition in all the other, unobserved, possible worlds. This further bit of "connecting" information, Kripke contends, is knowable by *a priori* philosophical analysis. If the *K* and *I* mechanisms more or less accurately represent the way in which we generate *a posteriori* knowledge of modal propositions of the form "It is necessarily the case that such-and-such," then such generated knowledge is *a posteriori*—obtained at least partly by recourse to sensory experience—precisely because such knowledge is derived from an empirically verifiable nonmodal fact, together with the further connecting fact that if the nonmodal state of affairs obtains, then so does a corresponding modal state of affairs.[5] Given knowledge of this conditional "connecting statement," any empirical verification of the nonmodal proposition (e.g., that Woody the Table was in fact constructed from a hunk of wood, or that water is in fact H_2O) is indirectly, but automatically, verification of the modal proposition.[6] There is at least one important *a priori* element involved in generating the necessary *a posteriori* conclusion. This is the faculty of *reason,* which allows us to infer conclusions from premises. There may be other important *a priori* elements involved from the philosophy of language as well. But there is in addition an inescapable *a posteriori* element. The derived knowledge that Woody the Table necessarily does not originate from a hunk of ice, and that water is necessarily H_2O, is based in part on the empirical premises that Woody in fact originated from a hunk of wood, and that water is in fact H_2O. Hence, the derived knowledge is obtained only by ultimate recourse to sensory experience, specifically the sensory experience that verified the empirical premises. The immediate data of empirical investigation *directly* verifies only the nonmodal premises, but this data also *indirectly* verifies, *via* mechanisms like the *K* and *I* mechanisms, certain modal conclusions.

Of course, something very similar must be said about our knowledge of general essentialist principles such as (22′) and its analogues, if such knowledge is indeed ultimately *a posteriori,* as Donnellan suggests. For general essentialist principles of the form of (27) that are involved in the *K*-mechanisms are straightforwardly modal

---

[5]More accurately, the *K* and *I* mechanisms employ a premise to the effect that if a certain state of affairs *might* obtain, then it *must* obtain. The trivial consequence that if it *does* obtain, then it *must,* is all that is needed. See Chapter Six, footnote 2.

[6]Our notion of a "connecting statement" or "connecting fact" is similar in some respects to Hempel's notion of a *bridge principle.* See 1966, chapter 6, pp. 70–84, especially pp. 72–75.

261

propositions, and the very sorts of propositions that are not directly verifiable by the immediate data of empirical investigation. If (22′) and its analogues are knowable only by ultimate recourse to sensory experience, it seems that they must be only indirectly verified by empirical investigation, in some manner analogous to the way in which our knowledge that it is necessary that Hesperus is identical with Phosphorus is apparently only indirectly verified by empirical investigation. Even if the nonmodal counterparts of (22′) and its analogues obtained by deleting the modal operators are verified completely empirically, so that both they and their modal counterparts are *a posteriori,* it seems that we shall still require some connecting principle to take us from the nonmodal versions of these principles to the modal versions if we are to use the immediate empirical data to verify the modal versions.

Let us suppose for instance that it is indeed empirically discovered that substances are in fact distinguishable by chemical structure. Then (22′) is also knowable only *a posteriori,* if at all, since it yields the former fact as a logical consequence. But if we are to use the direct empirical data involved in verifying the nonmodal fact to verify also the modal fact, then it seems that we still need to know that if substances are in fact distinguishable by chemical structure within the actual world, then substances are also distinguishable by chemical structure across distinct possible worlds, so that the chemical structure of a substance is an essential feature of that substance. Even if the nonmodal version of (22′) is knowable only *a posteriori,* involved in our *a posteriori* knowledge of the truth of (22′) itself is the epistemically prior knowledge of the connecting fact that (22′) is true if its empirically verifiable nonmodal consequence is true. A similar situation obtains with respect to the analogues of (22′) for the cases of species and elements. Even if (22′) and its analogues are knowable only *a posteriori,* involved in their empirical confirmation are, respectively, the following three connecting principles:

> Given that substances are *in fact* distinguishable by unique chemical structures, every substance is such that if it *might have* a certain chemical structure, then it *must* have that chemical structure.

> Given that biological species are *in fact* individually completely subsumed under biological classes, every species is such that if it *might* be subsumed under a certain

biological class, then it *must* be subsumed under that biological class.

Given that chemical elements are *in fact* distinguishable by the number of protons in their component atoms, i.e., by their atomic number, every element is such that if it *might* have a certain atomic number *n*, then it *must* have that atomic number *n*.

Without such conditional knowledge to connect nonmodal and modal states of affairs, the immediate data of empirical investigation that directly verifies the relevant nonmodal state of affairs shows nothing whatsoever about the corresponding modal state of affairs. We need connecting facts to take us from what we observe in the actual world to knowledge concerning all of the other possible worlds we do not observe. Induction will not do it for us.

32.2. *The Theoretical Status of the Connecting Statements*

If these connecting statements to the effect that "if this is so, then it must be so" are indeed a source of our knowledge of the general essentialist principles involved in the *K*-mechanisms, as it seems they must be if the latter knowledge is *a posteriori,* then we should also inquire into the theoretical status of these conditional statements. For unless it can be shown that they too are free of any ultimate reliance on an irreducibly metaphysical theory of essentialism, then the case has not been successfully made that certain nontrivial forms of essentialism are a product of science proper, rather than a product of science-cum-metaphysics.

This is a serious impasse for Donnellan's position concerning the theoretical status of (22′) and its analogues. For it is especially implausible that any one of the three essentialist connecting theses displayed above is entirely the product of science, with no reliance on a logically independent metaphysical theory. Each of these three **x** essentialist theses seem to be purely and irreducibly metaphysical. It is even plausible that, as with any purely metaphysical thesis, none of them is knowable *only* by ultimate recourse to sensory experience. If these theses are genuinely *knowable* at all, it seems that they are known *a priori,* by reflection on our concepts of *substance, element, chemical composition, species, biological class,* and so on. They are just the sort of metaphysical theses that give rise to armchair philosophical debate and controversy. Any philosopher who opposes

263

nontrivial essentialism is certain to reject them. This anti-essentialist position, even if incorrect, does not seem to conflict in any way with the findings of science proper. An anti-essentialist philosopher could wholeheartedly accept the findings of science, as well as the theory of direct reference as presented in Part I, and still reject these essentialist connecting theses.

33. Conclusion

It has not been argued here that Kripke is correct that essentialist principles like (22′) and its analogues are knowable *a priori,* nor has it been argued that Donnellan is correct in suggesting that they are knowable only *a posteriori.* Indeed we have found that the analogue of (22′) regarding species is plausibly regarded as *a priori* whereas the analogue of (22′) regarding elements is more plausibly regarded as *a posteriori.* But even if these various essentialist principles are *a posteriori,* involved in their empirical confirmation are certain essentialist connecting principles that are not the product of science proper, but irreducibly metaphysical and, perhaps, knowable *a priori.* Whereas Kripke's position concerning the theoretical status of (22′) and its analogues may be something of an overstatement, there does appear to be at least some metaphysics, as opposed to science proper, involved in our knowledge of them. The various forms of natural kind essentialism that have been the concern of Part II do not seem to be the product of science proper any more than they seem to be the product of the philosophy of language. Our final conclusion— and the main contention of the present work—is that there is no reason to suppose that nontrivial essentialism concerning natural kinds or concrete individuals is anything but what it appears to be: an irreducibly metaphysical doctrine, or set of doctrines, from a *sui generis* branch of philosophy.

Selected Bibliography

ACKERMAN, D.

    1976a.   "Propositional Attitudes and the Causal Theory of Names." Unpublished manuscript.

    1976b.   "Plantinga, Proper Names and Propositions." *Philosophical Studies* 30 (December): 409–412.

    1979a.   "Proper Names, Propositional Attitudes and Non-Descriptive Connotations." *Philosophical Studies* 35: 55–69.

    1979b.   "Proper Names, Essences and Intuitive Beliefs." *Theory and Decision* 11: 5–26.

    1980.   "Natural Kinds, Concepts and Propositional Attitudes." In French, Uehling, and Wettstein, eds., *Midwest Studies in Philosophy V: Studies in Epistemology* (Minneapolis: University of Minnesota Press), pp. 469–485.

ADAMS, R. M.

    1971.   "The Logical Structure of Anselm's Arguments." *The Philosophical Review* 80 (January): 28–54.

    1974.   "Theories of Actuality." *Noûs* 8 (September): 211–231; also in Loux, 1979, pp. 190–209.

    1979.   "Primitive Thisness and Primitive Identity." *The Journal of Philosophy* 76 (January): 5–26.

BLACKBURN, S.

    1975.   "The Identity of Propositions." In S. Blackburn, ed., *Meaning, Reference and Necessity* (Cambridge: At the University Press), pp. 182–205.

BURGE, C. T.

    1972.   "Truth and Mass Terms." *The Journal of Philosophy* 69 (May 18): 263–282.

    1974.   "Demonstrative Constructions, Reference, and Truth." *The Journal of Philosophy* 71 (April 18): 205–223.

    1977.   "Belief *De Re.*" *The Journal of Philosophy* 74 (June): 338–362.

    1979a.   "Individualism and the Mental." In French, Uehling, and Wettstein, eds., *Midwest Studies in Philosophy IV:*

Studies in Metaphysics (Minneapolis: University of Minnesota Press), pp. 73–121.

1979b.   "Sinning Against Frege." *The Philosophical Review* 88: 398–432.

CARNAP, R.
1947.   *Meaning and Necessity: A Study in Semantics and Modal Logic.* Second edition. Chicago: The University of Chicago Press.

CARTWRIGHT, R.
1968.   "Some Remarks on Essentialism." *The Journal of Philosophy* 65 (October 24): 615–626.

CASULLO, A.
1977.   "Kripke on the A Priori and the Necessary." *Analysis* 37 (June): 152–159.

CHANDLER, H. S.
1975.   "Rigid Designation." *The Journal of Philosophy* 72 (July 17): 363–369.

1976.   "Plantinga and the Contingently Possible." *Analysis* 36 (January): 106–109.

CHISHOLM, R.
1967.   "Identity Through Possible Worlds: Some Questions." *Noûs* 1 (March): 1–8; also in Loux, 1979, pp. 80–87.

1973.   "Parts as Essential to their Wholes." *Review of Metaphysics* 26: 581–603.

1975.   "Mereological Essentialism: Some Further Considerations." *Review of Metaphysics* 28: 477–484.

1976.   *Person and Object.* London: George Allen and Unwin.

CHURCH, A.
1943.   "Review of Carnap's *Introduction to Semantics.*" *The Philosophical Review* 52: 298–304.

1951.   "A Formulation of the Logic of Sense and Denotation." In Henle, Kallen, and Langer, eds., *Structure, Method and Meaning: Essays in Honor of Henry M. Sheffer* (New York: Liberal Arts Press), pp. 3–24.

1956.   *Introduction to Mathematical Logic I.* Princeton: Princeton University Press.

1973.   "Outline of a Revised Formulation of the Logic of Sense and Denotation." Part I, *Noûs* 7 (March): 24–33; part II, *Noûs* 8 (May): 135–156.

COOK, M.
    1979.   "Singular Terms and Rigid Designators." *Southwest Journal of Philosophy* 10 (Spring): 157–162.

DAVIDSON, D.
    1967.   "Truth and Meaning" *Synthese* 17 (September): 304–323.
    1969.   "On Saying That." In D. Davidson and J. Hintikka, eds., *Words and Objections: Essays on the Work of W. V. Quine* (Dordrecht: D. Reidel), pp. 158–174.
    1979.   "The Method of Truth in Metaphysics." In French et al., 1979, pp. 294–304.

DAVIDSON, D., DENNETT, D., et al.
    1974.   "Second General Discussion Session." Transcription of a discussion session held at a conference on "Language, Intentionality, and Translation-Theory," the University of Connecticut, March 1973, *Synthese* 27 (July/August, 1974): 509–521. (Participants: D. Davidson, D. Dennett, M. Dummett, G. Harman, D. Kaplan, S. Kripke, D. Lewis, C. Parsons, B. Partee, H. Putnam, W. V. O. Quine, and W. Sellars.)

DEL CARRIL, M. F.
    1978.   "Designation and Identity." *Critica* 10 (April): 57–73.

DEVITT, M.
    1974.   "Singular Terms." *The Journal of Philosophy* 71 (April 18): 183–205.

DONNELLAN, K. S.
    1962.   "Necessity and Criteria." *The Journal of Philosophy* 59 (October 25): 647–658.
    1966.   "Reference and Definite Descriptions." *The Philosophical Review* 75 (July): 281–304; also in Schwartz, 1977, pp. 42–65.
    1968.   "Putting Humpty Dumpty Together Again." *The Philosophical Review* 77: 203–215.
    1972.   "Proper Names and Identifying Descriptions." In D. Davidson and G. Harman, eds., *Semantics of Natural Language* (Dordrecht: D. Reidel), pp. 356–379.
    1973a.   "Substances as Individuals." Abstract of Donnellan, 1973b, *The Journal of Philosophy* 70 (November 8): 711–712.

1973b.   "Substances and Individuals." Unpublished commentary on Putnam, 1973b, delivered at the 1973 American Philosophical Association Eastern Division Symposium on Reference.

1974a.   "Speaking of Nothing." *The Philosophical Review* 83 (January): 3–31; also in Schwartz, 1977, pp. 216–244.

1974b.   "Rigid Designators, Natural Kinds, and Individuals." Unpublished expansion of Donnellan, 1973b, delivered at a UCLA Philosophy Colloquium, October 1974.

1977.   "Review of K. Gunderson, ed., *Language, Mind, and Knowledge*." *Language* 53 (September): 714–722.

1978.   "Speaker Reference, Descriptions and Anaphora." In P. Cole, ed., *Syntax and Semantics 9: Pragmatics* (New York: Academic Press), pp. 47–69; also in French et al., 1979, pp. 28–44.

1979.   "The Contingent *A Priori* and Rigid Designators." In French et al., 1979, pp. 45–60.

DUMMETT, M.

1973.   *Frege: Philosophy of Language.* New York: Harper and Row.

1974.   "The Social Character of Meaning." In Dummett, *Truth and Other Enigmas* (Cambridge, Mass.: Harvard University Press, 1978), pp. 420–430.

1975.   "Frege's Distinction Between Sense and Reference." In Dummett, *ibid.,* pp. 116–144.

EVANS, G.

1978.   "Can There Be Vague Objects?" *Analysis* 38: 208.

1979.   "Reference and Contingency." *The Monist* 62 (April): 161–189.

FELDMAN, F.

1973.   "Kripke's Argument Against Materialism." *Philosophical Studies* 24 (November): 416–419.

1974.   "Kripke on the Identity Theory." *The Journal of Philosophy* 71 (October 24): 665–676.

FINE, K.

1977a.   "Prior on the Construction of Possible Worlds and Instants." Postscript to A. N. Prior and K. Fine, *Worlds,*

> *Times and Selves* (Amherst: University of Massachusetts Press), pp. 116–161.

1977b.   "Properties, Propositions and Sets." *Journal of Philosophical Logic* 6 (June): 135–192.

1978a.   "Model Theory for Modal Logic I." *Journal of Philosophical Logic* 7 (May): 125–156.

1978b.   "First Order Modal Theories I: Modal Set Theory." Forthcoming in *Noûs*.

FITCH, G. W.

1976.   "Are There Necessary *A Posteriori* Truths?" *Philosophical Studies* 30: 243–247.

FORBES, G.

1980.   "Origin and Identity." *Philosophical Studies* 37: 353–362.

1981a.   "On the Philosophical Basis of Essentialist Theories." *Journal of Philosophical Logic* 10 (February): 73–99.

1981b.   "Thisness and Vagueness." Unpublished manuscript.

FREGE, G.

1892.   "On Sense and Reference." In Frege, 1970, pp. 56–78.

1918.   "The Thought: A Logical Inquiry." A. M. and Marcelle Quinton, trans., *Mind* 65 (July 1956): 289–311; also in P. F. Strawson, ed., *Philosophical Logic* (Oxford: Oxford University Press, 1967), pp. 17–38.

1970.   *Translations from the Philosophical Writings of Gottlob Frege.* P. Geach and M. Black, eds. Oxford: Basil Blackwell.

1979.   *Posthumous Writings.* H. Hermes, F. Kambartel, and F. Kaulbach, eds. Chicago: University of Chicago Press.

1980.   *Philosophical and Mathematical Correspondence.* G. Gabriel, H. Hermes, F. Kambartel, C. Thiel, and A. Veraart, eds. Abridged by B. McGuinness and translated by H. Kaal. Chicago: University of Chicago Press.

FRENCH, P., UEHLING, T., and WETTSTEIN, H., eds.

1979.   *Contemporary Perspectives in the Philosophy of Language.* Minneapolis: University of Minnesota Press.

FUMERTON, R. A.

1978.   "Chandler on the Contingently Possible." *Analysis* 38: 39–40.

GIBBARD, A.
   1975.   "Contingent Identity." *Journal of Philosophical Logic* 4 (May): 187–221.

GÖDEL, K.
   1944.   "Russell's Mathematical Logic." In Paul A. Schilpp, ed., *The Philosophy of Bertrand Russell,* The Library of Living Philosophers, Evanston, Illinois (New York: The Tudor Publishing Company), pp. 125–153.

HAZEN, A.
   1976.   "Expressive Completeness in Modal Language." *Journal of Philosophical Logic* 5: 25–46.
   1979.   "Counterpart-theoretic Semantics for Modal Logic." *The Journal of Philosophy* 76 (June): 319–338.

HEMPEL, C. G.
   1966.   *Philosophy of Natural Science.* Englewood Cliffs: Prentice-Hall.

HIRSCH, E.
   1976.   *The Persistence of Objects.* Philadelphia: Philosophical Monographs.

HUDSON, J., and TYE, M.
   1980.   "Proper Names and Definite Descriptions with Widest Possible Scope." *Analysis* 40: 63–64.

HUGHES, G. E., and CRESSWELL, M. J.
   1968.   *An Introduction to Modal Logic.* London: Methuen and Co.

KALISH, D., and MONTAGUE, R.
   1964.   *Logic: Techniques of Formal Reasoning.* New York: Harcourt, Brace, and World.

KAPLAN, D.
   1964.   "Foundations of Intensional Logic." Doctoral dissertation, UCLA.
   1967a. "Trans-World Heir Lines." In Loux, 1979, pp. 88–109.
   1967b. "Individuals in Intensional Logic." Unpublished manuscript (September).

1969.   "Quantifying In." In D. Davidson and J. Hintikka, eds., *Words and Objections: Essays on the Work of W. V. Quine* (Dordrecht: D. Reidel), pp. 206–242; also in L. Linsky, ed., *Reference and Modality* (New York: Oxford University Press, 1971), pp. 112–144.

1970.   "Dthat." In P. Cole, ed., *Syntax and Semantics 9: Pragmatics* (New York: Academic Press, 1978), pp. 221–243; also in French et al., 1979, pp. 383–400.

1973a.   "Bob and Carol and Ted and Alice." In Hintikka, Moravcsik, and Suppes, eds., *Approaches to Natural Language* (Dordrecht: D. Reidel), pp. 490–518.

1973b.   "On the Logic of Demonstratives." In French et al., 1979, pp. 401–412.

1975.   "How to Russell a Frege-Church." *The Journal of Philosophy* 72 (November 6): 716–729; also in Loux, 1979, pp. 210–224.

1977.   "Demonstratives." Unpublished manuscript, UCLA Department of Philosophy.

KIM, J.
1977.   "Perception and Reference Without Causality." *The Journal of Philosophy* 74 (October): 606–620.

KING, J. L.
1978.   "Chandler on Contingent Identity." *Analysis* 38 (June): 135–136.

KRIPKE, S.
1961.   "Quantified Modality and Essentialism." Unpublished manuscript.

1963.   "Semantical Considerations on Modal Logic." *Acta Philosophica Fennica* 16: 83–94.

1971.   "Identity and Necessity." In M. Munitz, ed., *Identity and Individuation* (New York: New York University Press), pp. 135–164; also in Schwartz, 1977, pp. 66–101.

1972a.   "Naming and Necessity." In D. Davidson and G. Harman, eds., *Semantics of Natural Language* (Dordrecht: D. Reidel), pp. 253–355, 763–769. Also published as a book, with a substantive preface (Cambridge, Mass.: Harvard University Press, 1980); all page references given in this work are to the book.

271

1972b.   Untitled, unpublished transcript of a seminar on fictional entities (University of California at Berkeley).
1979a.   "Speaker's Reference and Semantic Reference." In French et al., 1979, pp. 6–27.
1979b.   "A Puzzle About Belief." In Margalit, 1979, pp. 239–275.

LEWIS, D.
1968.   "Counterpart Theory and Quantified Modal Logic." *The Journal of Philosophy* 65 (March 7): 113–126; also in Loux, 1979, pp. 110–128.
1970.   "Anselm and Actuality." *Noûs* 4 (May): 175–188.
1973.   *Counterfactuals*. Cambridge, Mass.: Harvard University Press.

LINSKY, L.
1967.   *Referring*. London: Routledge and Keagan Paul.
1977.   *Names and Descriptions*. Chicago: University of Chicago Press.

LOCKWOOD, M.
1971.   "Identity and Reference." In M. Munitz, ed., *Identity and Individuation* (New York: New York University Press), pp. 199–211.
1975.   "On Predicating Proper Names." *The Philosophical Review* 84 (October): 471–498.

LOUX, M., ed.
1979.   *The Possible and the Actual*. Ithaca: Cornell University Press.

LYCAN, W. G.
1974.   "Kripke and the Materialists." *The Journal of Philosophy* 71 (October 24): 677–689.

McGINN, C.
1976.   "On the Necessity of Origin." *The Journal of Philosophy* 73 (March 11): 127–135.

MACKIE, J. L.
1974.   "Locke's Anticipation of Kripke." *Analysis* 34 (June): 177–180.

MARCUS, R. B.
1962.   "Modalities and Intensional Languages." *Synthese* 27:303–322.

1967.   "Essentialism in Modal Logic." *Noûs* 1 (March): 91–96.
1971.   "Essential Attribution." *The Journal of Philosophy* 68 (April 8): 187–202.
1978.   "Review of Linsky, 1977." *The Philosophical Review* 87 (July): 497–504.

MARGALIT, A., ed.
1979.   *Meaning and Use.* Dordrecht: D. Reidel.

MELLOR, D. H.
1977.   "Natural Kinds." *British Journal for the Philosophy of Science* 28 (December): 299–312.

MILL, J. S.
1843.   "Of Names." Book I, chapter II, *A System of Logic* (New York: Harper and Brothers, 1893), pp. 29–44.

ODEGARD, D.
1976.   "On A Priori Contingency." *Analysis* 36 (June): 201–203.

PARFIT, D.
1971.   "Personal Identity." *The Philosophical Review* 80 (January): 3–27.

PARKS, Z.
1972.   "Classes and Change." *Journal of Philosophical Logic* 1 (May): 162–169.

PARSONS, T.
1969.   "Essentialism and Quantified Modal Logic." *The Philosophical Review* 78 (January): 35–52.
1970.   "An Analysis of Mass Terms and Amount Terms." *Foundations of Language* 6 (August): 362–388.

PERRY, J.
1977.   "Frege on Demonstratives." *The Philosophical Review* 86: 474–497.
1979.   "The Problem of the Essential Indexical." *Noûs* 13: 3–21.

PLANTINGA, A.
1974.   *The Nature of Necessity.* Oxford: The Clarendon Press.
1975.   "On Mereological Essentialism." *Review of Metaphysics* 28: 468–476.

1978. "The Boethian Compromise." *American Philosophical Quarterly* 15 (April): 129–138.

PRIOR, A. N.
1960. "Identifiable Individuals." *Review of Metaphysics* 13 (June): 684–696; also in Prior, *Papers on Time and Tense* (Oxford: Oxford University Press, 1968), pp. 66–77.
1971. *Objects of Thought.* Oxford: Oxford University Press.

PUTNAM, H.
1962. "It Ain't Necessarily So." *The Journal of Philosophy* 59 (October): 658–671; also in Putnam, 1975c, pp. 237–249.
1965. "How Not to Talk about Meaning." In R. Cohen and M. Wartofsky, eds., *Boston Studies in the Philosophy of Science II: In Honor of Phillip Frank* (New York: Humanities Press); also in Putnam, 1975d, pp. 117–138.
1966. "The Analytic and the Synthetic." In H. Feigl and G. Maxwell, eds., *Minnesota Studies in the Philosophy of Science III* (Minneapolis: University of Minnesota Press); also in Putnam, 1975d, pp. 33–69.
1970. "Is Semantics Possible?" In H. Kiefer and M. Munitz, eds., *Language, Belief and Metaphysics* (Albany: State University of New York Press), pp. 50–63; also in Putnam, 1975d, pp. 139–152; also in Schwartz, 1977, pp. 102–118.
1973a. "Explanation and Reference." In G. Pearce and P. Maynard, eds., *Conceptual Change* (Dordrecht: D. Reidel), pp. 199–221; also in Putnam, 1975d, pp. 196–214.
1973b. "Meaning and Reference." *The Journal of Philosophy* 70 (November 8): 699–711; also in Schwartz, 1977, pp. 119–132.
1974. "Comment on Wilfrid Sellars." *Synthese* 27 (July/August): 445–455.
1975a. "The Meaning of 'Meaning'." In K. Gunderson, ed., *Minnesota Studies in the Philosophy of Science VII: Language, Mind, and Knowledge* (Minneapolis: University of Minnesota Press); also in Putnam, 1975d, pp. 215–271; all page references given in this work are to the latter.

1975b. "Language and Reality." In Putnam, 1975d, pp. 272–290.

1975c. *"Philosophical Papers I: Mathematics, Matter, and Method.* Cambridge: At the University Press.

1975d. *Philosophical Papers II: Mind, Language, and Reality.* Cambridge: At the University Press.

1978. "Reference and Understanding." In Putnam, *Meaning and the Moral Sciences* (Boston: Routledge and Kegan Paul), pp. 97–119; also in Margalit, 1979, pp. 199–217.

1979. "Comments on Kripke." In Margalit, 1979, pp. 284–288.

QUINE, W. V. O.

1948. "On What There Is." In Quine, 1953b, pp. 1–19.

1951. "Two Dogmas of Empiricism." In Quine, 1953b, pp. 20–46.

1953a. "Reference and Modality." In Quine, 1953b, pp. 139–159.

1953b. *From a Logical Point of View.* Second edition. New York: Harper and Row.

1953c. "Three Grades of Modal Involvement." In Quine, *The Ways of Paradox* (New York: Random House, 1966), pp. 156–174.

1960. *Word and Object.* Cambridge, Mass.: The M.I.T. Press.

1962. "Reply to Professor Marcus." In Quine, *The Ways of Paradox,* pp. 175–182.

1969. "Replies." In D. Davidson and J. Hintikka, eds., *Words and Objections: Essays on the Work of W. V. Quine* (Dordrecht: D. Reidel), pp. 292–352.

1972. "Review of M. Munitz, ed., *Identity and Individuation."* *The Journal of Philosophy* 69 (September 7): 488–497.

RORTY, R.

1973. "Kripke on Mind-Body Identity." Unpublished manuscript.

1979. *Philosophy and the Mirror of Nature.* Princeton: Princeton University Press.

RUSSELL, B.

1903. *Principles of Mathematics.* New York: W. W. Norton and Co.

1905. "On Denoting." *Mind;* also in Russell, 1956, pp. 41–56.

275

1911.   "Knowledge by Acquaintance and Knowledge by Description." In Russell, *Mysticism and Logic and Other Essays* (London: Longmans, Green and Co.), pp. 209–232.

1912.   *The Problems of Philosophy.* Oxford: Oxford University Press.

1918.   "The Philosophy of Logical Atomism." In Russell, 1956, pp. 177–281.

1956.   *Logic and Knowledge.* R. C. Marsh, ed. London: George Allen and Unwin.

SALMON, N. U.

1979a.   "Review of Linsky, 1977." *The Journal of Philosophy* 76 (August): 436–452.

1979b.   "How *Not* to Derive Essentialism from the Theory of Reference." *The Journal of Philosophy* 76 (December): 703–725.

1979c.   "Essentialism in Current Theories of Reference." Doctoral dissertation, UCLA.

SCHIFFER, S.

1978.   "The Basis of Reference." *Erkenntnis* 13 (July): 171–206.

1979.   "Naming and Knowing." In French et al., 1979, pp. 61–74.

SCHWARTZ, S. P., ed.

1977.   *Naming, Necessity, and Natural Kinds.* Ithaca: Cornell University Press.

SEARLE, J.

1958.   "Proper Names." *Mind* 67 (April): 166–173.

1967.   "Proper Names and Descriptions." In P. Edwards, ed., *The Encyclopedia of Philosophy, Volume 6* (New York: Macmillan Publishing Co. and the Free Press), pp. 487–491.

SELLARS, W.

1963.   "Abstract Entities." *Review of Metaphysics* 16 (June): 627–671.

SHARVY, R.

1968.   "Why a Class Can't Change Its Members." *Noûs* 2 (November): 303–314.

SMULLYAN, A. F.
1948.   "Modality and Descriptions." *The Journal of Symbolic Logic* 13 (March): 31–37.

STRAWSON, P. F.
1959.   *Individuals: An Essay in Descriptive Metaphysics.* London: Methuen and Co.
1979.   "May Bes and Might Have Beens." In Margalit, 1979, pp. 229–238.

TELLER, P.
1975.   "Essential Properties: Some Problems and Conjectures." *The Journal of Philosophy* 72 (May 8): 233–248.

THOMASON, R.
1969.   "Species, Determinates and Natural Kinds." *Noûs* 3 (February): 95–101.

UNGER, P.
1980.   "The Problem of the Many." In French, Uehling, and Wettstein, eds., *Midwest Studies in Philosophy V: Studies in Epistemology* (Minneapolis: University of Minnesota Press), pp. 411–467.

VAN CLEVE, J.
1978.   "Why Do Sets Contain Their Members Essentially?" Unpublished manuscript.

WHEWELL, W.
1840.   *Philosophy of the Inductive Sciences Founded upon Their History, I.* London: J. W. Parker and Son.

WHITEHEAD A. N., and RUSSELL, B.
1927.   *Principia Mathematica.* Second edition. Cambridge: At the University Press.

WIGGINS, D.
1974.   "Essentialism, Continuity, and Identity." *Synthese* 28 (November): 321–359.
1980.   *Sameness and Substance.* Cambridge, Mass.: Harvard University Press.

WILSON, N. L.
1959.   "Substances Without Substrata." *Review of Metaphysics* 12 (June): 521–539.

WITTGENSTEIN, L.
    1953.   *Philosophical Investigations.* Third edition. G.E.M. Anscombe, trans. New York: The Macmillan Co.

WOLTERSTORFF, N.
    1970.   *On Universals: An Essay in Ontology.* Chicago: The University of Chicago Press.

Index of Labeled Expressions

For expressions (1) through (38), prime numerals label the English translation of the corresponding numbered expression given below. The 'λ'-operator is used here as a variable binding *property abstraction operator* which transforms any open sentence into a predicate designating the corresponding property. In English, a 'λ'phrase $\ulcorner\lambda\alpha\urcorner$, where α is an individual variable, may be read loosely as "the property of being an individual α which is such that . . . ."

(1) $(\exists y)\Box[\alpha = y]$

(2) $(\exists y)\,(y = \beta \wedge \Box[\alpha = y])$

(3) $\Box[\alpha = dthat(\beta)]$

(4) $\alpha = \beta$

(5) $(\exists y)(y = \beta \wedge \Box(x)[\Pi_\nu(x) \leftrightarrow x \in y])$

(6) $\Box(x)[\Pi_\nu(x) \leftrightarrow x \in dthat(\beta)]$

(7) $(x)[\Pi_\nu(x) \leftrightarrow x \in \beta]$

(8) $(w)\,(x)\,(Exists_w(x)$
$\rightarrow [\Pi_{water_w}(x) \leftrightarrow Same_L(x\text{-}in\text{-}w, this\text{-}in\text{-}W_@)])$

(9) $(w)\,(x)\,(Exists_w(x)$
$\rightarrow [\Pi_{water_w}(x) \leftrightarrow Consubstantial_w(x, this)])$

(10) $(w)\,(x)\,(Exists_w(x) \rightarrow [\Pi_{water_w}(x)$
$\leftrightarrow Cross\text{-}world\text{-}consubstantial(x, w, this, W_@)])$

(11) $(w)\,(x)\,[Exists_w(x) \rightarrow (\Pi_{water_w}(x)$
$\leftrightarrow x \in_w (\imath z)[Substance_{W_@}(z) \wedge (this \in_{W_@} z)])]$

279

(12) $\square(x)(\Pi_{water}(x)$
$$\leftrightarrow x \in (\imath z)A[Substance(z) \wedge (this \in z)])$$

(13) $\square(x)[\Pi_{water}(x)$
$$\leftrightarrow x \in dthat((\imath z)[Substance(z) \wedge (this \in z)])]$$

(14) $\square(x)(\Pi_{\nu}(x) \leftrightarrow x \in (\imath z)A[K(z) \wedge (this \in z)])$

(15) $\square(x)[\Pi_{\nu}(x) \leftrightarrow x \in dthat((\imath z)[K(z) \wedge (this \in z)])]$

(16) $\square(x)(\Pi_{\nu}(x) \leftrightarrow x \in (\imath z)A[K(z) \wedge \phi(z)])$

(17) $\square(x)[\Pi_{\nu}(x) \leftrightarrow x \in dthat((\imath z)[K(z) \wedge \phi(z)])]$

(18) $H_2O(this) \wedge Chemical\text{-}structure(H_2O)$

(19) $(w_1)(w_2)\,(x)\,(y)(Exists_{w_1}(x) \wedge Exists_{w_2}(y)$
$$\rightarrow [(x \in_{w_1} (\imath z)[Substance_{w_2}(z) \wedge (y \in_{w_2} z)])$$
$$\rightarrow (F)(Chemical\text{-}structure(F) \rightarrow [F_{w_1}(x) \leftrightarrow F_{w_2}(y)])])$$

(20) $(w_1)(w_2)\,(x)\,(y)(Exists_{w_1}(x) \wedge Exists_{w_2}(y)$
$$[((\imath z)[Substance_{w_1}(z) \wedge x \in_{w_1} z]$$
$$= (\imath z)[Substance_{w_2}(z) \wedge y \in_{w_2} z])$$
$$\rightarrow (F)(Chemical\text{-}structure(F) \rightarrow [F_{w_1}(x) \leftrightarrow F_{w_2}(y)])])$$

(21) $\square(F)(\Diamond Chemical\text{-}structure(F)$
$$\rightarrow \square(z)[\Diamond(Substance(z) \wedge (\exists x)[x \in z \wedge F(x)])$$
$$\rightarrow \square(Substance(z) \rightarrow (x)(x \in z \rightarrow F(x)])])$$

(22) $\square(F)\square(z)[\Diamond Chemical\text{-}structure(F) \wedge \Diamond Substance(z)$
$$\rightarrow (\Diamond(\exists x)[x \in z \wedge F(x)] \rightarrow \square(x)[x \in z \rightarrow F(x)])]$$

(23) $\square(x)[\Pi_{water}(x) \rightarrow H_2O(x)]$

(24) $\square(x)(y)[(x \in (\imath z)[Substance(z) \wedge y \in z])$
$$\leftrightarrow (F)(Chemical\text{-}structure(F) \rightarrow [F(x) \leftrightarrow F(y)])]$$

280

(25) $\psi(this) \wedge \Psi[\lambda x \psi(x)]$

(26) $(w_1)(w_2)(x)(y)(Exists_{w_1}(x) \wedge Exists_{w_2}(y)$
$\rightarrow [(x \in_{w_1} (\imath z)[K_{w_2}(z) \wedge y \in_{w_2} z])$
$\rightarrow (F)(\Psi(F) \rightarrow [F_{w_1}(x) \leftrightarrow F_{w_2}(y)])])$

(27) $\Box(F)\Box(z)[\Diamond \Psi(F) \wedge \Diamond K(z)$
$\rightarrow (\Diamond(\exists x)[x \in z \wedge F(x)] \rightarrow \Box(x)[x \in z \rightarrow F(x)])]$

(28) $\Box(x)[\Pi_\nu(x) \rightarrow \psi(x)]$

(29) $(\exists x)[(x \in (\imath z)[K(z) \wedge \phi(z)]) \wedge \psi(x)] \wedge \Psi[\lambda x \psi(x)]$

(30) $\Box[Woody = dthat(\text{the table located } here)]$

(31′)   The table located *here* was originally constructed from hunk of wood *H*.

(32) $(w_1)(w_2)(x)(y)(Exists_{w_1}(x) \wedge Exists_{w_2}(y)$
$\rightarrow [(x =_{w_1} (\imath z)[Table_{w_2}(z) \wedge y =_{w_2} z])$
$\rightarrow (F)(Original\text{-}composition(F) \rightarrow [F_{w_1}(x) \leftrightarrow F_{w_2}(y)])])$

(33) $\Box(F)\Box(x)[\Diamond Original\text{-}composition(F) \wedge \Diamond Table(x)$
$\rightarrow (\Diamond[Exists(x) \wedge F(x)] \rightarrow \Box[Exists(x) \rightarrow F(x)])]$

(34) $\Box[Exists(Woody)$
$\rightarrow Woody$ was originally constructed from hunk of wood $H]$

(35) $\psi(\beta) \wedge \Psi[\lambda x \psi(x)]$

(36) $(w_1)(w_2)(x)(y)(Exists_{w_1}(x) \wedge Exists_{w_2}(y)$
$\rightarrow [(x =_{w_1} (\imath z)[I_{w_2}(z) \wedge y =_{w_2} z])$
$\rightarrow (F)(\psi(F) \rightarrow [F_{w_1}(x) \leftrightarrow F_{w_2}(y)])])$

281

(37) $\Box(F)\Box(x)[\Diamond\Psi(F) \wedge \Diamond I(x)$
$\rightarrow (\Diamond[Exists(x) \wedge F(x)] \rightarrow \Box[Exists(x) \rightarrow F(x)])]$

(38) $\Box[Exists(\alpha) \rightarrow \psi(\alpha)]$

(C1) $\sim\Diamond T(B,C)$

(C2) $\Box[T(D,C) \rightarrow D \neq B]$

(C3) $\Box(x)[T(x,C) \rightarrow x \neq B]$

(K1) $(x)(y)(z)[K(y) \wedge K(z) \wedge x \in y \wedge x \in z \rightarrow y = z]$

(K2) $(x)(K(x) \rightarrow \Box[Exists(x) \rightarrow K(x)])$

(Sp1) $(x)(y)(z)[Species(y) \wedge Species(z)$
$\wedge x \in y \wedge x \in z \rightarrow y = z]$

(Sp2) $(x)(Species(x) \rightarrow \Box[Exists(x) \rightarrow Species(x)])$

(Sub1) $(x)(y)(z)[Substance(y) \wedge Substance(z)$
$\wedge x \in y \wedge x \in z \rightarrow y = z]$

(Sub2) $(x)(Substance(x) \rightarrow \Box[Exists(x) \rightarrow Substance(x)])$

(I) $\sim\Diamond(\exists x)(\exists y)(\exists y')[T(x,y) \wedge T(x,y') \wedge y \neq y']$

(II) $\Box(y)\Box(y')(\Diamond(\exists x)[T(x,y) \wedge y \text{ does not overlap with } y']$
$\wedge \Diamond(\exists x')T(x',y') \rightarrow \Diamond[(\exists x)T(x,y) \wedge (\exists x')T(x',y')])$

(III) $\Box(x)\Box(x')\Box(y)\Box(y')(\Diamond[T(x,y)$
$\wedge y \text{ does not overlap with } y'] \wedge \Diamond T(x',y')$
$\rightarrow \Diamond[T(x,y) \wedge T(x',y')])$

(IV) $\Box(x)\Box(y)\Box(y')(\Diamond[T(x,y) \wedge y \text{ does not overlap with } y'$
$\wedge \Diamond(\exists x')T(x',y') \rightarrow \Diamond[T(x,y) \wedge (\exists x')T(x',y')])$

282

(V) $\Box(x)\Box(y)[\Diamond T(x,y) \rightarrow \Box(z)(T(z,y) \rightarrow z = x)]$

(V′) $\Box(x)\Box(y)\Box(P)[\Diamond(T(x,y)$ according to plan $P)$
              $\rightarrow \Box(z)([T(z,y)$ according to plan $P] \rightarrow z = x)]$

(V″) $\Box(x)\Box(y)\Box(P)[\Diamond(x = (\imath z')[T(z',y)$ according to
         plan $P]) \rightarrow \Box(z)(z = (\imath z')[T(z',y)$ according to plan $P]$
              $\rightarrow z = x)]$

Index of Subjects

Ackerman, D., 11n

actual, 27, 163, 218n, 234, 236n; chemical structure, 185–186; gamete, 209–210; individual, 144n; nature, 106; original composition, 238; original matter, 203, 230, 241, 243, 246, 248; paradigm, 148, 163–164, 180; referent, 38; sample of water, 112, 114, 149n, 164; species, 101n; state of affairs, 119–120, 239; substance, 145, 149; table, 240, 242, 245, 249

actuality operator, 44, 55, 188; persistent, 145n

actually, xiii, 15n, 27-28, 54, 100n, 109, 113, 145, 149, 165, 169, 180n, 185, 188–91, 188n, 197–98, 209, 209n, 211–212, 235, 238, 254, 260; denote, 30, 39n; exist, 39n, 40n, 137n; logic of, 28n 187; possible, 239

actual world, 27, 52, 75, 103, 107n, 112, 138, 161–163, 173, 180, 180n, 182, 197–198, 202, 207, 212, 238, 250n, 254–255, 260, 262; denotation with respect to, 149, 149n; exist in, 137n; individual constant denoting, 107, 107n; possible relative to, 239, 247–249, 249n; reference to, 54, 150, 154; same$_L$ in, 101–102, 108, 115; same species in, 139; statue-in-, 109

Adams, R.M., 20n, 21, 147n

addition argument, 203, 212–213, 224n, 229. *See also* Neat Argument

analytic, 25, 25n, 27–29, 59–61, 81, 88n, 89n, 101, 103, 166, 172n, 257–258

anti-essentialism, 86, 90n, 91n, 186, 209n, 215–216, 251n, 253, 264

a posteriori, 76–77, 79, 81, 163, 165, 168–169, 171, 174, 177, 193, 195, 217, 256–257, 260, 262–263; knowable only, 28, 253, 262, 264; knowledge, 194, 261; sentence, 187, 191; truth, 91n, 188, 188n, 256

apprehend, 9, 13n, 57–58. *See also* grasp

a priori, 28, 81–82, 95, 164, 168, 177, 195, 217, 256–258, 261; knowable, 27, 28n, 59–60, 76, 171, 196–197, 253, 258, 261, 264; knowledge, 28, 77, 166, 194-195, 263; necessary, 13, 29. *See also* contingent

Bacon, F., 20, 25, 25n, 28

Blackburn, S., 13n

Burge, C. T., 12n, 42n

Carnap, R., 24, 33n, 34, 45–46, 45n, 53, 53n, 55, 70. *See also* descriptional

Cartwright, R., 87n

Casullo, A., 78n, 196n

category, 45, 51–52, 53n, 71, 95, 100n, 154, 164. *See also* kind

causal theory of reference, xiii, 3, 5n, 8, 31–32

Chandler, H. S., 219–224, 220n, 223n, 224n, 226–229, 230n, 237n, 238, 241, 246, 251n

Chisholm, R., 230n, 233, 233n, 240n, 251n

Church, A., 50n, 55

common noun, 44–48, 50, 52–53, 55–56, 59, 74, 139, 148, 150, 151, 168–170, 173; phrase, 43, 45–50, 50n, 54, 74. *See also* general term

concept, 9, 10, 10n, 23, 27–28, 31, 65–67, 93–94, 96, 156. *See also* stereotypical

conceptual, 12, 23, 32, 68, 79, 97n

'consists in', 163–164, 166–168, 170–173, 176, 179, 182–183, 190, 253; vagueness of, 177–178

conspecific, 99, 124, 133–134, 141, 259

conspecificity, 116, 118, 131, 135–136, 147n; cross-world, 122, 147n, 154; definition of, 123, 133, 136, 138, 141–142

94–95, 100n; a haecceity, 31, 39; modally indexed properties, 28; a stereotype, 103, 153
—natural kind term, 172n
—relationally, 54–55, 70, 155, 157; *see also* singular term
—relative to, 21, 22n, 55–56, 64, 79, 81, 101, 172n
—rigidity, 35n
—singular term, 14, 15n, 18, 26n, 35, 43, 70
—theory, 21, 25n, 27, 30, 60, 60n, 90n
—thoroughly, 17–18, 17n, 20–23, 20n, 22n, 55–56, 70, 93, 155
designation, 42n, 45–46, 48, 50n, 51–54, 53n, 71–72, 74, 102, 104–106, 119–120, 154, 156, 167–169, 171n, 173, 191n; fix, 31, 75, 105–106, 112, 139, 148, 150, 151n; of a general term, 151n; of a natural kind term, 45, 100, 195; rigid, 5, 5n, 69–72, 80–81, 106, 112–114, 148, 151, 151n, 172–173, 176; with respect to a context, 35, 100, 100n, 107n; with respect to a possible world, 33, 53
designator, 45, 48, 53, 56; obstinate, 34–36, 37n, 40–41, 40n, 72, 73n, 89n, 90n, 145n, 172, 234; persistent, 34–35, 39–40, 72, 144n; rigid, 33–35, 33n, 69–70, 72–75, 80, 84–85, 85n, 88n, 97, 107, 150–151, 169, 172n, 173–174, 182, 188, 195, 197, 212, 217, 218n. *See also* natural kind
designatum, 55, 64, 71–72, 79
direct reference, 14n, 16, 19n, 56, 58, 58n, 63, 65, 68–69; to the actual world, 54; to an individual, 17, 19–20, 55; to a kind, 54, 55; to the species *Tiger,* 56, 59, 63, 65, 69
dominant claim, 220, 225. *See also* theory of dominant and recessive rival constitution claims; theory of dominant and recessive rival identity claims
Donnellan, K. S., 3, 3n, 5, 5n, 6, 10n, 18n, 20, 22–23, 22n, 29, 31–32, 69, 69n, 72, 80–81, 86n, 90, 91n, 92, 114, 149, 149n, 163–168, 171, 171n, 174, 176–177, 179, 181, 185–186, 185n,

192–193, 196, 253, 256, 259n, 261, 263–264
dthat, 15n, 35–36, 40, 41n, 74, 85n, 145–146, 145n, 148–152, 154–156, 166–170, 172–173, 178, 187; obstinacy of, 145n
Dummett, M., 26n, 33n, 55

epistemological argument, 15n, 23, 27–28, 30, 60
essentialism, xiv, xv, 4, 5, 17, 47n, 82, 84n, 89, 177, 180n, 190–191, 205, 209n, 210, 217, 224n, 229–230, 236
—Aristotelian, 84, 86, 209n
—commitment to, 83n, 84n
—concerning: abstract entities, 89n, 90n; artifacts, 227; concrete individuals, 6, 86, 88–90, 91n, 114, 174; natural kinds, 5–6, 47n, 84, 88–90, 91n, 174, 210, 260; origin, 5, 91n, 211; substances, 137, 137n; universals, 86n
—extreme, 235n
— -free, 177, 204
—general principle of, 191–192, 210, 263
—inflexible, 236n, 237, 240n, 251n
—metaphysical theory of, 82, 88, 208, 217, 260, 263
—nontrivial, xiii, xiv, 5–6, 84, 86, 88–90, 89n, 91n, 92n, 133n, 138, 174–175, 184, 186–187, 192–193, 196–198, 204, 208, 210, 213–214, 214n, 217, 218n, 260, 263–264
—"proof" of, 206
—with respect to haecceities, 40n, 214n
essentialist, 87n, 88n, 89n
—assertion, 177
—claim, xiii, 113
—conclusion, 186, 208n, 211, 213, 229
—import, 83–84, 83n, 84n, 89; nontrivial, 5, 83n, 84n, 167, 169, 175–177, 180n, 182–183, 185–186, 185n, 190n, 191n, 192, 196, 198, 205, 213–215, 217
—principle, 184, 186, 188–191, 195–

287

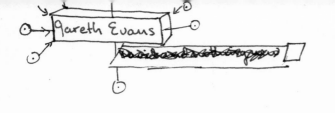

Gareth Evans